Beyond Four Walls

Australian College of Theology Monograph Series

SERIES EDITOR GRAEME R. CHATFIELD

The ACT Monograph Series, generously supported by the Board of Directors of the Australian College of Theology, provides a forum for publishing quality research theses and studies by its graduates and affiliated college staff in the broad fields of Biblical Studies, Christian Thought and History, and Practical Theology with Wipf and Stock Publishers of Eugene, Oregon. The ACT selects the best of its doctoral and research masters theses as well as monographs that offer the academic community, scholars, church leaders and the wider community uniquely Australian and New Zealand perspectives on significant research topics and topics of current debate. The ACT also provides opportunity for contributors beyond its graduates and affiliated college staff to publish monographs which support the mission and values of the ACT.

Rev. Dr. Graeme Chatfield
Series Editor and Associate Dean

Beyond Four Walls

Explorations in Being the Church

Edited by
MICHAEL D. O'NEIL
and
PETER ELLIOTT

WIPF & STOCK · Eugene, Oregon

BEYOND FOUR WALLS
Explorations in Being the Church

Copyright © 2020 Wipf and Stock Publishers. All rights reserved. Except for brief quotations in critical publications or reviews, no part of this book may be reproduced in any manner without prior written permission from the publisher. Write: Permissions, Wipf and Stock Publishers, 199 W. 8th Ave., Suite 3, Eugene, OR 97401.

Wipf & Stock
An Imprint of Wipf and Stock Publishers
199 W. 8th Ave., Suite 3
Eugene, OR 97401

www.wipfandstock.com

PAPERBACK ISBN: 978-1-7252-7890-5
HARDCOVER ISBN: 978-1-7252-7891-2
EBOOK ISBN: 978-1-7252-7892-9

Citations from the New American Standard Version (NASB) used with permission.

Citations from the New International Version (NIV) used with permission.

Citations from the New Revised Standard Version (NRSV) used with permission.

Manufactured in the U.S.A.   07/20/20

To Dr. Richard K. Moore

In grateful acknowledgement of your many years of service to the Baptist Theological College of Western Australia (Vose Seminary)

Contents

Contributors | ix

Introduction | xiii
—MICHAEL D. O'NEIL AND PETER ELLIOTT

1 Church as Gospel | 1
—SCOT MCKNIGHT

2 Being God's People Among the Nations: Gleanings from Kings | 17
—JOHN OLLEY

3 Jonah's Wail: The Death and Resurrection of a Recalcitrant Church | 31
—MICHAEL D. O'NEIL

4 The Church as Family in the Teaching of Jesus, and Today | 50
—MARGARET WESLEY

5 Leadership in Apostolic Perspective: Acts 20:17–35 | 64
—ALLAN CHAPPLE

6 The Pastor-Teacher and the Church | 79
—SCOT MCKNIGHT

7 I Am a Woman: Please Let Me Be Who I Am In God | 97
—KAREN SIGGINS

8 Living in God's Mission: Theses for a Systematic Ecclesiology | 113
—JOHN MCCLEAN

9   Trinitarian Apologetics: Participating in Communities of Surprise, Embrace, and Witness | 133
    —Brian Harris

10 Romancing the Church: Nineteenth-Century Romanticism in the Twenty-First Century Church | 147
    —Peter Elliott

11 Cultural Exegesis: Missiological Pragmatism or Theological Imperative? | 160
    —Stephen Garner

12 The Goldilocks Planet—When It's Just Not Right: Psalm 24, The Environment, and Human Responsibility | 176
    —David J. Cohen

13 Atonement and Church | 193
    —Scot McKnight

14 The Spirit—Beyond Christ? Christian Witness in a Plural World | 206
    —Carolyn Eng Looi Tan

15 Transcending Morality: The Church and Christian Living in a Post-Christian World | 223
    —Andre van Oudtshoorn

Contributors

Allan Chapple is Senior Lecturer in New Testament at Trinity Theological College, Perth, Western Australia. His doctorate in New Testament studies is from Durham University in the UK. He has previously served as a pastor in both Western Australia and the north-east of England, as a faculty member of the Seminari Theoloji Malaysia, and as a staff worker for the Australian Fellowship of Evangelical Students.

David Cohen has been Head of Department of Biblical Studies, and Lecturer in Hebrew Bible and Language at Vose Seminary since 2004. He is a specialist in the book of Psalms and has published a number of articles especially on the psalms of lament. He is the author of *Praying Lament Psalms* and *Why O Lord? Praying our Sorrows*, and has edited a number of books.

Peter Elliott has been lecturing in theological institutions for nearly a quarter of a century, primarily in Church History. His recent research interests have focused on Edward Irving, the Catholic Apostolic Church, and Pentecostal precursors. His PhD was published as *Edward Irving: Romantic Theology in Crisis* (2013). Peter is currently an adjunct lecturer at Sheridan College, a research supervisor at Alphacrucis College, and an Honorary Research Fellow at Murdoch University.

Stephen Garner is Academic Dean and Senior Lecturer in Theology at Laidlaw College in Auckland, Aotearoa New Zealand. With a background in both computer science and theology, his teaching and research focuses upon the intersection of theology, science, technology, and media, as well as public and contextual theology. His publications include the edited volume *Theology and the Body: Reflections on Being Flesh and Blood* (2011) and *Networked Theology: Negotiating Faith in Digital Culture* (2016) with Heidi Campbell. He is married to Kim with four children and worships at Massey Presbyterian Church in West Auckland.

Brian Harris, an internationally regarded teacher and communicator, has served as Principal of Vose Seminary since 2004. He leads the Department of Ministry and Practice. Originally from South Africa, Brian has pastored churches in his home country, New Zealand, and Australia. He has published many journal articles and is the author of a number of books, especially his trilogy, *The Tortoise Usually Wins*, *The Big Picture*, and *When Faith Turns Ugly*. Brian blogs at https://brianharrisauthor.com/.

John McClean is Vice-Principal at Christ College, the Presbyterian theological college in Sydney where he teaches systematic theology and ethics. He has published an introduction to the thought of Wolfhart Pannenberg, a short introduction to Christian doctrine (*Real God for the Real World*), as well as a wide range of articles and book chapters. He is an elder at Springwood-Winmalee Presbyterian Church and serves the wider Presbyterian Church in the areas of ethics, apologetics, and social policy.

Scot McKnight is an internationally regarded New Testament scholar, a sought-after speaker with a global following, and author of numerous articles, biblical commentaries, and books on a variety of topics. He is the Julius R. Mantey Chair of New Testament at Northern Seminary in Chicago, and a recognized authority on the historical Jesus, early Christianity, and the New Testament. His *Jesus Creed* is a leading Christian blog.

John Olley served as Principal of Baptist Theological College of Western Australia (now Vose Seminary) for thirteen years, and as Head of Old Testament for twenty-five years, retiring in 2003. John has published many articles and books including *Ezekiel* in the Septuagint Commentary Series, and *The Message of Kings* in the Bible Speaks Today series. John continues as a Research Fellow of Vose Seminary, serves as Chair of the Missiological Advisory Committee of Global Interaction, and on the board of Carey Baptist Church in Perth.

Michael O'Neil has been teaching Christian Thought and History at Vose Seminary since 2010, after serving as a pastor in several churches over a twenty-year period. He has published articles and a book (*Church as Moral Community*) on the theology of Karl Barth, as well as articles and chapters on matters to do with the Christian life and ethics. Michael is married to Monica, and together they have three adult children, and a growing number of grandchildren.

Karen Siggins is Senior Minister of Lesmurdie Baptist Church and Chair of the Board of the Council of Baptist Churches of Western Australia. As a minister her aim is to be part of a church family who would be immediately missed by its community if it were to close its doors. Karen lives her life according to the principle that God is love and everything else is a theological footnote. Karen is married to Hadyn and together they have three adult children and a cadre of six marvellous grandchildren.

Carolyn Eng Looi Tan, whose background is Malaysian-Singaporean, previously worked as a paediatric surgeon. She came to Perth in Western Australia to pursue theological studies at the Baptist College of Western Australia (later renamed Vose Seminary). She graduated with a Master of Divinity in 2009, and subsequently engaged in doctoral research into the role of the Holy Spirit at the cross. Her contribution in this book is part of that research. Carolyn was awarded her Doctorate of Theology in 2017, and her thesis has been published in the ACT Monograph Series in a volume entitled "The Spirit at the Cross: Exploring a Cruciform Pneumatology." Meanwhile, she teaches New Testament Greek at Vose Seminary, is active in various leadership roles in Perth Baptist Church, looks after her aging parents, and whenever time allows, attends to her vegetable plot.

Andre van Oudtshoorn is the Academic Dean at Perth Bible College. He has written devotional books on divine election, theology of worship, and Christology. His latest book, *A Taste of Glory: An Introduction to Theological Studies* is a prescribed text in a number of theological colleges.

Margaret Wesley serves as an Anglican minister in Brisbane, after having taught at Mary Andrews College in Sydney for a number of years. She is the author of *Jesus, Son of Mary: The Family of Jesus and the Community of Faith in the Fourth Gospel*, and editor of *Loss and Discovery: Responding to Grief with the Compassion of Christ and the Skills of All God's People*.

Introduction

> "Jesus foretold the kingdom, and
> it was the church that came."[1]

ALFRED LOISY'S SOMEWHAT CAUSTIC or possibly disappointed statement from the early twentieth century captures something of the modern disquiet with the church that continues and has even increased into the early decades of the twenty-first century. Put simply, in many parts of the world the church is "on the nose," in some cases with good reason. We live in an environment in which trust in traditional institutions has fallen dramatically, especially those institutions associated with formal religion. In many places in the modern West, churches have shut their doors and sold their buildings, their congregations having dwindled to a level where it was no longer viable to continue ministry in that location. Ironically, those buildings are often situated in population centers with many people surrounding them but not entering them. It seems that the witness of the church, in these instances at least, has failed. The decline in church attendance among the young, and the rise of the "nones" in national census data have become topics of conversation not only in denominational meetings and academic journals, but in the newspapers.

And yet, there are still those who believe in the church the way those did who framed the Christian creed at Constantinople in 381 AD; that is, that the church itself is part of the gospel proclaimed by the church: "We

---

1. Loisy, cited in Marshall, "Church," 122. Loisy's statement is from *Evangile et l'Eglise*, published in Paris in 1902.

believe in one, holy, catholic, and apostolic church," just as we believe also in "One God, the Father Almighty . . . and in One Lord Jesus Christ, the Son of God . . . And in the Holy Spirit, the Lord and Giver of life." There are those who despite the very real, checkered history of the church, who despite its historical and present failures and foibles, still maintain the faith of the creed, that the church itself is an integral part of God's redemptive purposes being worked out in history, and that God's call to the church is now what it has always been: to be the faithful people of God, bearing joy-filled witness to the resurrection of Jesus Christ in word, worship, and work, in its corporate life, and in the lives of each of its members.

On the one hand, therefore, disquiet and even rejection of the church and all that it represents; on the other, a sobering recognition of the failures and unfaithfulness of the church, and yet a heartfelt yearning that the church might by divine grace be restored to the kind of faithfulness that does indeed bear a joyful and vibrant witness to Jesus Christ in every time and place. It should come as no surprise that the women and men who have contributed to this volume are amongst those who long for a better future for the church, and who have hope that this will, in fact, be the case. The basis of this hope is not the church's ability to rectify its mess or to generate its own faithfulness. Rather, this hope is grounded in Jesus Christ, the head of the church, in the ongoing work of the Holy Spirit to convict and convert the church that it might yet become what it is called to be, and in the power of the word of the gospel which continues to gather, renew, build up, and send forth the people of God. The mixed affair that is the history of the church has seen some very low points indeed. But Jesus Christ has never and will never abandon his people: "I will build my church and the gates of Hades will not overpower it" (Matt 16:18). The word of God is not bound; even if we his people have been unfaithful, he remains faithful and will deny neither himself nor his promise (2 Tim 2:8, 13). This is our hope for the church. Indeed, Jesus Christ is our *only* hope!

The papers in this volume had their genesis in a conference at Vose Seminary in Perth, Western Australia, a few years ago. The theme of the conference has given us the title of the book: *Beyond Four Walls*. The purpose of the conference was to explore what it means to *be* the church, with a particular recognition that the church is not an end in itself but exists for the service of God, and for participation in the divine mission of reconciliation and redemption in the world. The Vose Conference aims to equip the churches, ministers, and Christians in our region of the world with thoughtful, relevant, theological reflection on matters of primary importance. We aim to bridge the divide that sometimes emerges between the practice of theology in academic institutions and the work of the church in its everyday ministry.

Our guest for this conference was renowned speaker, author, and blogger, Scot McKnight. Scot and his wife Kris joined us a few days before the conference, enjoying a couple of days in the famed Margaret River area of Western Australia to recover from the long flight. Kris assured me that despite the jet lag, Scot managed occasionally to drive on the "right" side of the road! During his time in Perth Scot preached in a couple of churches, met with New Testament scholars from a number of theological institutions in the city, and presented several very well-received papers at the conference. We were delighted that he and Kris were willing and able to join us in Perth, and very glad that Scot has allowed us to reproduce his papers in this volume. We have retained, in his chapters, the informal nature of his presentations that communicated clearly, simply, and powerfully to our pastors and friends at the conference, and we hope that you gain a sense of the vitality of his sessions.

Scot's keynote sessions were supplemented by more than two dozen other papers given by scholars from Australia and New Zealand, a selection of which form the rest of this volume. Presenters were given freedom to reflect broadly on the nature and mission of the church, from biblical, historical, theological, philosophical, missiological, or practical perspectives. Some presenters focused very clearly on the life and role of the Christian community in its engagement with culture *beyond* the four walls of the church, while others explored what it means to *be* the church *within* the four walls, though still with a view to its broader responsibility in the world. We have chosen to organize the volume loosely around these two categories of paper. The first eight chapters lean a little more toward an exploration of the being and activity of the church "within the four walls," while the latter seven chapters turn more decisively to consider the being and activity of the church in its cultural context and engagement beyond its walls. The common theme provides an overall unity for the volume, while the range of particular topics and perspectives enriches and deepens our appreciation for the "manifold wisdom of God" which is given to the church as both a divine gift and task (Eph 3:10). Our hope is that you will find much to inform and interest, to consider and discuss, as you make your way through the various essays in this volume.

In the first of his three chapters, "Church as Gospel," Scot McKnight makes two fundamental claims. First, he argues that many Christians and traditions, including evangelical believers, have misunderstood what the gospel actually is, and so present truncated versions of the gospel. Second, after having established his own understanding of what the gospel is, he argues further that the church is to so inhabit the story and vision of the gospel as it is presented in the New Testament, that it *embodies* the gospel in its life in the world. It is true, of course, that we often embody things other than the gospel. King Solomon, for example, might be seen as an embodiment of wisdom, wealth, and power. Drawing on the depiction of Solomon's life in Kings, John Olley demonstrates that God's presence and provision flow in surprising ways between the powerful and the powerless—the outsiders—those "beyond the wall." Solomon's trajectory is depicted as a salutary reminder for leaders in any age, that what often appears to be glorious success may very well be the path to failure.

The relationship between the people of God and outside nations is also the focus of the book of Jonah. Michael O'Neil shows how the petulant prophet demonstrates the interplay between divine and human agency, while also highlighting that the purpose of God's people was (and is) to be a blessing to the nations. Jonah, Israel, and the church were or are called to move beyond self-serving security and comfort to become renewed and reflecting communities, embracing the fact that election *is* commission.

Everyday life in Christian community is influenced by a host of different variables, not least those personal and interpersonal dynamics brought by the person to their involvement in the congregation. Margaret Wesley shows that the New Testament uses the metaphor of family to describe the church and argues that the Christian family and family of origin are very alike in many ways. She explores the complexity of being in two families at once, and the healthy and unhealthy ways we can manage the tension between those two families.

Continuing a consideration of the dynamics of congregational life, Allan Chapple notes that for some years, pastors and church leaders have been deluged by material on the subject of church leadership. Should pastors be CEOs? Managers? "Ranchers"? Differences between biblical leadership models and management models are explored by Chapple, including the tension between authority *in* the church versus ownership *over* the church. Drawing on Paul's final words to the elders of Ephesus in Acts 20, the focus of Christian leadership is identified, and its comprehensive, costly, and countercultural aspects are highlighted. The focus on Christian leadership, together with a discussion of the power of spoken words, continues in Scot McKnight's second chapter. McKnight turns to the letter of James to examine the power of the tongue and the implications for pastor–teachers. Beneath the choice to opt for either words of wisdom or words as weapons is the deeper choice between humility and peace in the face of criticism or the desire for control.

Those outside the four walls of the church often notice the contradictions between the statements of churches and their actions. The paper by Karen Siggins focuses on the discrepancy between the stated position of many Baptist churches regarding women in senior ministry roles, and their praxis. Multigenerational churches contain multiple perspectives and assumptions about women's leadership, and Siggins warns that there is a real risk of losing the ministry of gifted women, ironically at a time when many congregations are in decline.

Each generation considers anew what it means to be the church, but how should we respond to ancient models from the Mediterranean world? John McClean argues that biblical descriptions of church are neither redundant nor straitjackets, but rather function as paradigms. In a series of argued theses he calls the church to be grounded in the mission of God, recognizing the value of culture without identifying with it. The church must function as a fractured foretaste of the kingdom if it is to fulfill its calling as an instrument of the kingdom.

Another factor affecting the faithfulness and response of the Western church to cultural challenges has been the tension between individuality and community, which has often resulted in the folly of the isolated self. Brian Harris exhorts the church to move beyond a social-club mentality, and to take its bearings from the activity of the three divine persons in the world, and in so doing to become a community of "surprise, embrace, and witness." Such a church will be hospitable and apologetic in its orientation toward the world, open to new ways and forms of life and service. Harris argues that an incarnational and Trinitarian ecclesiology will produce a church that is persuasive, inviting, and winsome.

An exaltation of individualism was also one of the characteristics of nineteenth-century Romanticism, which Peter Elliott examines, using the ministry of Edward Irving as a case study. Romanticism caused a seismic shift in the theological thought of the nineteenth century, and its ongoing (and often paradoxical) relevance to contemporary Christianity in the areas of spiritual gifts, hermeneutics, the ministry of the laity, and leadership roles is demonstrated.

The perennial dialogue between Christianity and culture is examined by Stephen Garner, who acknowledges that gospel always critiques culture, but goes beyond this to consider how culture critiques the church, and to argue that one responsibility of the church is to listen to, assess, and receive such critique. Popular-culture examples are used to demonstrate ways in which the church has failed to communicate effectively, as well as showing opportunities for doing so, leading to the view that cultural exegesis is a theological imperative.

In his essay, David Cohen takes one of contemporary culture's controversial topics—concern for the environment—and examines it through the lens of Psalm 24. The discussion is grounded firmly in the historical context of ancient Israel and focuses on the roles of Yahweh and humanity. With Yahweh acknowledged as agent and owner of creation, does this mean humanity is essentially left with a passive role concerning the natural world and its order? This chapter argues towards a more nuanced, complex, and deeply theological conclusion.

Scot McKnight's final chapter in this volume draws together several themes, including the distinctively missionary character of the apostolic church, the embodiment of Jesus in and through his people, and the powerful reimagining of temple imagery to show how revolutionary the church was (and is). Christians are exhorted to continue living the reality of the atonement, with special recognition of the power of baptism and eucharist.

Yet how can the distinctiveness of Christianity be maintained amidst a plethora of competing belief systems in a world clamoring for inclusiveness? Carolyn Tan assesses a recent argument posed by Amos Yong and Veli-Matti Kärkkäinen that the work of the Holy Spirit present in other religions is a sign of God's providential activity within those religions, and a sound basis for interfaith dialogue. Tan responds to these arguments with a close analysis of the New Testament's portrayal of the Holy Spirit as the Spirit of Christ.

The final chapter requires us to think through the implications of the life of faith for behavior and moral choice. Interacting with a variety of thinkers such as Socrates, Hume, Kierkegaard, and Nietzsche, Andre van Oudtshoorn challenges the idea that an objective standard can ever be reached for value-based ethics. Ethics cannot be contained by pure rationalism, and although it strives to be universal, cannot be divorced from subjectivity. Christian morality is presented as essentially theological and pneumatological, and thereby based on a radically subversive view of reality.

Vose Seminary is a member institution of the Australian College of Theology (ACT), and we would like to express our gratitude for the generous support the ACT has given both for the conference, and subsequently for assistance in preparing this volume for publication.

Finally, it is our privilege and delight to dedicate this volume to Dr. Richard K. Moore. Richard is a valued teacher, friend, and esteemed colleague who was Head of New Testament at the Baptist Theological College of Western Australia (now Vose Seminary) until his retirement in 2002, having served the college for twenty-four years. During this period Richard pursued a lifelong quest to understand and explicate the apostle Paul's doctrine of justification, taught New Testament, and supervised candidates undertaking research degrees in New Testament. He has published a number of books, including a three-volume treatment of *Paul's Doctrine of Rectification* (Edwin Mellen), works on the history of Baptists in Western Australia, including a biography of Dr. Noel Vose, the founding principal of the seminary and former President of the Baptist World Alliance, and *Under the Southern Cross: The New Testament in Australian English* (2014). In retirement Richard, together with his wife Kath, have remained active in scholarship, and in the life of the seminary and the Baptist churches of Western Australia, contributing generously to the ongoing work of the church both within and beyond its four walls. We, and many others, are the richer for his scholarship, support, and encouragement.

Michael D. O'Neil

Peter Elliott

Perth, 2020

Bibliography

Marshall, I. Howard. "Church." In *Dictionary of Jesus and the Gospels*, edited by Joel B. Green et al., 122–25. Downers Grove: IVP, 1992.

I

Church as Gospel

Scot McKnight

You probably know that I am from Illinois in the United States, and so I want to introduce you to an Illinoisan expression. When we wonder in Illinois if something is credible and real, practicable and true, we ask "But will it play in Peoria?" If it plays in Peoria, an ordinary blue-collar community in Illinois, it will play everywhere. My claim today is that the proposal being made today about the gospel is the sort of thing that will play in Peoria. My two claims are these: As evangelicals, and even more broadly, *we have misdefined the gospel*. And second, *the church—both the universal and the local—is the gospel*. Both of these, of course, need nuances, and I shall proceed now to make my case for both.

The Gospel

An irony in the contemporary (American, at least) evangelical scene is that there's a genuine battle for the gospel. It's the one thing we ought to have figured out by now but it's one of the elements of our faith that genuinely is being debated today. In broad strokes I think I can say there are two poles to this discussion in the US. On the left pole one finds people like Peter Gomes, the well-known preacher at Harvard's Memorial Church, or Brian McLaren's *The Secret Message of Jesus* which was then clarified sociopolitically in

Everything Must Change.[1] Keeping to a broad brush, the left pole is to one degree or another a social justice or liberation theology gospel, and in this framework the gospel means more or less justice. Justice, I fear, means what the French handed on to moderns: freedom, fellowship, and equality, and tied into them a sense of human rights. I banked on each of these in our trip from Chicago to Perth, and I value these elements of a Western sense of justice, and each of them in some ways flows directly from what the Bible says about justice, but the earliest Christian rock band, Peter, Paul, and Jesus, would simply not recognize this sense of justice as what they meant by "gospel." These forms of justice may well be good for society today, but they simply aren't what the word "gospel" means. The essence of liberalism is to colonize the Bible, theology, and the gospel into culture. This left pole is guilty of colonizing the gospel into Western values.

If the left understands the gospel as justice, the right considers it as justification. From John Piper, who asked if Jesus preached Paul's gospel—and by that wondered if Jesus preached justification by faith alone, to Greg Gilbert's new book *What is the Gospel?*, this group of pastors and theologians believe the gospel is justification by faith, and by this they mean justification as understood in the Reformation. Without a hint of reductionism, the essence of this gospel is double imputation and the necessity for the sinner to dig deeply into his or her own dark heart to see the glory of this truth in order truly to be saved or to have comprehended the gospel.[2] Still, Gilbert's book perfectly meshes with the standard understanding of the gospel that one hears in most forms of evangelism, from John Stott and Billy Graham, to Nicky Gumbel: God is creator, God is loving but holy, humans are made in God's image but are sinners under God's wrath, Jesus came to die so that wrath can be averted, and all one must do is to believe that message—faith alone—and so attain salvation to spend eternity with God. Gilbert's approach is more nuanced, but he has four points: God (and love is minimized in his sketch), man as sinner, Christ, and faith. Yes, each of these elements is true and can be found in the Bible but Jesus, Peter, and Paul would not recognize that gospel as their gospel. In other words, I'm unconvinced either of these gospels will play in the Peoria of the New Testament. I am convinced they *do* play in modern Peorias because both are forms of colonizing the gospel to the agendas of our own culture. Those are strong claims and they will be supported in what follows.

---

1. See Gomes, *Scandalous Gospel*; McLaren, *Secret Message*; *Everything Must Change*.

2. See Piper, *God is the Gospel*, and Gilbert, *What is the Gospel?*

Before I sketch how Jesus and the apostles understood the gospel, I want to make three brief points. The first is that many of us, and I include myself, *came to Christ when someone preached that gospel as the gospel*. So, whatever I have to say in what follows does not diminish that this gospel *has worked, works, and will probably continue to work*. Second, this word "works" deserves attention. The correlation of those who respond to that four- or five-step gospel and those who follow Christ as disciples is not high. David Kinnamon, who is now President of the Barna Research organization, showed me some numbers once wherein it was clear that about 90 percent of children who grow up in evangelical homes "make a decision for Christ" but only about 20 percent can be said to be "following Christ" when they are in their thirties. The research doesn't show this, but does anyone doubt that the gospel those 90 percent heard was more or less the gospel we sketched above? The third point now will begin to scrape the chalkboard: *the four-point approach in the standard evangelical gospel is our doctrine of salvation arranged into a compelling, convicting, guilt-producing, rhetorical bundle*. What drives this gospel, though, has begun to change in the last decade or so, with a marked decline in the idea that God is the kind of judge who will send someone to suffer consciously in hell for all eternity if they don't respond to the offer of the good news. What many of us grew up with then was a rhetorically effective bundling of the doctrine of salvation shaped to precipitate decisions that would relieve our deepest angst about God and our eternal state, and what drove that bundle was the threat of judgment and hell. Jesus, then, was sent to give us a chance to escape the wrath of God.

Again, I do not question any of the four points or anything I've said about salvation in the previous comments. I believe in God's judgment, and I believe that Jesus saves us, and I believe that God loves us. But, and here's the scraping part, *this is not what Jesus, or Peter, or Paul meant when they used the word "gospel."* What, then, did they mean?

Leg One: 1 Corinthians 15

To answer this question, we have to ask *how* we are to answer this question. In good Protestant fashion we have to go to the Bible, and that means we are in search of a text that *defines* gospel, and happily we've got one: 1 Corinthians 15. But when we go to 1 Corinthians 15, something in the text immediately jumps up at us and says "Surprise, surprise!" Why? Because the one text that defines gospel in the entire New Testament tells us that the gospel is neither "justice" nor "justification." Instead, it tells us that the gospel announces the resolution to a story. To be sure, that story saves, effecting both justification and justice, but what drives the gospel according to 1 Corinthians is neither the injustice of this world that needs to be set aright, nor our sins—Adamic and personal—that need to be forgiven. And neither does it suggest that the problem the gospel resolves is God's wrath. What drives the justice gospel is social systems gone awry and what drives the justification gospel is personal rebellion leading to guilt, but what drives the apostolic gospel of 1 Corinthians 15 is something else.

I will make seven observations about the apostolic gospel, and I will then suggest that this fresh perspective on the gospel throws piercing light on church praxis and mission in our world today. Rerun: what played in the original Peoria of the New Testament will play as well in modern and postmodern Peorias. But it will require that we make some adjustments in our minds and praxis.

First, a historical claim: before there was a New Testament, before the apostles wrote letters, before the Gospels were written, there was the gospel. When it comes to the Christian faith, in the beginning was the gospel. The gospel created the church, and the Gospels. The gospel created the Epistles, and the gospel created the New Testament, and the canon.

Second, there is dispute about which verses of this text are the gospel. Some say only verses three to five refer to the gospel while others see it extending from verse three through to verse eight. But in light of what we will see of the gospel elsewhere in the New Testament, and all the way to the Nicene Creed, we might do ourselves the favor of thinking that Paul, though he can chase a few tangents here and there, never left the gospel and that it extends from verse three through to verse twenty-eight.

Third, the gospel of 1 Corinthians 15 is not Paul's gospel as if he were the first to articulate it. The gospel of 1 Corinthians 15, made clear in Paul's own words in verses 1–3, is *the one and only apostolic gospel that was passed on in oral form from the very beginning by all apostolic Christians.* This is not Paul's gospel; this is the *apostolic* gospel and therefore Paul's gospel.

Fourth, the gospel is defined *by events in Jesus's life*. In crisp formulae we find four rapidly narrated events in verses 3–5: he died, he was buried, he was raised, and he appeared. If we continue to verse 28, we need to add that he was exalted, and he will reign, and he will return, and he will hand over to the Father. Instead of four *spiritual laws*, we get four (or more) *events in the life of Jesus*. I cannot emphasize this contrast enough. The gospel of evangelicalism is an abstracted system of salvation and even transaction; the gospel of the apostles was a story about Jesus. I'm not saying this to be cute or provocative; I'm saying this because it's what 1 Corinthians 15 says.

Fifth, the word "gospel" means to "announce" or to "declare," and what is declared according to 1 Corinthians 15 is that *Israel's story has come to its fitting completion in the story of Jesus.* "To gospel," then, was to announce that Jesus of Nazareth was the Messiah and the destined goal of the story of Israel. This is made clear in verses 3–5 in the words "according to the Scriptures" but it is found in the constant resonances of verses 3–28 to the Old Testament narrative. What drives this story is neither injustice nor the need for personal salvation but the need for a king for Israel. Jesus is that king.

Sixth, this story about Jesus *saves.* Or better, Jesus saves, but the Jesus who saves is the Jesus of this story of Israel. He's the Savior of Israel. But the defining word for Jesus in the gospel is that he is *Messiah and Lord.* As Messiah and as Lord he is Savior. Once a young man wrote me an e-mail and asked this question: what does Jesus being Messiah have to do with the gospel? We've got a problem if we are asking that question. We're so far from the original Peoria we don't even know where it is! The reason the e-mailer asked that question was because he understood the gospel not as justice but as personal salvation from God's wrath and his personal sin, and Jesus being a Jewish Messiah had so little to do with it, he was having trouble making sense of the only narrative that the Bible tells. But, still and without any reduction, this story saves. In verse 3, Paul says Jesus "died for our sins." There is no explicit atonement theory here because for the apostles the effect of the gospel was salvation, however it happened.

Seventh, the gospel is a complete story of Jesus. It has been said, and it deserves to be said often, that for most Christians, and here I blanket the entire church—Orthodoxy, Catholicism, and Protestantism—the only event in the life of Jesus of significance was his death. They have a Good Friday gospel. But the gospel of the apostles included his life as well as his death and his burial, and his resurrection and his exaltation. It's a complete life that has to be told if we wish to announce the gospel.

Before I push on, a tangent for you to think about. I grew up reading the Bible through a salvation hermeneutic that went something like this: Creation, Fall, Redemption, and Consummation, sometimes abbreviated C-F-R-C. One year while teaching the whole Bible to a group of first year college students it dawned on me, that no one in the Bible revealed that he or she read the Bible like that until Romans 5 and 1 Corinthians 15. Furthermore, if we are bound to restrict the gospel to verses 3–5 or 3–8, then we will have to admit that the C-F-R-C narrative is not the gospel but a salvation story. But, as I said earlier, it is wiser to extend the gospel to verse 28, and if we do that, there is at least the reality of the C-F-R-C in the apostolic gospel statement. But there the focus is not so much on the death of Christ but the resurrection of Christ.

Let me now summarize: we have seen that in the one and only place where the term is actually defined the gospel refers to the narration of the entire story of Jesus as the completion of the story of Israel and that this narrative story of Jesus saves us from our sins. To "gospel," then, means to tell this story of Jesus as the saving story. I believe we've got the saving part down pat, and we've ignored the story almost entirely.

Leg Two: The Sermons in Acts

But it is the story that is precisely what two other major elements of the New Testament understanding of the gospel tell us as well. If the first leg in our stool is the apostolic definition of the gospel in 1 Corinthians, the *second element is the apostolic gospel sermons in Acts*. There are in fact seven of them, unless you count Stephen's speech, in which case there are eight. I don't, but that's because it ends with finger pointing instead of a call to conversion.

Sit down some day and read Acts 2, 3, 4, 10–11, 13, 14, and 17. Then read them all over again carefully with this question: If these two apostles, Peter and Paul, are gospelling in these passages, what was *their* gospel? What was the gospel of their gospelling sermons? I hope you conclude what I concluded a few years back, and I hope you don't do what I did. I was writing books on the gospel and atonement, one of which was popular, called *Embracing Grace*, and one for a more pastoral context, *A Community Called Atonement*. When I was working on those books, I was convinced that the gospel was the message of salvation, and in that work I happened quite often onto the sermons in Acts and kept saying to myself: *but these apostolic sermons don't do what I'm doing.* I didn't think the apostles were wrong, but they didn't fit how I was describing a salvation and atonement theory. Because I didn't think that I might be wrong, I ignored Acts. But for a lecture on the book of Acts I was to give at the University of Stellenbosch, I decided to work on the gospel in the book of Acts, and I have to confess it was one of the rare academic experiences where everything fell into place, not unlike the way Chesterton described his conversion. Formerly I couldn't quite figure out what to make of the apostolic gospel sermons in Acts, but I thought I had salvation more or less figured out. But in working on that lecture for South Africa, it suddenly dawned on me that what I was calling "gospel" was not what Peter and Paul would have called gospel. Instead, the word "gospel" refers to something else.

What was that? Go ahead, read Acts 2, 3, 4, 10–11, 13, 14, and 17[3] and you will no doubt conclude what I concluded. The gospel of the apostles

---

3. More precisely: Acts 2:14–39; 3:12–26; 4:8–12; 10:34–43 with 11:4–18; 13:16–41;

was not the "plan of salvation" or "how to get saved" or atonement theory or anything like what the "left" or the "right" said it was. Instead, those seven apostolic sermons had one and the same perception of the gospel: it is *the announcement that the narrative of Israel's story had come to completion in the story of Jesus as Israel's Messiah and Lord*. In other words, the sermons in the book of Acts take the gospel of 1 Corinthians 15 and make it sing and sting in real, live preaching. Seven sermons are hard to digest at once and they are also hard to synthesize into a few words, so I'll just make a couple observations. But before I do that let me quote from the heart of Peter's gospel sermon to Cornelius, who lived in Caesarea Maritima, the newly fashioned city built by Herod the Great. We were in Caesarea recently and it struck me as a really good place to explain the gospel to gentiles, which is just what Peter did.

> Then Peter began to speak: "I now realize how true it is that God does not show favoritism but accepts from every nation the one who fears him and does what is right. You know the message God sent to the people of Israel, announcing the good news of peace through Jesus Christ, who is Lord of all. You know what has happened throughout the province of Judea, beginning in Galilee after the baptism that John preached—how God anointed Jesus of Nazareth with the Holy Spirit and power, and how he went around doing good and healing all who were under the power of the devil, because God was with him.
>
> "We are witnesses of everything he did in the country of the Jews and in Jerusalem. They killed him by hanging him on a cross, but God raised him from the dead on the third day and caused him to be seen. He was not seen by all the people, but by witnesses whom God had already chosen—by us who ate and drank with him after he rose from the dead. He commanded us to preach to the people and to testify that he is the one whom God appointed as judge of the living and the dead. All the prophets testify about him that everyone who believes in him receives forgiveness of sins through his name." (Acts 10:34–43)

First, the gospel in Acts is driven by the story of Israel coming to completion in the story of Jesus, and in particular in the glories of his resurrection and exaltation. Observe as you read the texts in Acts how frequently the apostles Peter and Paul are using Old Testament texts. In the text I just quoted, Peter caps it off with this: "All the prophets testify about him" (10:43). Second, these apostolic gospel sermons declare the whole story about Jesus:

14:15–17; 17:22–31. If we add Stephen's speech, 7:2–53.

life, death, burial, resurrection, and vindication. Third, they make claims about Jesus, calling him Messiah, Lord, Prince, Servant, Holy and Righteous One, the Author of Life, and the Prophet. Peter said in Acts 2:36, at the concluding point of his sermon, that "God has made this Jesus, whom you crucified, both Lord and Messiah." It can be said, in other words, that gospelling is about hermeneutics: it's about how to make sense of history in light of *who Jesus is*. My fourth point, which would take weeks to unpack, is that Paul's gospelling involves adaptation to gentile contexts in such a way that the story of Israel is extended into new categories and new terms. In Acts 17 one needs to read the lines and between the lines when Paul is preaching on the Areopagus. What we discover here is that Paul keeps the story about Jesus and his resurrection, he anchors it in the story of Israel, and he points his fingers at his listeners to tell them they are accountable to God. Which leads to my fifth and final point: gospelling in the book of Acts leads to a summons to repent, to believe, and to be baptized. No gospelling is complete unless it calls people to turn from self-control to surrender to what God tells us in the story of Jesus.

To sum up again: what is the gospel in the gospelling sermons in Acts? Plain and simple, it is that the story of Israel is now fulfilled in the story of Jesus's life, in his messianic ministry, his death, his burial, his resurrection, and his vindication by being exalted to the right hand of God. It's the same gospel that we find in 1 Corinthians 15. This gospel is not driven by the need for personal salvation; it is not driven by an atonement theory; it is not even driven by the grace or love or holiness of God. Instead, it is driven from beginning to end by the story of Israel coming to completion in Jesus. "To gospel" is to announce that Jesus is the Messiah and Lord. That story, if this needs to be said, awakens people to their own life, to their own usurpation of God's role in their life, and to their need to repent, confess, believe, and be baptized. But notice that the apostles did not manipulate their audience in order to manufacture decisions; instead, they were confident in the story of Jesus and they declared that gospel boldly.

Third Leg: The Gospels and the Gospel

One more point and then we'll consider what it means for the church to be the gospel today. If we want to understand the gospel, we have to go to the apostolic definition, 1 Corinthians 15. And we have to go to the apostolic gospel sermons, for the apostles ought to know what the gospel is and how to preach it, and those are found in Acts. The third leg is almost cheeky in how it surprises us. Here it is, and I make this point by asking a question:

Why do you think the Gospel writers and especially the early churches called the first four books of the New Testament *the gospel*? The answer is simple, and it virtually clinches our case: they called Matthew, Mark, Luke, and John "*the gospel according to . . .*" because *the first four books of the New Testament are the gospel.* They were not using the term "gospel" as a genre, as we do today. They were marking the *substance and content* of the first four books, and they called them the gospel.

The point needs emphasis. Again, when we say they are gospels we are not speaking of a kind of literature, a genre. Instead, we're saying that they called Matthew "the gospel" because Matthew's Gospel *is the gospel.* Why are they the gospel? Did they preach justification by faith? Penal substitution? Double imputation? A new kind of justice? A new kind of peace? Well, you can try hard as you want to show they did, but the honest soul knows that when he or she is done trying to wrestle the first four books into those terms that it could only be accomplished with force and coercion and twists and pleadings to make them say those things. I'm suggesting this is wrongheaded. If you equate gospel with justification by faith, as the right does, you will be disappointed with the Gospels, and that is one reason why some today avoid the Gospels when they preach and why some are wondering if they are preliminary to the gospel. In other words, though I'm putting cheeky words in their mouths, they are saying, "Poor Jesus, born on the wrong side of the cross, didn't get to preach the full gospel." What I'm saying is that some are driven to this because they have failed to ask basic questions and go to the basic texts. They failed to ask if it plays in the original Peoria. My friend, I'm appealing to you to reconsider the original gospel. The gospel is defined in 1 Corinthians 15, it is preached in the book of Acts, and it is *detailed in the four Gospels.*

So here is our conclusion: the Gospels are called the gospel (always singular, never plural) because they are preeminently the gospel. I quote an Australian, John Dickson, which ought to clinch my point: "All of the Scriptures point to the gospel, but *only the Gospels recount the gospel in all its fullness. The Gospels and the gospel are one.*"[4] If Dickson is right, and our sketch above suggests he is, do you realize what this means for evangelism? What this means for the basic framework of theology?

We need not delay: if we are right on 1 Corinthians 15 and the gospel sermons in Acts, you can see why the Gospels are called *The Gospel*: because they, too, tell the story of Israel coming to completion in the complete story of Jesus as King and as the one who saves us from our sins. To make this point one other way: when asking if Jesus preached the gospel, it is

---

4. Dickson, *Best Kept Secret*, 140, emphasis added.

customary to show how Jesus's *soteriology* fits ours, or Paul's soteriology. After wrangling with the texts long enough to show they fit, we stand up with a flag of victory and say, "See there, Jesus preached the gospel." But this is mistaken if we are right about the gospel. Instead, we need to be asking this: "Do the Gospel writers, and does Jesus himself, make sense of life by showing that Jesus is himself the completion of Israel's story?" We don't ask first, "Does Jesus preach justification?" We ask first, "Does Jesus preach himself?" I could go on, my point has been made.

Church as Gospel

Our aim today is not just to argue this theological point about what the gospel was in the original Peoria, even if it is arguably the single-most important theological point that needs to be made. Instead, I want to tie the church to the gospel by saying *the church is designed to be the gospel*. This immediately connects us with the idea of the *missio Dei*,[5] that is, the idea that the church does not have its own mission, but that its task is to join in God's mission. Speaking of God's mission invokes words like Israel, kingdom, and church as well, although we can't resolve all these issues in this setting.[6] Probing this discussion through the window of gospel will permit us to see enough to know our task.

I'm going to circle around now and say that the church *is* the gospel *to the degree that it embodies the gospel* of 1 Corinthians 15, the sermons in Acts and the Gospels themselves. That gospel is a story—a story about Israel coming to fulfillment in the story of Jesus. In essence, then, the gospel is about Jesus, and the church is to declare that story in word and in deed. The operative word for us is "embody." But to embody that story, we have to learn the story, we will have to indwell the story, and only then can we embody the story in our world today. To each term we now turn.

Learn the Story

If we are to become truly "gospelized" people, we will have to become people of the Book, or people of the story, people who find the Bible's story about Israel, Jesus, and the church to be their defining story. We live in a biblically available culture though not a biblically literate culture. You and I have the Bibles at our fingertips, whether in "hard copy" or on our computers and

---

5. Jenson and Wilhite, *Church*, 153–91.
6. Wright, *Mission of God*.

smartphones. The Bible is available, but we don't know the Bible's story or stories. To remedy this we are going to have to read the Bible for ourselves and draw others into that Bible; and we will have to stop preaching our favorite texts and start preaching the whole Bible, and a lectionary is a good place to start; and we might begin doing more reading from the Bible during our Sunday morning services, learning the art of the public reading of large chunks of Scripture.

I want to take Mary as an example of learning to read the Bible aright, which means a good place to start is at the low point of her life as recorded in Scripture, at Mark 3:21, 31–35:

> Then Jesus entered a house, and again a crowd gathered, so that he and his disciples were not even able to eat. When his family heard about this, they went to take charge of him, for they said, "He is out of his mind." . . . Then Jesus' mother and brothers arrived. Standing outside, they sent someone in to call him. A crowd was sitting around him, and they told him, "Your mother and brothers are outside looking for you." "Who are my mother and my brothers?" he asked. Then he looked at those seated in a circle around him and said, "Here are my mother and my brothers! Whoever does God's will is my brother and sister and mother."

Mary hears of the good and unconventional deeds of Jesus down on the Sea of Galilee at Capernaum. She, along with her sons and daughters (Mark 6:3), comes to the conclusion that Jesus "is out of his mind." Dick France, after sorting out the evidence, renders the scene in these words: "Jesus' people back home [i.e., his family] have heard reports on the rowdy scenes in Capernaum, and decide that it is time to take Jesus in hand for his own sake and for the family's reputation, on that assumption that, to use a modern idiom, he has 'flipped.'"[7] We, together with the second evangelist, know Mary has got her facts wrong. Yes, she's probably worried Jesus could lose his life; yes, from what she knows, her son, who is born to be Messiah, is losing favor fast with those in power; but, no, this isn't contrary to God's will. But Mary doesn't know that.

Why? Because she believed every word the angel told her: that her son was destined to occupy the throne of David forever. Why? Because the song she sang, the *Magnificat*, sings of an imminent victory of God over the Romans and the disestablishment of injustice and the establishment of justice and peace. Why? Because her relative priest, Zechariah, said what amounts to the same thing. Why? Because whatever Simeon meant by a sword, Mary

---

7. France, *Gospel of Mark*, 167.

knew that her son was designed by God to bring the consolation of Israel. Why? Because not long ago she had seen, down the hill in Cana, a miracle beyond miracles. At the heart of each of these *why* questions was an answer that involved her son, Jesus: he would be king, he would bring justice, he would kick out the Romans, he would bring consolation, and God's power was upon him unlike anything Israel had ever seen. That was her story, and she was sticking to it. That's why Jesus was out of his mind; he evidently wasn't living out the same story.

But God had another story, and she had to learn it if she was to *learn Israel's story so that it led to her Son in the way God designed it*. She had to go back and listen again to what Simeon meant when he said a sword would pierce her own heart; she had to go back in time to Jerusalem when after traveling an entire day, perhaps all the way to Scythopolis, a Roman city over which stood the tel on which Saul was brutally exhibited, she and Joseph realized Jesus wasn't with them. So they retraced their steps, and having climbed up to the temple, they found the young messianic boy teaching the leaders of Israel. At that time, he taught Mary that he had to be about his Father's business, and Mary began to ponder what kind of boy he might be. But she knew because she had heard the angel and had sung the song and seen the miracles. She also had to go back and think of how he first responded to the request for more wine. Instead of saying "Sure, mom, check the clay pots," Jesus said, "Not now." At that moment Mary surrendered to Jesus's plans. There were, in other words, hints, but nothing was as clear as this silliness of attracting hookers and toll collectors, of hanging with fishermen and family members, and of exorcising demons and troubling the Pharisees.

Mary had to learn a different story, and eventually she did, but it may not have been until her son was publicly and humiliatingly crucified in Jerusalem, no doubt stark naked, with a mocking title over his head that Mary gained the chutzpah to believe. When did she learn? We don't know, but by the time Jesus was raised and exalted, she had come to terms with the story more completely because she was with the followers of Jesus in Acts 1 and she was there at Pentecost, and she no doubt played a role in the early fellowship in Jerusalem, and it was no doubt in part from her that Luke was able to tell the stories of Luke 1–2 and that one of her other sons, James, was able to lead the church in Jerusalem.

What was the story she had to learn? That God's story is Jesus's story. That making sense of Jesus's story is the way to make sense of God's story in this world. That her son, Jesus, was indeed the Messiah, but that he was a Messiah who would reign not by force or by coercion or by violence, but by suffering under the force, coercion, and violence of the political, military, and religious leadership of Jerusalem. But that God, her God, could raise her son back to life and exalt him above every other name, and that this story, the story of living faithfully, dying unjustly but redemptively, and being raised was the story that needed to be learned.

It's told over and over in the pages of the Bible, beginning of course with Adam, and Abraham, and Joseph, and Moses, and David, and the prophets, who in their own ways anticipate the fulfillment of God's story in the story of Jesus. But we can't become gospelers until we learn this story the way Mary had to learn it. When we do, the gospel comes alive and we can expand beyond the reductive boundaries of the gospel that so many of us learned, and learn to embrace the kind of gospel Jesus and the apostles preached.

Indwell the Story

Learning the story is the first part. It is when we *indwell* the story that we, as the church, *become the gospel by embodying it*. I'd like to take Paul the apostle, and especially as seen in Galatians, to illustrate what I mean by "indwelling" the story.

We will assume the conversion story of Paul in Acts 9. What we find is that Paul's encounter with Jesus, the resurrected, vindicated, and now speaking-to-Paul Jesus, was a one-of-a-kind explosive encounter and from that point on, Paul reframed Israel's story as a story that was fulfilled in Jesus. Allow me, though, to retrace steps by saying that Paul's conversion story is not the story of "how he got saved" so much as how he came to the conviction that Jesus was Messiah. Anyone who has studied the stories of Jews who convert to Jesus know that the conversion story is essentially one of exploring whether or not Jesus is Messiah.[8] That, I am contending, is the archetypal gospel story and gospel response.

How then did Paul "indwell" this story? He not only had learned the story inside and out, as the many references to the Old Testament and his exegesis of the Old Testament reveal, but he had learned to indwell this story. I want to draw our attention to one text, Galatians 2:15–21, which can be read as the central theological text of the entire letter.

> We who are Jews by birth and not sinful Gentiles know that a person is not justified by the works of the law, but by faith in Jesus Christ. So we, too, have put our faith in Christ Jesus that

---

8. See McKnight and Ondrey, *Finding Faith*.

> we may be justified by faith in Christ and not by the works of the law, because by the works of the law no one will be justified.
>
> "But if, in seeking to be justified in Christ, we Jews find ourselves also among the sinners, doesn't that mean that Christ promotes sin? Absolutely not! If I rebuild what I destroyed, then I really would be a lawbreaker.
>
> "For through the law I died to the law so that I might live for God. I have been crucified with Christ and I no longer live, but Christ lives in me. The life I now live in the body, I live by faith in the Son of God, who loved me and gave himself for me. I do not set aside the grace of God, for if righteousness could be gained through the law, Christ died for nothing!"

For our purposes the opening lines of verses 15–16 are nothing short of monumental. Here is Paul, a Jew, dragging Peter, also a Jew, into the same circle, and *openly confesses that justification before God comes by faith and not by adherence to the Torah*. However, one comprehends Judaism and Paul's relationship to Judaism, and how one comprehends justification, whether it is exclusively a soteriological word or also an ecclesiological word, what matters here is that *Paul indwells this story of Jesus as the saving story*. I take the "we" and the "I" of this entire passage to be about the Jewish experience (and not the gentile experience).

The story of Israel has become, in the hands of Paul, the story of Jesus who saves both Jews and gentiles on the basis of faith. The Torah has served its purpose; the Torah that divided the Jew from the gentile has now lost its divisive power. Paul is indwelling this story of a Jew *and* gentile church, a free *and* slave church, and a male *and* female church, and this church's unity is found *100 percent in Christ alone*. (That's another *sola* for our Protestant theology: unity in Christ alone.)

Furthermore, Paul personally indwells this story because he's died with Christ on the cross; so much has the cross become central to Christ and his story that he has climbed Golgotha and died with Christ. Yet more, the life he now lives is a resurrection life; so much has the resurrection penetrated his theology that the very Christian life he now indwells is a resurrection life that taps into the resurrected life of Christ. Thus, "Christ lives in me."

His entire life is now a Christ-life. That story has so impacted him that his life is now indwelt by Christ and he indwells Christ, and his life is the Christ-life lived out in the Roman Empire for the sake of Christ. Paul's life is thoroughly gospelized: he has learned the story and he is indwelling the story.

Embody the Story

Enough theory. What about today? How can we embody the gospel today? How can we make the story visible to our communities? I want to suggest that one word will tie this into a coherent whole for us, and that one word is *witness*. We are called to be witnesses.

But of what? That's one of our problems. We are witnesses to so many things, perhaps too many things. Let me call attention to American Peoria for a minute. I'm sure that most people know about the Republicans and the Democrats, and you probably know that many evangelicals are Republicans, and if you listen to some—not all, mind you—you would think some evangelicals are witnesses to Republican politics. And we are witnesses also to, for many, a preferred lifestyle. We need to hear again the searching words of Jesus in the Sermon on the Mount, not the least of which would be those found in Matthew 6:25–34, which probe us and say, "You are way too wealthy, you are holding on to too many things, and you are wearing fine clothing and jewelry, and you . . . you . . . you." Power and money. All we need is sex and we've got the devilish trinity.

But I want to contend that the way we most embody the story is to *witness* to Jesus Christ:

> But you will receive power when the Holy Spirit comes on you; and you will be *my witnesses* in Jerusalem, and in all Judea and Samaria, and to the ends of the earth. (Acts 1:8)

> Beginning from John's baptism to the time when Jesus was taken up from us. For one of these must become a *witness* with us of his resurrection. (Acts 1:22)

> God has raised this Jesus to life, and we are all *witnesses* of the fact. (Acts 2:32)

> You killed the author of life, but God raised him from the dead. We are *witnesses* of this. (Acts 3:15)

> We are *witnesses* of these things, and so is the Holy Spirit, whom God has given to those who obey him. (Acts 5:32)

> We are *witnesses* of everything he did in the country of the Jews and in Jerusalem. They killed him by hanging him on a cross. (Acts 10:39)

> He was not seen by all the people, but by *witnesses* whom God had already chosen—by us who ate and drank with him after he rose from the dead. (Acts 10:41)

> And for many days he was seen by those who had traveled with him from Galilee to Jerusalem. They are now his *witnesses* to our people. (Acts 13:31)
>
> You will be his *witness* to all people of what you have seen and heard. (Acts 22:15)
>
> Now get up and stand on your feet. I have appeared to you to appoint you as a servant and as a *witness* of what you have seen and will see of me. (Acts 26:16)

Of all these statements, the first and last are the most important to me: We are witnesses and we are called to be a witness "of what we have seen and will see" of Jesus. We embody the gospel when we convert churches from lifestyle organizations and from political powerhouses into places where people can hear about Jesus, find Jesus, and learn to live under him, with him, and behind him. We are witnesses when the entire church becomes enraptured with the story of Jesus and lets that story shape everything: everything we think, everything we say, and everything we do.

Do you want to embody the gospel? Tell people about Jesus. Point people to Jesus. Live Jesus. With others.

Bibliography

Dickson, John. *The Best Kept Secret of Christian Mission: Promoting the Gospel with More than Our Lips.* Grand Rapids: Zondervan, 2013.

France, R. T. *The Gospel of Mark.* New International Greek Testament Commentary. Grand Rapids: Eerdmans, 2002.

Gilbert, Greg. *What is the Gospel?* Wheaton: Crossway, 2010.

Gomes, Peter J. *The Scandalous Gospel of Jesus: What's So Good about the Good News?* New York: HarperOne, 2007.

Jenson, Matt, and David E. Wilhite. *The Church: A Guide for the Perplexed.* New York: T. & T. Clark/Continuum, 2010.

McKnight, Scot, and Hauna Ondrey. *Finding Faith, Losing Faith.* Waco: Baylor University Press, 2008.

McLaren, Brian. *Everything Must Change: When the World's Biggest Problems and Jesus' Good News Collide.* Nashville: Nelson, 2007.

———. *The Secret Message of Jesus: Uncovering the Truth That Could Change Everything.* Nashville: Thomas Nelson, 2006.

Piper, John. *God is the Gospel: Meditations on God's Love as the Gift of Himself.* Wheaton: Crossway, 2005.

Wright, Christopher. *The Mission of God: Unlocking the Bible's Grand Narrative.* Downers Grove, IL: IVP Academic, 2006.

2

Being God's People Among the Nations

Gleanings from Kings

JOHN OLLEY

FROM THE BEGINNING, BY placing the call of Abraham after Genesis 1–11, the Bible situates the life of God's people in the midst of God's purposes for the whole of creation, including all humanity. The call of Abraham culminates in a promise of blessing for "all the families of the earth."[1] The next mention of blessing to "all nations on earth through him" is immediately followed by "for I have chosen him, so that he will direct his children and his household after him to keep the way of the Lord by doing what is right and just, so that the Lord will bring about for Abraham what he has promised him."[2] Blessing comes to the nations through the God-like lifestyle of his people. In contrast to the lifestyle of Babel/Babylon which is concerned for issues of security and self-protection (a "city" is walled), and of reputation

---

1. Gen 12:3; *mišpāḥôt* "extended families, clans" is also in the table of nations, 10:5, 18, 20, 31, 32, and the description of creatures that came out of the ark, 8:19 (NIV "peoples," "clans," and "kind" respectively). *ʾădāmāh* "earth, ground" features prominently throughout Gen 1–11 (28 times), echoing the commonality of all people as *ʾādām*, more basic than any family or ethnic identity. Bible quotations are from the NIV unless otherwise specified.

2. Gen 18:18–19; here the terminology is the more common "nations" (*gôyim*) and "earth, land" (*ʾereṣ*).

and remembrance through a building ("a name"),[3] Abraham is promised a name and God's protection through a journey of trusting, risk-taking obedience.[4]

The rest of the Old Testament tells the story of God's people in the midst of the "peoples" and "nations." The narrative provides many examples of common occurrence: God's people do not always experience blessing, nor do they always bring blessing to others! The Old Testament is nevertheless an account of God's ongoing presence working out divine purposes for all the earth in and through imperfect people. The twofold combination of God's presence and provision and his people's lifestyle amongst the nations is explicit in the exhortation before entry into the land:

> See, I have taught you decrees and laws as the LORD my God commanded me, so that you may follow them in the land you are entering to take possession of it. Observe them carefully, for this will show your wisdom and understanding to the nations, who will hear about all these decrees and say, "Surely this great nation is a wise and understanding people." What other nation is so great as to have their gods near them the way the LORD our God is near us whenever we pray to him? And what other nation is so great as to have such righteous decrees and laws as this body of laws I am setting before you today? (Deut 4:5–8)

The Old Testament provides a rich resource that can be a mirror for exploring features of Christian life and witness today around the globe. For several centuries following Abraham, the people lived as a minority in the land of Canaan and then in Egypt, and even later with some measure of political autonomy there was continual influence from surrounding nations, not always benign. Importantly, the accounts of the kingdoms of Israel and Judah as we now have them are addressed initially to people in exile under the dominance of wealthy, powerful Babylon (1 and 2 Kings) or living in a province of the even greater Persian Empire (1 and 2 Chronicles).[5] The final bringing together of what we now call the Old Testament was by people who lived under foreign rule, as were the early Christians who have given us the New Testament. Indeed, in contradistinction to much reading of the Bible in past centuries within "Christendom," the whole Bible is best read as God's

---

3. Gen 11:1–9; English versions transliterate the Hebrew *bābel* only in v. 9, elsewhere using the later Greek form "Babylon."

4. Gen 12:2; 15:1.

5. While recognizing incorporation of earlier material, implying selection and editing, our attention is the context of recipients of the present form of the books: what is the writer/editor communicating in that setting?

word to a minority people living in the midst of larger communities and under pagan rule—the context of most Christians today.

First and Second Kings is that part of the Bible which most tells of situations familiar in the world today: a mixture of material prosperity, political maneuvering, dominant military powers, pragmatic national alliances and international trade, mixed religious affiliations with compromised worship, violent *coup d'états*, famine, wars, oppressive rule, children dying. With these topics often dominating news, Kings becomes a major resource to explore how to live as God's people in the arena of everyday life, the place where God is present fulfilling his mission. Here we consider only two broad topics: a focus on lifestyle, not temple or wealth or political astuteness, and two instances of blessing to non-Israelites. These are aspects that are explicitly taken up in the New Testament.[6]

Putting the Temple and "Success" in their Place

The early readers were exiles in Babylon, surrounded by splendid palaces and impressive temples that would have made the Jerusalem royal buildings and temple seem insignificant even if they had not been recently demolished by the Babylonians! Present readers in Western countries might see some similarities in our own context: previously church buildings were the focal point of towns, their spires dominating the skyline, but now they are dwarfed by towers of financial institutions and alluring large shopping complexes. The ever-visible dominant symbols are those of the gods of the empire of commerce and pleasure. How are the people of God to live in this new context? An answer comes in the place of the temple and Solomon's buildings in the narrative of Kings and the ways in which their importance is relativized. There are potent narrative illustrations of what happens when people seek to serve both God and the counterfeit gods of money, sex, and power, rather than following God's ways wholeheartedly.[7]

Throughout the ancient Near East, kings as a priority built and funded temples for the nation's or the capital's god. David had thus been acting like any king of "the nations" in seeking to build an appropriately magnificent temple for the Lord in his capital Jerusalem. Surprisingly God seems to be unenthusiastic, being more interested in promising a "house" (dynasty) for David than in a "house" (temple) for himself. Nevertheless, he does tell David that his son will build a temple (2 Sam 7:1–16). With this background

---

6. In Olley, *Message of Kings*, I explore several ways in which Kings shines light into current faith and lifestyle issues.

7. Keller, *Counterfeit Gods*.

it may surprise readers that David's final charge to Solomon says nothing about a temple, but rather enjoins, "Observe what the LORD your God requires: Walk in obedience to him, and keep his decrees and commands, his laws and regulations, as written in the Law of Moses." The path that will "prosper"[8] for David's successors is to "walk faithfully before me with all their heart and soul" (1 Kgs 2:3).

The first mention in Kings of a temple is in the introductory setting of the scene after Solomon is established as king. Again, contrary to what we may expect, even after the comment that "a temple had not yet been built for the Name of the LORD" (1 Kgs 3:1, 2), when God appears to Solomon there is silence concerning a temple. Rather the focus is "a wise and discerning heart to administer justice" (3:11–12). Immediately follows an account of justice being given in the case of two prostitutes and their children, and the concluding statement is that "all Israel . . . saw that he had wisdom from God to administer justice" (3:16–28). Not until Hiram of Tyre sends envoys to Solomon does Solomon's return message center on his intention to "build a temple for the Name of the LORD my God" (5:5). Obeying God and doing justice come first in the telling of the reign of Solomon.

A related motif in the opening chapters is "wisdom." Solomon asked God for "a discerning heart to govern your people and to distinguish between good and bad"[9]—God adds the word "wise" (3:9, 12). Previously, like a movement from the idealism and piety of a Sunday sermon to the *Realpolitik* of weekday life, David's words to Solomon switched dramatically after the charge to obey God's commands. He instructed Solomon to remove certain people who might be threats: "deal according to your wisdom . . . you are a man of wisdom; you will know what to do" (2:6, 9). Solomon ensured the death of these and more, removing "adversaries." There is thus a certain irony in God's subsequent words that Solomon had "not asked for the death of your enemies" (3:11), and that later Solomon links building the temple with his now having "no adversary" (5:4).[10] The wisdom given by God for the administering of justice, discerning good and bad, stands over against Solomon's pragmatic wisdom that removes opposition. Here

---

8. So NIV. The verb *hiśkîl* may also be translated "be successful" (as in Josh 1:7–8) or "understand, gain insight" (so LXX; cf. Gen 3:6). Success and wisdom, along with prosperity, flow from trusting obedience.

9. My translation; NIV's "right and wrong" obscures the echoes of the narrative of Genesis 3 and the "tree of the knowledge of good and bad," with its fruit "desirable for gaining wisdom" (*hiśkîl*).

10. Gordon, "A House Divided," 94–105. Gordon notes also that the last recorded activity of Solomon is seeking the life of his rival Jeroboam (11:40). The narrator there pointedly says 'the Lord raised up adversaries' (11:14, 21).

is a stark example of the contrast James describes between wisdom that is "earthly, unspiritual, demonic" and "the wisdom that comes from heaven" that is "first pure; then peace-loving, considerate, submissive, full of mercy and good fruit, impartial and sincere." It is "peacemakers who sow in peace (who) reap a harvest of righteousness" (Jas 3:13–18). It is as Solomon proposes equitable friendly arrangements with the Tyrian Hiram for the supply of timber for temple-building, that Hiram responds by praising God "for he has given David a wise son to rule over this great nation" (5:7).

The temple building and dedication is described in much detail, with four chapters (5–8) in the center of chapters 1–11. Its beauty is evident. God authenticates by the presence of "the glory of the LORD" as at the time of completion of the tabernacle (8:10–11; cf. Exod 40:34–45), and affirms by a word to Solomon in a vision (9:3). Features of the account, however, provide a tempering perspective.

As Solomon begins to build, the word of the LORD came to Solomon: "As for this temple you are building," and then God says nothing about the temple! Rather the word is a promise that God's presence depends not on a temple but on "following my decrees and observing my laws" (6:11–13). God appears again to Solomon after the temple dedication. As the message moves through three components there is an ominous doubling in length: one verse is a statement regarding the temple, two verses deal with obedience "with integrity of heart and uprightness," and then four verses are a warning of destruction and exile if the people worship other gods (9:3–9). The temple is no substitute for obedience in life.

The priority and the implied criticisms in the warning of 9:6–9 suggest another look at the preceding account of the temple building. Crane has commented that detail is mainly of "the ornateness and splendor of the temple" rather than features "having cultic value." Further, when Solomon responds to the presence of "the glory of the LORD" (8:11), his early words are "I have indeed built a magnificent temple for you" (8:13) and in the following prayer he "frequently mentions that he built the Temple (8:20, 27, 44, 48)."[11] Solomon's focus appears to be on the magnificence of the building under his patronage rather than its worship aspects.

The writer suggests Solomon's priorities also by the surprising center of the temple narrative mention of Solomon's building his own palace.[12] In contrast to later chapter divisions, the Hebrew Masoretic Text sharpens the contrast in having no division between 6:38 and 7:1:

---

11. Crane, "Solomon," 34, 40.

12. It is also the centre of the chiastic structure of the whole narrative, chs. 1–11. See Olley, "Pharaoh's Daughter," 355–69.

> ... the house[13] was completed according to all its matters and specifications
>> and he built it in seven years
>> and his house Solomon built in thirteen years
> and he completed all his house [my translation].

The parallel between two houses is reinforced by the central section ending which points to similar structures (7:12). The priority is hinted at earlier: in 3:1 Solomon's "house" is mentioned before the "temple." Is this a clue as to why, on the several later occasions when temple wealth is given to, or taken by, invading kings, God apparently does nothing to protect such wealth?[14] The writer is saying to people in exile, and beyond, that God's interest is not in the material wealth supplied but in heart allegiance shown in obedience.

A further dimension of what is important to God in his relationship with his people is evident in other features of the narrative structure. The central account of Solomon's building of his palace mentions his building a palace for "Pharaoh's daughter" (7:8), and two other key locations mention "Pharaoh's daughter" (3:1–3; 9:24–25). What is the writer communicating in this structure? Associated is reference to the exodus "out of Egypt" framing the temple narrative: "In the four hundred and eightieth year after the Israelites came out of Egypt . . . he began to build the temple" (6:1) is matched by the account of temple dedication, "since the day I brought my people out of Egypt" (8:16), "the covenant of the Lord that he made with our ancestors when he brought them out of Egypt" (8:21), "they are your people and your inheritance, whom you brought out of Egypt" (8:51), and "you sovereign Lord brought our ancestors out of Egypt" (8:53). Sadly, after his death, Solomon's subjects describe his rule in language echoing Pharaoh's oppression of the Israelites, a "heavy yoke and harsh labor" (12:4).[15] What is going on here?

Positively, we see repeated affirmation that the temple is secondary to the covenantal relationship evident in the exodus, a powerful message to people in exile after the temple has been destroyed. Negatively, there is a contrast between the Lord who brought the people out of Pharaoh's bondage in Egypt and Solomon who sealed an alliance with Pharaoh by marrying his daughter and whose own buildings are made possible by oppression that

---

13. *bāyit* "house" is commonly translated "palace" when it is a king's "house" and "temple" when reference is to God or a god.

14. The first such instance is as early as the fifth year of the reign of Solomon's son, Rehoboam (1 Kgs 14:25–26); cf. 1 Kgs 15:18; 2 Kgs 12:18; 14:14; 18:14–16.

15. Cf. Exod 1:14; 2:23; 5:9; 6:6, 9 with "yoke" used in Lev 26:13.

is the opposite of the justice seen earlier in his reign. Solomon's apparent "success" is described as a reversal of the exodus.

Where is Solomon's Heart?

Intertwined with the relativizing of the temple, with priority given to the exodus and formation of a redeemed people who are to live according to covenantal laws, there is critique of material prosperity evidenced in buildings, military power, and trade.

The detail within 1 Kings 9:10–19 is often seen as a catalog of "Solomon's Other Activities,"[16] a miscellany of projects in international relationships, buildings in Jerusalem and beyond, efficient organization of non-Israelite labor, fulfillment of temple obligations, and trade.

> On the face of it, the text is a celebration of the king and his remarkable achievements. If we remember that Israel, only two generations before, was a disadvantaged hill country with a peasant population, the work of Solomon must necessarily be received as exotic and astonishing.[17]

It is this which attracts the Queen of Sheba; is this how Israel is to be a blessing to the nations? One might compare the material splendor of many centers of "Christendom."

The context provides a different perspective. It is common to speak of Solomon being led astray by "foreign women" (11:1, 4),[18] but here are signs that he is being led astray by material wealth and power, with "conspicuous consumption"[19] that enhances his status. In 9:1 it states more than "when Solomon had finished building the temple of the LORD." It continues "and the royal palace and had achieved all he had desired to do" [lit., "and every desire ($hēšeq$) of Solomon which he delighted ($hāpēṣ$) to do/make"]. The noun $hēšeq$ is rare[20] but the related verb (used along with the noun in v. 19) is a strong word describing strong affection towards a person or God.[21] In

---

16. The heading in NIV; also Wiseman, *1 and 2 Kings*, 125.

17. Brueggemann, *1 and 2 Kings*, 127–28.

18. Cf. NIV's insertion of "however" in 11:1 (not in Hebrew), so suggesting that the marriages were the sole factor in Solomon's failure.

19. The term was coined by Veblen to describe the use of money or resources to display a higher status than others; see *Leisure Class*.

20. The noun is only here in v. 19 (par. 2 Chr 8:6) and in Isa 21:4, "longing for" twilight, probably as relief.

21. A person "desiring" a woman (Gen 34:8; Deut 21:11) or God (Ps 91:14; NIV "love") and God "setting his affection on" Israel (Deut 7:7; 10:15).

contrast, Solomon's "desire" is towards things: the listing in verses 10–19a is summarized as "Solomon's desire (*ḥēšeq*) which he desired (*ḥāšaq*) to build in Jerusalem, in Lebanon and throughout all the territory he ruled" (v. 19b). He is able to build "all" he desires (9:1) and his "desires" are all matters of status, power, and wealth. Later the Queen of Sheba will say of Solomon's wealth and wisdom that "the LORD has delighted (*ḥāpēṣ*) in you." God has kept his promise, but 9:1–19 shows that Solomon's "delight" is not in God but in his magnificent buildings. At what cost? The people themselves experienced oppressive labor policies (12:4).

Reading the listing (vv. 10–19) after God's words of promise and warning (vv. 2–9) is salutary. God provides his criteria for success (vv. 3–9) which include "nothing about trade or buildings or alliances or organization. It all turns on the single point of Torah obedience . . . If Torah has to do with *love of God* and *love of neighbor*, then the massive expansionist enterprise of Solomon is to be judged harshly as a deep failure."[22] Verses 1–9 provide a piercing light to reveal what may be overlooked in the dazzling list of accomplishments. Solomon's chosen path led initially on his death to the division of the kingdom and ultimately to the end of the Davidic dynasty.

How is Israel to be a blessing to the nations? Solomon begins with much that is commendable. His early actions were praised by Hiram, but later Hiram complains about shoddy treatment (9:11–14).[23] The Queen of Sheba is attracted, most likely by the possibilities of a lucrative trade, yet readers will see unexpected irony in her words. After praising Solomon's achievements, evidenced by the wealth of the court, and his wisdom, as seen in his answers to her questions, she praises "the LORD your God . . . Because of the LORD's eternal love for Israel, he has made you king to maintain justice and righteousness" (10:9; cf. Gen 18:19). She affirms God's intention, but the preceding narrative has shown how far Solomon has departed from "justice and righteousness."

The rest of chapter 9 and chapter 10 detail a clear negative parallel to the Deuteronomic laws relating to the king (Deut 17:16–17):

> The king, moreover, must not acquire great numbers of horses for himself or make the people return to Egypt to get more of them, for the Lord has told you, "You are not to go back that way again." He must not take many wives, or his heart will be led astray. He must not accumulate large amounts of silver and gold.

---

22. Brueggemann, *1 and 2 Kings*, 128.

23. There is also a reversal of the exodus and settlement of the land in that Solomon gives some of the land away to a foreign ruler.

The details of horses—the acquisition of military resources—including trade with Egypt, and "much gold" are given before we come to the wives.

People in exile, feeling insignificant and powerless amongst the material grandeur and economic strength of Babylon are reminded that Solomon's "glory" was the path to failure. The allure of material grandeur of places of worship, of great political structures and economic power through trade, and of this being achieved through pragmatic wisdom, continues today.

A New Testament perspective is evident in its explicit references to Solomon. Matthew 6:29, "not even Solomon in all his splendor was dressed like one of these," is part of 6:19–34 commencing "do not store up for yourselves treasures on earth" and warning that "you cannot serve both God and money"; rather God supplies what is needed and so our priority is to "seek first his kingdom and his righteousness." The parallel comparison in Luke 12:27 is in a block (12:13–34) which commences with the parable of the rich fool, and goes on to enjoin "sell your possessions and give to the poor," concluding "for where your treasure is, there your heart will be also." Solomon's glory becomes warning, with the implication that in the end he was a "rich fool."

Other references to Solomon in the Gospels are in the genealogy of Jesus (Matt 1:6–7), pointing to Jesus as the fulfillment of the promise concerning the Davidic king, reinforced by the statement that the "Queen of the South" came to "listen to Solomon's wisdom, and now something greater than Solomon is here" (Matt 12:42; Luke 11:31). The only other New Testament mention of Solomon is in Stephen's provocative retelling of the history of God's people: his inclusion of Solomon's building the temple is immediately followed by "however, the Most High does not live in houses made by human hands" (Acts 7:47–48). In saying "made by human hands," Stephen may be deliberately echoing the LXX's derogative description of idol worship,[24] as well as the quoted words of Jesus, "I will destroy this temple made by human hands and in three days will build another, not made with hands" (Mark 14:58).[25]

The New Testament endorses features of the Kings narrative: the primacy of wholehearted following of God's ways, the dangerous allure of wealth and desire for security and status symbols, and the secondary position of places of worship and associated ritual. How often are these aspects of Solomon referred to in preaching? New Testament allusions direct us to pay attention to the Solomon narrative and so reflect on the complexities of

---

24. Greek *cheiropoiētos* is in LXX Lev 26:1, 30; Isa 2:18; 10:11; 19:1; 21:9; 31:7, etc., overwhelmingly of idols.

25. Marshall, *Acts*, 146. See also Acts 17:23; Heb 9:11, 24.

decisions to be made in everyday life and to see clearly the temptations to misuse God's good gifts, turning aside after counterfeit gods.

Early in his reign Solomon is commended for his "love" of God (1 Kgs 3:3) and for his answer to God's question, "Ask for whatever you want me to give you" (3:5), but later "all he had desired to do" (9:1) is related to royal buildings and "he held fast to them (foreign women) in love" (11:2). A thousand years later Christ says to his disciples, "Ask and it will be given to you" (Matt 7:7), significantly in the context of the Sermon on the Mount which contrasts the priorities of Solomon (6:29), a reminder of ways in which Solomon misused the generous gifts of God. How will Christ's followers respond to that generous offer today? We are promised all that we need so that our "good works" lead others to "glorify your Father in heaven" (5:16).[26]

Blessing to Other Nations

Apart from Solomon, Jesus refers to only two incidents from 1 and 2 Kings, both telling of blessing to someone outside God's people: Elijah and provision for a widow in Zarephath, and Elisha and the healing of Naaman.[27] These reminders were a scandal to the hearers in the Nazareth synagogue (Luke 4:25–30): behavior and attitudes that are commended by God often are controversial and unwelcome.

God's Grace in Unexpected Places

Elijah boldly confronts King Ahab, but the first person to whom God tells Elijah to "go" is not the king but a non-Israelite widow (1 Kgs 17:1, 8–9). The God who had "directed the ravens to supply you with food there" (v. 4) now "directed a widow there to supply you with food" (v. 9). Here is a claim to sovereignty outside the land and his people—"Zarephath in the region of Sidon" is the home not only of Jezebel but of her god!—and a widow outside of Israel will learn to her life-continuing gain that indeed "the LORD your God lives" (v. 12). Far away from centers of power and wealth she will be the first to affirm that "the word of the LORD from your mouth is the truth" (v. 24).

Jesus's introduction, "no prophet is accepted in his hometown" (Luke 4:24), shows that he has more in view than simply pointing to God's grace

---

26. I have developed this in Olley, "Light of the World," 9–28.
27. The only other New Testament allusion to Kings is Elijah's prayer for rain (James 5:17–18; cf. 1 Kgs 18:41–46).

to gentiles, although that aspect is important. The widow is an example of an "outsider," someone on the fringe, who, when given opportunity to respond to God's gracious saving provision, believes and lives, whereas "insiders" are not willing to believe or have a compromised faith and may be critical when "outsiders" are welcomed. How ready is the church today to see God graciously at work in people outside certain boundaries and perhaps to see that as a challenge to our own actions and attitudes? Konkel[28] tells of Lamin Sanneh, an Islamic scholar, originally from Gambia, who became a follower of Christ but met suspicion and skepticism from various churches. He persevered because "Jesus was for real in spite of the prevarications of the church" and from 1989 until his death in 2019 was Professor of Missions and World Christianity at Yale Divinity School. The story of the widow of Zarephath encourages us to open our eyes and hearts to God's grace in unexpected people and places, and to allow their response to challenge our own.

Here is also a story where the person of God does not come with all the resources but rather depends on help from the "outsider." A striking comparison is Jesus asking for a drink of water from the woman at the well in Samaria, and she too, an "outsider," became the first to see that he could be the Messiah and told others (John 4:7, 25–29).[29]

Naaman is Also a Human Being Like Us

The story of Naaman and his cleansing from a skin disease (2 Kgs 5) is familiar and Christians have seen many analogies with the gospel of Jesus Christ and cleansing from sin. Is this the main reason for the story being here? A number of features aid reflection on varying responses of God's people in living amongst the nations.

From the start it challenges self-centered (or rather *God's people-*centered) attitudes. It opens with simple, but unexpected, statements: "Now Naaman was commander of the army of the king of Aram. He was a great man in the sight of his master and highly regarded, because through him the LORD had given victory to Aram" (2 Kgs 5:1). How might an Israelite receive these words? "Here is an archenemy. It can't be true that the Lord gave Aram victory; God is supposed to give *us* victory." Yet the narrator asserts God's sovereignty and freedom to act on the side of Aram against

---

28. Konkel, *1 and 2 Kings*, 317–19.

29. Cf. the crucial role of the "worthy person" or "someone who promotes peace" who supplies the needs of the itinerant disciples who take nothing with them (Matt 10:11; Luke 10:6).

Israel and continues to praise Naaman, "he was a valiant soldier" but he "had leprosy" (one of a number of possible skin diseases). An Israelite could give three reasons for detesting Naaman: a foreigner, head of the army that has defeated them, and a leper. Further, as a result of raids, a captured Israelite girl is now servant of Naaman's wife. An Israelite might hope and pray for the freeing of the slave girl through the defeat of Aram. The narrator sees differently.

First, we read of the captive girl, a person on the fringe, seemingly insignificant as a member of God's people. Yet here shines an example of concern for the enemy that leads ultimately to his full participation in communal life. Surprising inversions of human expectations continue: an Aramean king is genuinely and generously open to the possibility of an Israelite prophet healing, while the king of Israel is fearfully concerned for his own security. Next we read how Elisha is not overawed by the importance and possible generosity of this foreign army commander, simply sending a message as to the way to wholeness. He later refuses a very large gift of thanks, sending Naaman away "in peace" (v. 19).

We might expect the story to end there, but the narrator turns to Gehazi, Elisha's assistant. The principle that a laborer is worthy of their hire is biblical (Matt 10:10; 1 Tim 5:18), and prophets relied upon the gifts of people (e.g., 1 Sam 9:8). Like Paul much later (1 Thess 2:9), Elijah however knows that claiming personal rights and material advantage is not as important as seeing people grow in faith in the life-giving God. Gehazi thinks otherwise. He sees an opportunity to live much more comfortably. He may well have justified his actions (as have many since), but the use of a lie and asking for only some of the gift is a standard form of graft. Elisha pinpoints not only Gehazi's deceit, but his self-seeking at a time of hardship for others (v. 26).

Gehazi's attitude to Naaman is evident in his "Naaman, this Aramean" (v. 20). He fails to have the breadth of compassion of Elisha—and God. Further, "with the derogatory epithet, 'this Aramean,' Gehazi impugns the man who has declared his faith in YHWH and who is about to act on it."[30] Naaman's seed of faith is belittled rather than nurtured. By branding Naaman as "this Aramean," Gehazi lessens his responsibility to care for a fellow human being, also made in the image of God. Gehazi's attitude is reflected in countless contexts of human relationships, the labelling of the other in a way that regards them as of less worth than one's own kind. This becomes particularly relevant in times of conflict or hardship, when all too readily there is division between "us" and "them."

30. Cohn, 2 Kings, 40.

The story of Naaman involves four members of God's people. The Israelite king saw Naaman as a threatening enemy while Gehazi saw an outsider to be used for personal advantage. A servant girl and Elisha were agents of God's compassion so bringing blessing. Here "the other" came to Elisha, while Elijah was sent to the widow of Zarephath. In both cases the result was wholeness, and the stories are told to shape the attitude and actions of exiles amongst the nations.

When Jesus highlighted the otherness of the widow of Zarephath and of Naaman the Syrian as recipients of God's favor, the people in the synagogue of Nazareth were "furious" and wanted to throw Jesus off the cliff (Luke 4:28–29). To show compassion and understanding to those who are "different from us" is risky! If this is how Christ was treated, should we be surprised?

In Light of the Past, Living in the Present among the Nations

It is easy to say in abstract that God's people are to be a means of blessing to the nations by doing what is right and just. Biblical narrative provides stories of success and failure in doing so in the complexities of daily life at personal, family, and community levels. As the exiles in Babylon struggled to make sense of their current position and sought a way forward, the Kings narrative was more than a reminder of the past. As the story was told of the golden period of Solomon's reign hearers found their gaze was turned from the temple, magnificent buildings, wealth, and brilliant wisdom to look rather at the cost to the community of the failure to have at the center, obedience to God's covenantal requirements. They also saw in other stories examples of how it was possible to show God's compassion for those outside his people and of how they too might come to faith in him.

We have had occasion already to refer to Jesus's Sermon on the Mount, to which could be added other blocks of teaching in Matthew. Significantly, the final words in Matthew are Jesus's commission to "make disciples of all nations," linked with "teaching them to obey everything I have commanded you" (Matt 28:19–20). God's purpose to bless all nations still places at the center his people's priorities in living his way, showing in their lives his own character of compassion and justice.

Bibliography

Brueggemann, Walter. *1 and 2 Kings*. Smyth and Helwys Bible Commentary. Macon, GA: Smyth and Helwys, 2000.

Cohn, Robert L. *2 Kings*. Berit Olam. Collegeville, Minnesota: Liturgical Press, 2000.

Crane, Ashley. "Solomon and the Building of the Temple." In *Text and Task: Scripture and Mission*, edited by Michael Parsons, 33–49. Milton Keynes: Paternoster, 2005.

Gordon, Robert P. "A House Divided: Wisdom in Old Testament Narrative Traditions." In *Wisdom in Ancient Israel*, edited John Day, Robert P. Gordon, and H. G. M. Williamson, 94–105. Cambridge: Cambridge University Press, 1995.

Keller, Tim. *Counterfeit Gods*. New York: Dutton Adult, 2009.

Konkel, August H. *1 and 2 Kings*. NIV Application Commentary. Grand Rapids: Zondervan, 2006.

Marshall, I. Howard. *Acts*. Tyndale New Testament Commentaries. Leicester: Inter-Varsity, 1980.

Olley, John W. *The Message of Kings*. The Bible Speaks Today. Nottingham: Inter-Varsity, 2011.

———. "Pharaoh's Daughter, Solomon's Palace and the Temple: Another Look at the Structure of 1 Kings 1–11." *Journal for the Study of the Old Testament* 27 (2003) 355–69.

———. "'You are Light of the World': A Missiological Focus for the Sermon on the Mount in Matthew." *Mission Studies* 20, no. 1 (2003) 9–28.

Veblen, Thorstein. *The Theory of the Leisure Class*. New York: Macmillan, 1899.

Wiseman, Donald J. *1 and 2 Kings*. Tyndale Old Testament Commentaries. Leicester: InterVarsity, 1993.

3

Jonah's Wail

The Death and Resurrection of a Recalcitrant Church

MICHAEL D. O'NEIL

Jonah in Context

THE BOOK OF JONAH is a marvel. Though only forty-eight verses, its artistry, narrative drama, heart-stopping action, and astonishing reversals have captured the imaginations of poets and novelists, artists and children, philosophers, and preachers across many generations. As an inspired piece of human literature, it is a *tour de force*. And yet, for peoples ancient and modern, far more is evident here than simply human inspiration and ingenuity, as its inclusion in the biblical canon testifies. Jonah combines profound theological insight and prophetic sensitivity to set forth a majestic vision of God as sovereign creator and merciful redeemer. The divine presence, power, and sovereignty are universal in scope, and God's mercy is directed toward all God's creatures. The book of Jonah explores the inexplicable interplay of divine and human agency, and probes the mysteries of fallen human existence, salvation, and vocation. The story of Jonah is often noted with reference to its foreshadowing of the death and resurrection of Jesus Christ, primarily, of course, by Jesus himself (Matt 12:39–41). But even this does not exhaust the prophetic message of the book, for just as the book was relevant for the community of God's people in ancient times, so it continues to speak to the people of God in every generation.

Scholars will no doubt continue to debate the critical questions that swirl around the book of Jonah, threatening to drown this prophetic text in a stormy sea of conjecture and assertion. Historicity, genre, provenance, and setting are all important, and one's perspective here influences what one finds in the book. This chapter assumes that Jonah is a postexilic composition, addressing the community of God's people as they seek to reestablish their identity and national life in the aftermath of devastating conquest and exile.[1] Israel has long since gone into exile and captivity, and Judah too, has been judged and cast out of God's presence, and yet restored.

In the biblical story, Jonah—the character—is brought low, his very life ebbing away, until finally he is brought "down" to death and hell.[2] Wiped from the face of the earth and expelled from the sight of all but God, Jonah is beyond all human hope. In utter desolation and hopelessness, reaping the harvest of his own disobedience and unfaithfulness, Jonah determines to "look again" toward the holy temple of God, to remember the Lord and to pray to God—even while still within the belly of the fish (2:4). And here, the stunning reversal: God commands the fish and Jonah is vomited onto dry land—his death overturned in the gracious wonder of resurrection! Judged under the dreadful wrath of God, and rescued in the tender mercy of God, Jonah is restored to his call and commissioned afresh as a prophet to Nineveh, even as Paul would later affirm, "For the gifts and calling of God are irrevocable" (Rom 11:29).

Jonah, however, lacks enthusiasm for his task. Indeed he fulfills his commission, but only in the very barest of terms; his proclamation to Nineveh

---

1. It is not my intent in this paper to canvass these matters which are treated extensively in the literature. For discussion of the issues from different perspectives, see the commentaries by Allen, *Joel, Obadiah, Jonah*, 185–91; Wolff, *Obadiah and Jonah*, 76–78; and Cary, *Jonah*, 32, 36, for a defense of the view in this chapter. For perspectives that view the book in terms of an eighth-century provenance associated with the "historical Jonah" of 2 Kings 14, see Stuart, *Hosea–Jonah*, 432–33, 440–42; *Jonah, Book of*, 457, 460–61; and Timmer, *Gracious and Compassionate*, 60–67.

2. The narrative and poetic sequence of chapters one and two portray Jonah fleeing, in chapter 1:3, from the presence of the Lord and going "down" to Joppa, "down" into the boat, into the sea, into the fish, and finally, to the "depth of Sheol" (2:2). The imagery is evocative and imaginative, rather than literal. Sheol refers not to hell per se but to the world of the dead, but it may be and has been likened to the exclusion from God's presence identified by the concept of hell. Allen, for example, suggests that Jonah has been "in Sheol's belly . . . The gates of hell prevailed against him, clanging shut with a terrible finality—or so it seemed." Allen, *Joel, Obadiah, Jonah*, 216–17, original emphasis; see also Carey, *Jonah*, 85.

consists of one brief sentence—just five words in the Hebrew[3]—which does not even mention God, and is wholly concerned with the destruction of the city.[4] Imagine his chagrin, then, when this reluctant proclamation results in revival, conversion, and deliverance amongst the Ninevites. Seething with anger and furious at God, Jonah would rather be dead than see the pagan enemies of his people forgiven. But God ignores his wail that "death is better to me than life" (4:4), and begins the slow process of educating Jonah, and with Jonah, the community of God's people.

The figure of Jonah is thus representative of God's people and symbolically portrays their fate, their call, and their challenge.[5] Like Jonah, Judah had been called by God, but she has rejected her commission, and in her unfaithfulness has fallen under the terrible judgment of God. Like Jonah, Judah has been "cast into the deep," swallowed whole by a pagan empire, and has suffered "in the belly of the beast." And like Jonah, a remnant has been returned to the land, a small and marginalized people in the midst of a sea of hostile and seemingly godless paganism. Out of the "death" of conquest and exile, however, the recalcitrant people have been "raised" to a new existence in which their life is wholly a matter of divine grace and mercy. What is her role in this context, her mission among the nations? What will it mean for this people to live again as *God's* people, a priestly people and holy nation in the midst of a hostile and pagan environment? Like Jonah, Judah needs to learn again her obligations as God's people in the midst of the nations. This education consists not in the amassing of new information about God, Israel, and the nations, but rather in a deeper and more consistent appropriation of the revelation already given to Judah and Israel in their traditions, history, and Holy Scriptures.

It was for this purpose, then, that Jonah was written, its prophetic message recalling Judah to their original call and purpose, and challenging them

3. Timmer, *Gracious and Compassionate*, 41.

4. Cary, *Jonah*, 111.

5. Wolff, *Obadiah and Jonah*, 99, insists that, "Jonah as prophet and Jonah as a typical representative of Israel can hardly be separated from one another in the story." More expansively, Cary, *Jonah*, 86, argues that, "Jonah is the representative Israelite for the original audience of Jewish readers thinking about the meaning of their captivity in Babylon, which is their time in the belly of the beast. Jonah swallowed up in the heart of the sea represents Judah swallowed up in Babylon, descending into a kind of national death. Nations don't return from exile, any more than people return from the dead. Yet the Judeans in Babylon pray and sing psalms as if they were simply there to be disciplined by their loving father, not destroyed. It is indeed there that they become a people dedicated to obedience to the law of God. They emerge from the depths of exile a new and reborn people, as if baptized in Babylon. Their time in exile is the time of their salvation, transformation, and renewal. So Jonah praying in the guts of the fish is to remind us of the people of Judah singing the songs of Zion by the waters of Babylon . . ."

to renewed faithfulness. The prophetic message comes in the form of a narrative filled with allusions, references, and echoes from Israel's Scriptures. These intertextual references lead the hearers and readers into the deeper appropriation of the revelation already given to Israel. By attending to these hints and clues within the narrative itself, Judah might learn what it means to be God's people in the midst of the nations, and how they might fulfill the commission given to them by God. So, too, readers of Jonah in the post-Christian and sometimes hostile environment of the contemporary West can also attend to these hints and clues within the narrative and also learn how they too might live as a priestly people and holy nation in their time, place, and context. In what follows, I explore three aspects of the Jonah narrative which I find provide rich and timely instruction for the contemporary Western church as it faithfully pursues its call as God's people.

The Elect Community

The first intertextual allusion in Jonah occurs in the opening scene of the book, as the word of the Lord comes to the prophet: "Arise, go to Nineveh the great city and cry against it, for their wickedness has come up before me." There is, in this verse, an echo of Genesis 18:20–21 where the Lord says to Abraham,

> The outcry of Sodom and Gomorrah is indeed great, and their sin is exceedingly grave. I will go down now, and see if they have done entirely according to its outcry, which has come to me; and if not, I will know.[6]

There is widespread agreement amongst commentators that Jonah draws upon the Genesis story of Sodom and Gomorrah, especially in Jonah 3:4 where the same Hebrew verb is used in Jonah's proclamation as is used to describe the destruction of the two cities of the plain.[7] That the story shows up here at the beginning of Jonah is also noted, but the significance of the allusion is left undeveloped in some, although Allen certainly sees it, noting that the expression "recalls the divine statement in Gen 18:20, 21 . . .

---

6. Note: all Scripture citations in this chapter are taken from the New American Standard Version of the Bible.

7. See, for example, Allen, *Joel, Obadiah, Jonah*, 222, and Stuart, *Hosea–Jonah*, 485, although Stuart suggests the verb might better be interpreted to mean that "in forty days Nineveh will have a *change of heart*" (489). The verbal link between the two passages, *hpk*, is found in Gen 19:25 (cf. Deut 29:22–23, and Amos 4:11).

Nineveh is another Sodom, an unhallowed haunt of *wickedness* meriting destruction."[8]

Despite verbal differences between the two texts, in both cases the wickedness of a great city has come to the attention of Yahweh. In the Genesis text, the wickedness of the city has come to Yahweh through the "outcry" of others. Yahweh's apprehension of Nineveh's wickedness in the Jonah text does not preclude the same kind of outcry, though it is not mentioned. The significance of the Genesis passage, however, is not merely in the imagery used to express the divine cognition, but the way in which it presents the connection between the election of Abraham and the redemptive purposes of God, including Israel's role within those purposes. Yahweh recalls the prophetic pronouncement given in Genesis 12:3 that in Abraham "all the nations of the earth will be blessed" (Gen 18:18). It is evident that God's election of Abraham—and of Israel—was for the sake of the nations, as Vriezen insists:

> Israel was only elected in order to serve God in the task of leading those other nations to God. In Israel God sought the world. Israel was God's point of attack on the world. When from the knowledge that it is God's people Israel derived the certainty of its special election, and because of that considered itself to be superior to the other nations, the prophets must contradict this and recall the people to the living God, whose mercy is great for Israel but also for the world. For in His mercy He called Israel to the service of His kingdom among the nations of the earth.[9]

In Genesis 18:19 this responsibility is particularly developed in terms of God's ethical requirement for his people: "For I have chosen him, so that he may command his children and his household after him to keep the way of the LORD by doing righteousness and justice, so that the LORD may bring upon Abraham what he has spoken about him."

Over against the "outcry" (*tseaqah*) against Sodom—the term used "for the crying out of those suffering from oppressions and cruelty"—God requires righteousness (*tsedaqah*) and justice, the wordplay indicating the

---

8. See Allen, *Joel, Obadiah, Jonah*, 203, original emphasis. Wolff notes the allusion with the comment only that the *immediacy* of Yahweh's knowledge shows his intimate closeness to human affairs in the story (*Obadiah and Jonah*, 100). Stuart, in line with his approach to the message of the book, notes the connection to Gen 18:20–21, but prefers to understand the divine command as saying Nineveh's *misfortune* has risen to God's notice (444, 449; cf. Wolff, 95, n. 2c). Carey seems aware of the connection though he does not develop this thought or its implications explicitly (*Jonah*, 37–38).

9. Vriezen, *Outline*, 88.

contrast that is to exist between the community of God's people and the "Sodoms" of this world. Thus, Chris Wright argues that,

> Simply to be Israel meant having an ethical agenda and mission in the midst of the world. To be an Israelite was to be called to respond to God's covenant purpose for the nations by living as the people of God in their midst... In the midst of a world characterized by Sodom, God wants a community characterized by his own values and priorities, *i.e.* righteousness... and justice.[10]

Wright goes on to insist that being an ethical community was *constitutive* of Israel's mission to the nations:

> Abraham was chosen, not *because* of his righteousness, but *in order to* be the fountainhead of a righteous community. Election means election to an *ethical* agenda in the midst of a corrupt world of Sodoms... What is therefore highly significant in the structure of this verse [*i.e.* Genesis 18:19], syntactically as well as theologically, is the way ethics stands as the middle term between election and mission. The distinctive quality of life of the people of God, committed to his way of righteousness and justice, stands as the purpose of election on the one hand and the means to mission on the other. It is the fulcrum of the verse.[11]

Israel's destiny was to be such a community that in and through their existence all the nations would be blessed by God. It was their failure to be such a community that caused them to fall under the judgment of the exile. Indeed, shortly before this awful judgment, Jeremiah called Judah to repentance in language recalling the Abrahamic promise and mission from the Genesis narrative:

> "If you will return, O Israel," declares the Lord, "Then you should return to me. And if you will put away your detested things from my presence, and will not waver, and you will swear, 'As the LORD lives,' in truth, in justice and in righteousness; Then the nations will bless themselves in him, and in him they will glory." (Jer 4:1–2)

Again we see God's concern for the integrity of Israel as a community living in accordance with God's truth, justice, and righteousness, with

---

10. Wright, "Old Testament Ethics," 50.

11. Wright, "Old Testament Ethics," 50, 51. See also Wenham, *Genesis 16–50*, 42–44, 50.

the divinely intended result that *then* the Abrahamic promise would find fulfillment.[12]

With this initial allusion, then, the book of Jonah sets the entire story within the compass of God's covenantal dealing with Abraham and his people—and therefore with all the nations of the earth also in view, and reminds its readers of their status and responsibility as God's elect community. So, too, it offers its message also to the contemporary reader. In modern parlance we might say that *being* the church—that is, *being* a community of truth, righteousness and justice—is the means by which we realize our identity and mission as God's people in the midst of the nations.

A Kingdom of Priests

The Genesis 18 passage bears witness against Jonah in a further matter: the contrast between the response of Abraham and that of Jonah to Yahweh's revelation. Jonah "rose up to flee . . . from the presence of the LORD" (1:3), while Abraham "came near" and began to intercede for the people of Sodom (Gen 18:22–23).

It is noteworthy how prominent the theme of prayer is in the book of Jonah, although it is a theme rich in irony and parody.[13] In the first chapter of the book Jonah does not pray at all, even when called upon by the pagan captain of the ship: "Get up and call on your god. Perhaps your god will be concerned about us so that we will not perish" (Jonah 1:6). Jonah, however, does not pray; instead he sleeps. As yet he is unwilling to acknowledge that God is concerned about these heathen sailors. Later in the book it becomes evident that Jonah was indeed concerned about this very thing: that God might indeed have compassion on the pagans, and Jonah is wholly unprepared to share God's concern or to offer prayer on their behalf (see Jonah 4:2). Jonah only prays when he is brought to the very precipice of death at the gates of Sheol. His prayer, however, recorded in the beautiful psalm of chapter two is a model psalm of thanksgiving for deliverance.[14] In fact, Jonah 2:1 records the detail that (finally!) Jonah prayed, while the psalm itself is written from the perspective of a later time.

---

12. See Thompson, *Jeremiah*, 213.

13. For reflections on the theme of prayer in Jonah, see, for example, Allen, *Joel, Obadiah, Jonah*, 229, and Perry, *Honeymoon is Over*, 109–119.

14. Eugene Peterson makes much of Jonah's use of existing psalms in his prayer, in a reflection on pastoral spirituality and ministry. See Peterson, *Unpredictable Plant*, 99–115.

But Jonah's joy in his salvation is short-lived. After he fulfills his commission and Nineveh, contrary to his message, is spared, he again prays, though this time in anger and self-pity. Through these accounts, therefore, we observe that Jonah's prayer was self-centered and mean-spirited, a perversion of true prayer. On no occasion does he pray for the mariners or for Nineveh. This stands in stark contrast to Abraham in Genesis 18 whose intercession on behalf of Sodom is bold, insistent, and deeply concerned. Of even greater import than Abraham's intercession is Yahweh's response to Abraham's prayer, mercifully conceding to the parameters Abraham sets, within which Yahweh will act in judgment upon Sodom.[15]

The imagery of powerful, sacrificial, and heart-felt intercessory prayer lies also in the background in Jonah 4, where the parody of the prophet reaches its climax.

> But it greatly displeased Jonah and he became angry. He prayed to the LORD and said, "Please LORD, was not this what I said while I was still in my own country? Therefore in order to forestall this I fled to Tarshish, for I knew that you are a gracious and compassionate God, slow to anger and abundant in lovingkindness, and one who relents concerning calamity. Therefore now, O LORD, please take my life from me, for death is better to me than life" (Jonah 4:1–3).

In 4:3 Jonah is citing Exodus 34:4–7, Yahweh's self-revelation given to Moses where the Lord proclaimed his name after Moses had asked to see his glory. The divine self-description became something of a creedal statement in later biblical writings.[16] In Jonah this citation functions to provide a true understanding of Yahweh's character, and thus to establish the *imitatio Dei* as the content of God's ethical requirement in a new context. This is Yahweh's true nature and true glory; that is, his merciful and compassionate character, especially in the face of human sinfulness. God can deal with human sinfulness in one of two ways: he might judge and punish the one who sins, or he might have mercy and forgive. In response to Moses's intercession God indeed pardons the people.

But Jonah's citation also contains a phrase not found in Exodus 34: "one who relents concerning calamity." The additional phrase follows the version of the creedal formulation found in Joel 2:13. Further, the language of God "relenting" concerning intended disaster pronounced upon an

---

15. See Wenham, *Genesis 16–50*, 51–53, 63.

16. See Num 14:18; Neh 9:17; Pss 86:15; 103:8; 111:4; 145:8–9; Joel 2:13; Nah 1:3. See Allen, *Joel, Obadiah, Jonah*, 228, and Durham, *Exodus*, 453–55.

ungodly nation is also found in Jeremiah 18:8. These texts coalesce in Jonah 3:9–10 to describe Nineveh's repentance and deliverance:

> "Who knows, God may turn and relent and withdraw his burning anger so that we will not perish." When God saw their deeds, that they turned from their wicked ways, then God relented concerning the calamity which he had declared he would bring upon them. And he did not do it.

Moreover, the idea of God "relenting" concerning disaster is not altogether absent from the Exodus context. Jonah's citation conflates Exodus 34 with the incident in Exodus 32 where the people committed sacrilege, worshipping the golden calf. Here, too, God's wrath was "burning hot" against his people so that he threatened to destroy them (Exod 32:9–10). Into this breach of relationship Moses stepped, interceding on behalf of the people, and imploring God to "turn from [his] burning anger and change [his] mind about doing harm to [his] people," with the result that "the LORD changed his mind about the harm which He said He would do to His people" (Exod 32:12, 14).[17] Moses continued his intercession for the people in Exodus 32:31–32; 33:12–17; and 34:8–9. Through Moses's intercession God relented of his destruction of the people, forgave them, and dwelt amongst them, taking them as his people in spite of their sin.

Moses's intercession for the people—like that of Abraham—was constant, persistent, and bold. He identifies and stands in solidarity with his people at great personal risk: "Alas, this people has committed a great sin, and they have made a god of gold for themselves. But now, if you will, forgive their sin—and if not, please blot me out from your book which you have written!" (Exod 32:31–32).

Such self-sacrificial intercession stands in stark contrast to the self-centered and self-indulgent prayer of Jonah. Jonah never once prayed for the gentiles. His prayer in chapter four is a wail of anger and self-pity. Whereas Moses is prepared to sacrifice his life and accept damnation in solidarity with his people, Jonah would rather die than have God's compassion extended to the gentiles, and especially to the Ninevites.

What is evident in Jonah's prayer is that at the core of his being, Jonah did not really know the heart of God. Or perhaps better: he knew it only too well and did not agree with it ("I *knew* that you were a gracious and compassionate God"); he was not *aligned* with the heart of God, but was more committed to his view of Israel's uniqueness and privilege, and his disdain and hatred for her enemies. He knew the word of God, and he

---

17. The NIV uses the term "relent" in both verses twelve and fourteen.

knew the creedal formulation of Israel. His heart, however, was committed to his own security, comfort, and belief structure. He had no fundamental identification with the people that God loved—all people, and as a result he missed his *raison d'etre*.

A Community of the Word

Thus far, my exposition has focused largely on the figure of Jonah, and the message of the book of Jonah in light of the intertextual references we have examined. While this is not inappropriate, it is crucial to recall that the primary message of the book is not about Jonah at all, but about God, and about God's character, and God's redemptive will—not to mention also God's utter sovereignty over nature, people, and nations, a sovereignty which nevertheless encompasses a sphere in which human persons have genuine agency, with all the ambiguity and consequences associated with such privilege.[18] The climax and decisive message of the whole is surely Jonah 4:11, the final verse of the book in which God puts the fundamental question to the prophet about his compassion for all his creatures, both human and nonhuman, a compassion which judges the people of Nineveh not as utterly wicked pagans deserving of judgment, but more as naive children who have not yet learnt the rudimentary realities of existence, such as distinguishing between one's right and left hand. God *loves* the Ninevites and yearns over them in spite of their history of idolatry, violence, and injustice. That this view is so very different from that of other Old Testament texts such as Nahum, needs hardly to be said, and it is on this ground that Jonah makes

---

18. The ambiguity of the sphere of freedom may be observed in the mariners' dilemma in chapter one: whatever they do with respect to Jonah, is bound to be wrong. They are placed in a circumstance in which they must *act* but can do so only in the committal of themselves and their action to divine judgment: they cannot *know* the right and the good ahead of their action (vv. 10–14). The consequences of the sphere of freedom are, of course, dramatically portrayed in Jonah's story: he uses his genuine agency to flee from the presence of the Lord, and God allows him to do so—and to suffer the consequences. Yet his sphere of freedom is wholly enclosed and surrounded on every side by the greater and more dynamic freedom of God, who rescues his prophet and restores his commission! So, too, the agency of the Ninevites in chapter three is genuine: their choice either for or against God will have *decisive* consequences for them (vv. 9–10). To observe these features of the narrative does not, of course, solve or resolve the age-old mystery of the relation of divine and human agency; rather, it is merely a descriptive tool that shows that the ancients also wrestled with these impenetrable mysteries of our faith, and perhaps also gives some pastoral guidance for those grappling with moral, and other difficult life issues and questions, in the modern world.

its most compelling and fruitful contribution to Old Testament faith and theology.[19]

Thus God is educating Jonah, treating Jonah, too, as a willful and wayward child requiring instruction in the meaning of his own faith, tradition, and vocation. The instruction aims at the inculcation of the same attitude toward the pagan nations that God has, an attitude—and no doubt, for contemporary readers, a practice—of tender compassion, seeking the repentance and renewal of the Ninevites rather than their otherwise inevitable judgment and destruction. Jonah, too, as the recipient of a salvation utterly grounded in the mercy of the gracious God, can but—or at least *should* (cf. also the note of obligation in Matt 18:33)—have similar mercy towards those who are no more undeserving than himself. *Salvation is from the Lord!* (Jonah 2:9).

If, in the narrative, God is educating Jonah, the book of Jonah itself serves to educate the people of God. In his story, postexilic Judah see a reflection of their own experience of "death and resurrection," of their own unaccountable salvation at the hands of a merciful God, of their deliverance from exile and their restoration to the land, and with it, the restoration of their vocation as the people of God among the nations. And just as the "word of the Lord" came mercifully but insistently to Jonah "a second time" (3:1), so God's call upon his people has not been revoked. Nevertheless, becoming the people of God is a work beset with obstacles and detours, and God's people must learn again what it means to be his elect community, a kingdom of priests, and a holy nation. And such learning requires a return to the seminal sources of their faith, a deeper and more thorough-going apprehension of their identity as God's covenant people, as well as a clearer vision of the character and purposes of the God whose people they are. In short, such learning requires them to become a community of the word once spoken to Israel, and to reappropriate afresh in their common life, the saving truth of that word, and the moral and missional vision, which are the implications of that truth.

Part of the genius of the book of Jonah is not merely its inspired narrative, or the scope and beauty of the prophetic vision presented in it, but the *way* in which the prophet has set forth the message. The book itself is an exercise in theological reappropriation of the ancient traditions and Scriptures that shape Israel's identity and calling.[20] It plumbs the foundational

---

19. It is of interest that Nahum 1:2–3 also cites Exodus 34:6–8, though with a quite different emphasis and perspective. Whereas Nahum is typical in his ascription of the divine mercy to Israel, he insists that God "reserves his wrath for his enemies"—in this case, Nineveh (1:2)!

20. It is interesting to observe the use of the adjective *didactic* in the various genre

stories of Abraham and Moses to set forth a compelling vision of God and his intent for the people. It explores the prophetic witness of Jeremiah and Joel, with echoes of other prophetic figures such as Elijah. It introduces a psalm—whether written by the prophet or "borrowed" from Israel's liturgical tradition, we cannot tell—but which invites comparison with similar psalms and similar imagery in the Psalter. The book is structured around the familiar idea of the "the word of the Lord coming" to the prophet (1:1; 3:1) as it did to Joel, Hosea, and Ezekiel, among others. The scriptural echoes and resonances developed in the book stand in contrast to the prophet who, decidedly, is *not* Abraham, Moses, Elijah, or Jeremiah; *and*, presumably, in contrast to the prophet's contemporaries in Judah who also fall short of the vision of who they might be—are called to be—as God's servant and "light to the nations" (Isa 49:6).

Also embedded in the text and therefore part of the didactic structure and function of the book are confessional and theological materials from the tradition which synthesize the faith of the ancient people of God. I have noted already the role of Exodus 34:6–7 in the Hebrew Bible. Another confessional element is found in Jonah 1:9 where Jonah confesses the "Lord God of heaven who made the sea and the dry land." Not only is God the sovereign creator but, as the narrative makes clear, he rules and guides his creation, intimately involved especially in human affairs. God is also the judge who holds the nations to account, and finally the merciful redeemer, as the climax of the psalm makes clear: "Salvation is from the Lord" (Jonah 2:9). The book reflects at length on the relation of Israel and the nations, on prayer, on the nature of repentance, and as I have argued, on what it means to be the people of God.

Israel, therefore, is an elect people, called to be a kingdom of priests and a holy nation in the midst of all the nations (Exod 19:4–6), and as noted, a "light to the nations." Some care is required here if we are to avoid over-reading the book of Jonah, particularly with respect to the idea of mission. According to Ronald Clements, the theology of election was a conscious attempt to relate the special bond between Yahweh and Israel to the existence of the surrounding nations, an attempt carried out in a period characterized by crisis and threat.[21] What is intriguing in Deuteronomy is, that "although

---

descriptions commentators apply to the book of Jonah. For Allen, the work is a *didactic parable* (*Joel, Obadiah, Jonah*, 186), for Wolff, a *didactic novella* (*Obadiah and Jonah*, 83–84), and for Stuart, a *sensational, didactic, prophetic narrative* (*Hosea–Jonah*, 435). Despite the different genres ascribed to the text, the commentators agree that the book aims to *teach* and *instruct*. I suggest that it does so by its deliberate intertextual retrieval of core elements of Israel's covenantal tradition.

21. Clements, *Old Testament Theology*, 89.

it consciously considers Israel's position in relation to the nations, it does not develop from this any role or service that Israel is to play in regard to them."[22] Horst Preuss concurs, saying, "any possible significance attributed to the chosen people's responsibility toward the foreign nations is passed by in silence. *Israel, first of all, must and ought to discover itself again.*"[23] According to Preuss, then, the first responsibility Israel has is to live in accordance with its own identity and purpose as the elect of God. Yahweh's redemptive activity on Israel's behalf has the purpose "of other nations coming to know and acknowledge him as God. Thus YHWH's activity on his people's behalf is exemplary of his intention for his world."[24] In effect, Preuss wants to maintain a distinction between active and passive mission as the nature of Israel's calling. Israel is not called as an active missioner toward the nations, even in the case of the book of Jonah. Rather, Yahweh's "activity on behalf of his people shall possess the power of attraction that works outwardly in an enticing fashion to demonstrate the truth of YHWH before the rest of the world."[25] Israel mediates by what it is and what it experiences, that is, passively, a wider participation in its own community with God.[26]

The picture in the New Testament is, of course, quite different, because the church *is* commanded to "go, therefore, and make disciples of all nations" (Matt 28:19)—mission in the active sense. The church can take encouragement, however, from the book of Jonah with respect to its proclamation. The message of Jonah in 3:4, as terse and as unhelpful as it was—a declaration of impending doom rather than an announcement of good news and a call to salvation—nonetheless became the catalyst of a remarkable revival in the lives of the hearers. "It is clearly not Jonah but the word of God

22. Clements, *Old Testament Theology*, 95.

23. Preuss, *Old Testament Theology*, 1:33 (emphasis added).

24. Preuss, *Old Testament Theology*, 2:300.

25. Preuss, *Old Testament Theology*, 2:292. For Preuss's comments on the book of Jonah specifically, see page 303: "The Book of Jonah is also misunderstood, if one interprets it as a call to undertake a mission to the heathen. Much more, it has to do with Israel's not standing as a barrier between YHWH and the nations, due to its proud and egotistical certainty in its own salvation. Further, YHWH's compassion toward the heathen is not to be indignantly contested or undervalued."

26. Preuss, *Old Testament Theology*, 2:302. Thus, on page 305 Preuss goes on to comment, "The servant *was not to be* a light to the nations, and this is not mentioned as his mission, but rather he *is* this light; that is, his influence consists in the fact that 'light,' that is, salvation, is to be transmitted to the nations" (original emphasis). See also Clements, *Old Testament Theology*, 96, who arrives at a similar conclusion, stating that "the light that God had given to Israel would become a light by which other nations also might live . . . The picture is not that of a 'mission' in the strict sense of a going out to the nations, but rather that, when Israel returns to its homeland, it will bring the faithful of other nations in its train."

that converts Nineveh."²⁷ The great revival of chapter three resulting in the repentance of Nineveh had nothing to do with Jonah's depth of spirituality, degree of consecration, passionate ministry, spiritual anointing, prayerful preparation, learned exposition, eloquent rhetoric, love for the people, or dedication to God. On all counts, Jonah fails. The only reason that can be given for the spiritual awakening that grips Nineveh is the sovereign work of God accomplished through the proclamation of his mighty word. As is the testimony of Acts, so here: "The word of God kept on spreading . . . The word of the Lord continued to grow and to be multiplied . . . So the word of God was growing mightily and prevailing" (Acts 6:7; 12:24; 19:20). Jonah is, of course, a parody, and preachers should *not* seek to emulate him in his lack of spirituality, preparation, consecration, and so on! But the community of God's people, as a community of the Word, will necessarily also be a community that heralds the message of Christ, confident not in its own power or eloquence, but in the grace of the one who has called them to this service.

Nevertheless, Jonah's aim is not the creation of a company of preachers or missioners but the formation of a renewed covenant community, an elect people, a kingdom of priests whose lives together are grounded in and shaped by the Holy Scriptures and the confessional materials deriving from them: a community of the Word. For this is a presupposition of mission, even in the New Testament. And the book of Jonah models how such a community might be nurtured: by means of creative retrieval of the sources of the faith, mined in Holy Scripture, and by theological reflection on and interpretation of those sources, aiming at a "conversion of the imagination" such that the people of God are wrested as it were, from the confining ideologies and belief structures of the surrounding culture, and empowered and envisioned to inhabit the world *differently*, as the people of the God whose world it is.²⁸ Walter Brueggemann has written that,

> The prophetic tradition is not so much about scolding and threat as it is a massive act of imagination that asserts that the world could be different . . . I suggest that the recovery of the biblical text is urgent, the most urgent "social action" that can

---

27. Cary, *Jonah*, 111.

28. I was first introduced to the idea of the "conversion of the imagination" via Peterson, *Christ Plays*, where in his reflection on the plagues narrative in Exodus, Peterson writes that "If Moses led them out of Egypt with their imaginations still controlled by Egypt, it wouldn't be long before they would be repeating the 'way of Egyptian success' themselves" (162). He argues that the peoples' imaginations required exorcising, "clearing the mind to accept God's revelation reality, energizing their spirits to live in the world of salvation . . . mentally free of the evil imagination that had crushed the life out of them for so long" (163).

be undertaken. For it is only when the past is brimming with miracle and the future is inundated with fidelity that the present can be re-characterized as a place of neighborliness . . .[29]

A full account of how a community of the word might be nurtured is not possible in this chapter. I will, however, provide a few pointers in that direction. The first pointer comes from William Willimon who observes that "the normative scriptural encounter for the church is in Sunday worship. Think of the church as primarily a place where we are taught to read in a way that is Christian."[30] In the context of worship Scripture is interpreted, expounded, and proclaimed in such a way that it narrates the new world of salvation and the lives of God's people within that world, locating them in that world, instructing them in its ways, and rescripting their lives so that they are "caught up in a great drama that is called salvation."[31]

While we might agree with Willimon that Sunday (weekly?) worship provides the normative scriptural encounter for the church, it is not sufficient by itself. The second pointer to becoming a community of the word is that God's people must become "reading communities," developing practices of instruction, reflection, and deliberation that allow the word to reshape, and to become embedded in, the daily lives of God's people. L. Gregory Jones argues that the church becomes deeply immersed in Scripture through practices of catechesis, critical study, and reflecting on Scripture in the light of our engagements in the world. The aim is to become wise and faithful readers of Scripture—in community—so that the members of the church might imaginatively appropriate and perform Scripture in their everyday world.[32] Allen Verhey provides similar guidance arguing that Christian communities must become sites of moral discourse, deliberation, and discernment, based on their extensive and vigorous engagements with the Scriptures. His "rules" for reading the Scriptures include reading Scripture *humbly*, in the community of the church, and as "canon," by which he means ecclesially and in accordance with the "rule of faith." They are also to be read with exegetical care, skill, and insight, as well as prayerfully, with what he terms "certain standards of excellence" or "virtues" appropriate to the nature and intent of Scripture: holiness and sanctification, fidelity and creativity, discipline and discernment.[33]

---

29. Brueggemann, *Word that Redescribes*, 16–17.
30. Willimon, *Pastor*, 81.
31. Willimon, *Pastor*, 82, 86, 83, 104. See particularly chapter five, 111–39.
32. See Jones, "Formed and Transformed," 18–33.
33. See Verhey, *Remembering Jesus*, 49–76.

Particularly important in these essays is the recognition of different modes of thought appropriate to our engagement with Scripture: reflective and deliberative. Oliver O'Donovan distinguishes the two modes of thought as follows:

> Reflection is "turning back" on something that is already there, "behind us" as it were; "deliberation" is "weighing up," facing an alternative, looking at possible courses of action that have not yet been resolved. More simply, we may speak of "thinking about" and "thinking towards."[34]

Reflection provides basis for deliberation, and both are essential if Christian communities are to become communities of the Word. Christians *reflect* on Scripture, thinking about its stories and teachings, its proverbs and songs, images and commands—*everything* they find in the Bible. They reflect also about everything in life, whether relationships, employment, leisure, possession, or politics—*everything!*—in the light of the Scriptures. Christians *deliberate*, however, when considering how to live in accordance with the Scriptures in particular instances, seeking to discern what it might mean to embody and enact the vision and virtues of the gospel, reconciliation, and hope in those circumstances. Hearing the proclaimed word at regular worship is important, but it must be supplemented by these additional disciplines of reflection and deliberation if the community is to become a community of the word.[35] And let me suggest also, how critical it is that children, youth, and young adults are also participants in these congregational practices, and inducted, as appropriate to their age and development, into the church as a "reading community." The mission of the church, after all, includes the evangelization and discipling of the next generation in its midst.

A final pointer is that already identified in the book of Jonah: the community of the word must hold forth the word of life in the midst of a "crooked and perverse generation" among whom they shine as lights (Phil 2:15–16); it must *proclaim* the word—the Word made flesh, Jesus Christ, as set forth in the words of Scripture. Proclamation, of course, can occur both formally and informally, and it is arguable that the informal proclamation of Christian people amongst their friends, families, and colleagues is indeed the most effective means of proclamation by which the word of God "grows mightily and prevails" in a community. Christian proclamation, however, arises from the community grounded in the word, taught the word, and

---

34. O'Donovan, *Self, World, and Time*, 31. See also O'Donovan, "Moral Reasoning," 122–27.

35. An excellent resource for Christians and churches toward the development of these practices is Stone and Duke, *How to Think Theologically*.

one that has learned to reflect deeply on the saving truths of God and the wonder of his redemptive work in Jesus Christ.

Conclusion

In this chapter I have adopted a theological and figural interpretation of Jonah to reflect on the nature and mission of the community of God's people in the world loved by God, and redeemed by God in Jesus Christ. I have explored several intertextual allusions from the book which mine earlier significant texts in Israel's Scriptures, in the attempt to understand how the prophet's story—which is the "message" of the book—might have been heard by the ancient community, and how that message might in turn be heard also by the church in our time and place.

Jonah's story is that of Judah, and of the church: each chosen and called to a ministry as priest, to witness the word of God to the nations, and to bear the nations in prayer before God. In the case of Jonah and Judah, their refusal to accept this ministry and this call led inexorably and inevitably to their death. Can it be otherwise for a recalcitrant church? Jonah insists that the church can exist only as it accepts and lives in humble and responsive obedience to its commission. To be the church is to be elect, and to be elect is to be commissioned. There is no election which does not issue in mission. And the church can have no existence other than by participation in the mission of God. According to Jonah, the witness and mission of the church in a hostile cultural environment consists in its moral existence, intercession, and proclamation. As a moral community the church exemplifies the character of God, exhibiting love and holiness, righteousness and justice, both in its common life, and in its relations to the broader society. As a kingdom of priests the church is a community of prayer and proclamation. It stands in costly identification and solidarity with all those created and loved by God, and bears them in earnest and persistent prayer before the Father, pleading for their deliverance. It also holds forth the word of life trusting God to watch over his word that it might be fruitful and that the number of disciples might be multiplied. As the community of the word, it is mindful that its first responsibility is to be itself, the people of God, in all the fullness of what that means. To cite Preuss once more: "*Israel, first of all, must and ought to discover itself again.*"[36] So, too, must the church. And the only way to that end is via extensive, imaginative, engagement with the sources of our faith, especially Scripture. The church can legitimately be what it is called to

---

36. Preuss, *Old Testament Theology*, 1:33 (emphasis added).

be beyond its four walls only when it is authentically what it is called to be within the walls. And in this, Jonah has showed the way.

Bibliography

Allen, Leslie C. *The Books of Joel, Obadiah, Jonah and Micah*. The New International Commentary on the Old Testament. Grand Rapids: Eerdmans, 1976.

Brueggemann, Walter. *The Word that Redescribes the World: The Bible and Discipleship*. Minneapolis: Fortress, 2006.

Cary, Phillip. *Jonah*. Brazos Theological Commentary on the Bible. Grand Rapids: Brazos, 2008.

Clements, Ronald. E. *Old Testament Theology: A Fresh Approach*. Marshall's Theological Library. London: Marshall, Morgan and Scott, 1978.

Durham, John I. *Exodus*. Word Biblical Commentary 3. Waco: Word, 1987.

Jones, L. Gregory. "Formed and Transformed by Scripture: Character, Community, and Authority in Biblical Interpretation." In *Character and Scripture: Moral Formation, Community, and Biblical Interpretation*, edited by William P. Brown, 18–33. Grand Rapids: Eerdmans, 2002.

O'Donovan, Oliver. "Christian Moral Reasoning." In *New Dictionary of Christian Ethics and Pastoral Theology*, edited by Atkinson, David J. and David H. Field, 122–27. Leicester: IVP, 1995.

———. *Self, World, and Time: Ethics as Theology, Volume 1, An Induction*. Grand Rapids: Eerdmans, 2013.

Perry, T. A. *The Honeymoon is Over: Jonah's Argument with God*. Peabody, MA: Hendrickson, 2006.

Peterson, Eugene H. *Christ Plays in Ten Thousand Places: A Conversation in Spiritual Theology*. Grand Rapids: Eerdmans, 2005.

———. *Under the Unpredictable Plant: An Exploration in Vocational Holiness*. Grand Rapids: Eerdmans, 1992.

Preuss, Horst Dietrich. *Old Testament Theology*. 2 vols. Translated by Leo G. Perdue. The Old Testament Library. Louisville: Westminster John Knox, 1995.

Stone, Howard W., and James O. Duke. *How to Think Theologically*. 3rd ed. Minneapolis: Fortress, 2013.

Stuart, Douglas. *Hosea–Jonah*. Word Biblical Commentary 31. Waco: Word, 1987.

———. "Jonah, Book of." In *Dictionary of Old Testament Prophets*, edited by Mark J. Boda and J. Gordon McConville, 455–66. Downers Grove: IVP Academic, 2012.

Thompson, J. A. *The Book of Jeremiah*. The New International Commentary on the Old Testament. Grand Rapids: Eerdmans, 1980.

Timmer, Daniel C. *A Gracious and Compassionate God: Mission, Salvation and Spirituality in the Book of Jonah*. New Studies in Biblical Theology. Nottingham: Apollos, 2011.

Verhey, Allen. *Remembering Jesus: Christian Community, Scripture, and the Moral Life*. Grand Rapids: Eerdmans, 2002.

Vriezen, Th. C. *An Outline of Old Testament Theology*. 2nd ed. Translated by S. Neuijen. Oxford: Basil Blackwell, 1970.

Wenham, Gordon. *Genesis 16–50*. Word Biblical Commentary 2. Waco: Word, 1994.

Willimon, William H. *Pastor: The Theology and Practice of Ordained Ministry*. Nashville: Abingdon, 2002.
Wolff, Hans Walter. *Obadiah and Jonah: A Commentary*. Translated by Margaret Kohl. Minneapolis: Augsburg Publishing House, 1986.
Wright, Christopher J. H. "Old Testament Ethics." In *New Dictionary of Christian Ethics and Pastoral Theology*, edited by David J. Atkinson and David H. Field, 49–56. Leicester: IVP, 1995.

4

The Church as Family in the Teaching of Jesus, and Today

Margaret Wesley

Family in the First Century Roman Empire

"Family" is one of the most powerful words in any language, and *oikos*[1] was one of the most powerful forces in the Roman Empire, where the emperor was *pater familias*[2] of the empire and fathers were emperors over their households. Over the past century the meaning of the word "family" has changed a great deal. It used to mean "mum, dad, and the kids" and that is still what dictionaries tell us, but in general usage it is much more elusive.

Whatever we mean by the word, there is no direct translation in Greek, Latin, Hebrew or Aramaic. *Oikos* included all who lived in the household, including slaves and dependent friends, as well as extended family and previous generations. The *oikos* was the basic unit of the empire,[3] and the most important reference point from which people found their identity and their place in the world.

In our time, genealogical research has become a popular interest for a number of psychological and sociological reasons. I suspect that a feeling of

---

1. Household
2. Father/head of household
3. See, for example, Cicero's *De Beneficiis* I.53–55, where the household is called the seedbed of the state.

dislocation and disconnection within our communities has driven people to look to their ancestors for answers to questions about identity and direction. In the Roman Empire published genealogies were ancestral curriculum vitae, drawing attention to the highlights of the family tree.[4] They tended to ignore the less honorable details[5] unless of course their purpose was to discredit the individual or the family.[6] The genealogies in Matthew and Luke are examples of how a man[7] could be introduced by his ancestry. The difference between the two genealogies illustrates how different authors might highlight different details to suit the claims they are making about the individual concerned.[8]

When Jesus used family language to talk about his disciples, he was not doing something entirely unprecedented. He was identifying the church as what anthropologists call a fictive kinship group. A fictive kinship group is, as the name suggests, a group that exhibits family-like structures and loyalties, but where relationship ties are not those of legal kinship.[9] In the ancient world, fictive kinship groups formed to provide mutual support among individuals who had no kin or who had been forced to leave their families to find work, or whose family was not sufficiently influential to support their career advancement.[10] In some of the trade guilds that flourished at this time members would call each other "brother." In these groups, the place of the *pater familias* was taken by a patron.[11] A powerful patron could expect group members to demonstrate the sort of loyalty usually devoted to the head of a household. This is probably one reason why emperors tended to view guilds and associations with suspicion. Such men were never eager to see their subjects' loyalties divided. The family nature of the early Christian community was one of the factors that made it political. Those who called God alone "Father" could not belong to the household of Caesar.[12]

---

4. Burridge, *What Are the Gospels?*, 141.

5. Note how Josephus begins his own genealogy in Josephus, "Josephi Vita," 1. See also Rohrbaugh, "Legitimating Sonship," 188.

6. Hellerman, *Ancient Church*, 52. See also Oakman and Hanson, *Palestine in the Time of Jesus*, 28.

7. Women tended to be treated slightly differently, but the complexities of gender in this culture are beyond the scope of this paper.

8. See Oakman, *Palestine*, 54, and Rohrbaugh, "Legitimating Sonship," 188.

9. I use the word "legal" here to denote both biological and adoptive kinship. See Hellerman, *Ancient Church*, 4.

10. Dixon, *Roman Family*, 115.

11. Duling, "Matthean Brotherhood," 162.

12. Oakman, *Palestine*, 127. See also Aristotle, *Pol.* 1.1 [1252a7–17]; Philo, *Jos.* 37–39.

Church as Family in the Gospels

The Gospels[13] present Jesus as calling disciples out of their families into a new type of kinship where they can look to a new genealogy to find their identity. Mark 3:31–35 (cf. Matt 12:46–50; Luke 8:19–21) is the key passage where the Synoptic Gospels[14] describe the community of disciples as a fictive kinship group distinct from biological family ties. The language here is of substitution, not addition.[15] Family-centeredness is replaced by church-centeredness; church is the new family.[16]

When Jesus speaks in Mark 10:29–30 of the sacrifices which may be expected from one who becomes his disciple, his primary image is that of leaving the family house (*aphēken oikian*), and therefore being removed from mother, father, brothers, sisters, and children.[17] Such a call does not strike us as overly demanding. We see leaving home and family as an indispensable part of growing up and working out for ourselves who we are.[18] Yet in first-century Palestine only young women left the family home.[19] Young men stayed in their father's home, pursuing the family trade and finding career advancement in kinship relationships and the family's social networks. The call to leave not just relatives but house and fields reminds us that it was not just emotional security that Jesus called them to forsake, but economic security as well.[20] Jesus called young men to abandon their stability, identity, and income for the (humanly speaking) insecure and unstable life of a disciple.

---

13. This theme is presented most clearly in the Synoptics but is not absent from the Gospel of John.

14. The Gospel of John treats this subject a little differently. See Wesley, "Family Fractured."

15. Moxnes, *Putting Jesus*, 60.

16. Pilch and Malina, *Biblical Social Values*, 73.

17. It is worth noting that there is no mention of leaving husband or wife. Following this through would be outside the scope of this discussion, but it may well be that the value placed by Jesus on the marriage bond (e.g. Neyrey, "Loss of Wealth"; Matt 19:3–9) precludes him from endorsing his disciples leaving their marriage partners for his sake. If that is the case, it is interesting to note that leaving children is not excluded in the same way, though we can reasonably assume that Jesus is speaking of adult children or children who will be cared for by those left behind. An unlikely alternative put forward by Hellerman is that the marriage relationship is not mentioned because it is the least valued of kinship bonds. See Hellerman, *Ancient Church*, 39.

18. See Moxnes, *Putting Jesus*, 46.

19. Hellerman, *Ancient Church*, 32–33. Perhaps Jesus is deliberately phrasing his call to discipleship in terms of a marriage proposal?

20. See Moxnes, "What Is a Family?," 23.

We hear echoes of Genesis 12:1 in Jesus's words about leaving home. Abraham was similarly called to leave house, kin, and land in order to form a new household, one in which Abraham was to be father but YHWH was to be head.[21]

Church Versus Family

Jesus's call to disciples to leave home is underlined by the account of the converse occurring in his own life. In Mark 6:4 and Matthew 13:54–58[22] household, family, and village unite in their failure to honor the prophet among them. They insult him by reminding him of his humble origins. Jesus responds in kind by questioning their ancestry.

For a man to be shamed by his own people was to be marginalized and dislocated; to be put outside of his own place.[23] Jesus shows by his response to their insult that he was not about to allow them to define him or to allocate or withhold honor from him, even though they were the people who should have known him best.[24]

While this story serves a number of functions within the four Gospels, one of its functions, in the Synoptics at least, is to reinforce Jesus's call on his disciples to leave family and hometown behind. If the teacher chose a life of dislocation from kin and village, the disciple should be willing to do the same.

Not only does Jesus call his potential followers to leave family behind, in Luke 14:25–33 (cf. Matt 10:34–39) he starkly warns them that the cost of discipleship includes a resolve to *hate* father and mother. Jesus says this to shame those who begin to follow him but who give up because it is too hard.[25] Yet there is more to Jesus's command here than merely "Make sure you know what you are getting yourself into." Neyrey comments:

> Both versions [Matthew and Luke] contain an exhortation to "take up one's cross" and become a member of Jesus' fictive kinship group. The "cross" must surely be a metaphor for negative

---

21. These words of Jesus also find resonance with Philo's description of the stranger who makes his home among the people of Israel: "he has made his own kinsmen, whom alone it was natural for him to have as allies and champions, his irreconcilable enemies, by quitting their camp and taking up his abode with the truth, and with the honour of the one Being who is entitled to honour." Philo, *Works of Philo*, 4.178.
22. Cf. Luke 4:16–30 and John 4:44 where kin and house are not mentioned.
23. Moxnes, *Putting Jesus*, 67.
24. Moxnes, *Putting Jesus*, 53, 68.
25. Pilch and Malina, *Biblical Social Values*, 101.

experiences, possibly physical sufferings (begging, hunger) and/or social ones (loss of family/shame). These sufferings are not the result of taxation, drought, or some other "misfortune" but precisely the results of becoming Jesus' disciple. There would be, then, shame from the family and honour from Jesus.[26]

The Gospel of Thomas (saying 16) extends the words of Jesus in Matthew 10 to say that the result of family conflict will be that one stands "solitary." This idea is completely absent from the Synoptic tradition. The disciple who is rejected by family because of loyalty to Jesus does not stand solitary but is embraced by a hundred times more "houses, brothers and sisters, mothers and children, and fields," along with persecutions (Mark 10:30). Forsaken kin are not replaced by solitude but by fictive kin—lots of them!

Here again, contemporary Christians may miss the point if we come to these passages with only our own experience of family and community. In the early church, the degree of social dislocation suffered by converts to Christianity could be extreme.[27] Of course, there are many Christians today who are in no danger of underestimating the dangers of conversion. Christians living in Northern Africa and across Asia could teach many Western Christians as much about dislocation, estrangement, and insecurity as could our sisters and brothers in first-century Palestine.

The Gospels speak of shame and estrangement from family for those who follow Jesus, and they speak of shame from Jesus for those who turn back, but they also speak of Jesus giving honor to those who choose to endure hardship for his sake. The primary function of the Beatitudes within the Gospels is to attribute public honor to those who are without honor.[28] The subjects of these blessings—the destitute, the marginalized, those who are desperate for justice—could easily be disciples who had found themselves in that state because they had left the security of home.[29] Subject to shame for the sake of Jesus, these brothers and sisters received honor from Jesus and, on account of this blessing becoming part of the Gospels, they received honor from their church family as well.

This perspective must cause us to question the extent to which we should see Jesus as an advocate of "family values." Jesus called his disciples to relegate their families to something less than their first loyalty. Should we then say that Jesus was anti-family? If not for a small number of important counterexamples in the Gospels, we almost could. These counterexamples

---

26. Neyrey, "Loss of Wealth," 150. See also Moxnes, *Putting Jesus*, 58.
27. Taylor, "Social Nature," 134.
28. Hanson, "How Honorable!"
29. Neyrey, "Loss of Wealth," 145.

must be taken into account. Jesus was adamant that though family loyalties should be relativized, the fifth and seventh commandments must not be. Parents must be honored (Mark 7:9–13) and marriage partners must be faithful (Matt 5:31–32; 19:3–9; Mark 10:2–9; Luke 16:18).[30]

An important distinction is being made here. Jesus called his disciples to be prepared to become estranged from their families for his sake, but he did not call them to initiate estrangement if their family was prepared to tolerate their discipleship. Be willing to be estranged, he says, but make sure it really is your discipleship that causes the estrangement, and not an abrogation of responsibility or a preference for more congenial company.

In Mark 1:16–20 we find Simon Peter leaving everything to follow Jesus; then nine verses later we find him back in his family home. He must have caused disruption by leaving the family business, but clearly in this case, the family has not responded by cutting this new disciple off.

At this point it might be useful to outline some implications of Jesus's use of family language that are outlined in the Gospels. These include:

1. *Forbidding the use of honorary titles* on the basis that "You are all brothers" (Matt 23:8–10). In this kinship group there is no human who corresponds to the all-powerful *pater familias* because all authority resides with the Father in heaven.[31] Many denominations honor the letter of this law by ensuring that ordained clergy are not called "Father." But what of the spirit of the law? How often do we see autocratic church leaders, who would never tolerate being called "Father" but who give the clear message that belonging to "their" church means following their vision, getting with their program, and doing ministry the way they dictate? How often do we observe whole churches in the thrall of powerful lay people who might have the best of intentions, but who achieve their goals through fear and intimidation? The church is a family, but there is only one Father over us all.

2. *A high priority for forgiveness, repentance, and reconciliation.* Peter's question concerning the number of times he should forgive (Matt 18:21–22) is couched in the language of brotherhood. Similarly, Matthew 5:21–26 records Jesus forbidding the harboring of anger against a brother, and calling his followers to be reconciled with "your brother" as a matter of the highest priority.[32] It is commonly known that reconciliation in the church can be messy and complex, and there are

---

30. Note that while Jesus often called people to leave their homes, he nowhere called them to leave their marriage partners.

31. See Duling, "Matthean Brotherhood," 165–66.

32. Duling, "Matthean Brotherhood," 169–170.

many historical instances of the church doing this very badly. So, what may Christians do now to resource their churches to do it well? How many churches have healthy reconciliation procedures that the whole community is committed to? Do denominations provide sufficient mediators to congregations at an affordable cost? Can modern Christian communities remove the stigma attached to requesting mediation and normalize the need for reconciliation?

3. *Providing for those in the family who are in need.* The sharing of resources is probably one of the most basic functions of any family.[33] In the first century, as in some parts of the world today, converts to Christianity could find themselves cut off from the resources of their legal families. The new family, formed around Jesus, would then be called upon to provide for those new members. It is no coincidence that the author of the Gospel of Luke, who so clearly warns that poverty is a possible consequence of following Jesus, presents readers of Acts, with a picture of a church where property is sold and given to the poor among them.[34] In an age of international mass communication, this is so much more complex than in the first century. What are our obligations within such an enormous, global family?

4. *Honoring faithfulness and perseverance among sisters and brothers.* Disciples who were shamed by their families were honored by Jesus. It is because Jesus's glory shone so brightly in his life, in his death, and in his resurrection, that disciples were able to follow his example: to despise the shame of discipleship for the sake of the glory and honor that was promised. Only a community that gives honor to the least honorable among them can stand in the place of the rejected/rejecting family for those who have lost all honor in the eyes of the world in order to follow Jesus.[35]

Today: Church as Repository of Family Intensity

We find ourselves today in a culture that is very different from that in which the Gospels were set. The word, "family" means something different now, so we need to be careful as we apply the family language of the Gospels to our churches.

33. See, for example, Levi-Strauss, *Elementary Structures*, 29–41.
34. See Hellerman, *Ancient Church*, 21–22.
35. All the material up until this point can be found in considerably more detail in Wesley, *Son of Mary*.

The first thing that needs to be said, though, is that much of the church exists in cultures that are not so different. In many parts of the world people who are attracted to Jesus know that conversion to Christianity is likely to bring at least estrangement from their family, and possibly discipline or even death. For them the message of the Gospel needs no cultural translation. They need to hear that if they are willing to lose their lives for Jesus's sake that they will gain life eternal. But we who are safe in the West have no right to say that to them until we have done everything in our power to protect and provide for them as our brothers and sisters.

Christians in Australia and other Western contexts do need more cultural translation, when we consider what it means in our context that the church is family.

I have space here to open only one line of inquiry into this multifaceted question, and I will do that via the family systems theory as developed by Murray Bowen. This is a theory that attempts to understand emotional processes in families in a way that is culturally unbiased.[36] Bowen's work was brought to the attention of the church in 1985 by Edwin Friedman's book, *Generation to Generation*, and since then has been expounded to the church by authors such as Roberta Gilbert, Jim Herrington, and Ronald Richardson.[37] I direct you to those authors for a wide range of applications of family systems theory to church life. For now, however, I will stay with the particular concerns that I have already been considering: the complexity of being in two families at once, and the healthy and unhealthy ways that we can manage the tension between those two families.

Friedman's introduction of family systems theory into church thinking was based on his observation that churches and synagogues are very much like families.[38] It might be imagined that this might make it easy for the church to operate as a healthy family. In reality, the similarity between church and family increases the difficulty and complexity of living as brothers and sisters in Christ. I will demonstrate this using a small amount of theory and a case study.

Emotional cutoff is one of the eight concepts that undergird Bowen's theory.[39] It relates to the way adult children separate themselves from their

---

36. To some extent the jury is still out on whether the theory is entirely unbiased culturally. I have been convinced by research I have examined that the theory, when properly applied, does work across cultures, but I am aware that such research is ongoing.

37. Friedman, *Generation to Generation*. See also, Gilbert, *Eight Concepts*, and Richardson, *Healthier Church*.

38. Friedman, *Generation to Generation*, 195–97.

39. In Wesley, "Angels and Devils," I consider another of the eight concepts,

family in order to become more autonomous. In a family with low levels of *chronic anxiety*,[40] the family relationship system is able to tolerate this separation, and adult children are able to decide their life direction for themselves while remaining in healthy contact with their family, even if their life direction is not what the family had wanted for them.

Many families are not like that. In a family with high levels of chronic anxiety, adult children have a tougher time separating themselves from their family and becoming autonomous. A desire to move in a direction the family disapproves of tends to lead to either compliance or cutoff. Adult children may go along with the family's expectations and deny their drive toward autonomy, or they may cut themselves off from their family in order to pursue their own life goals.[41] This cutoff can take many different forms: from maintaining contact with the family but refraining from discussing those points upon which they differ, to moving interstate or overseas or completely refusing to see or talk to family members.

Cutoff enables adult children to pursue their life goals in opposition to their family, but it has several undesirable side effects. First, it increases the intensity of relationships within their family. In an intense relationship each individual is constantly reacting to the others rather than freely and thoughtfully choosing their own actions. Cutting off from an intense family relationship, however, does not give more room to move, but less. Because they have set their life course in rebellion against their family, many of their decisions become reactions against the family, rather than autonomous choices.

This first side effect of cutoff is a particular struggle for people who become Christians or enter the ministry against their family's strong objections. Maintaining contact with their family while remaining firm in their convictions can be extremely difficult, but it is worth all the courage it requires, partly because of the second side effect of cutoff.

This is where the family emotional system seriously starts to interact with the church family emotional system. When people are cut off from their family of origin, to any extent, the intensity of relationships outside the family also increases.[42] A personal characteristic in another person, a role, or a situation can remind the adult child of their family relationships and can bring all the intensity of their family into the new relationship. Because

---

reciprocal functioning, in relation to church life.

40. *Chronic anxiety* is another of the eight concepts. It is anxiety that becomes part of the background noise of family life, as opposed to anxiety connected with a particular threat.

41. In reality, there is often a combination of these.

42. Bowen, "Toward the Differentiation," 462.

churches are so much like families, they tend to draw in all the intensity of the emotional cutoff of every member. And we wonder why church business meetings are so stressful!

I will present something of my own experience[43] here to give some concrete expression to this theory. I am the youngest of six children and I grew up in a highly intense family. My father turned eighteen in the middle of WWII and returned to Australia with post-traumatic stress disorder, which he managed through excessive drinking, smoking, and gambling. My mother was chronically ill, but she was universally recognized as a local saint. Though I was not able to separate myself geographically from my father, I cut myself off from him emotionally as much as I could through hiding and avoiding his touch. On the other hand, I stuck to my mother like superglue and competed intensely with my siblings for her attention.

So, from my earliest childhood I functioned in my family system with a bipolar relationship toward my parents (overly positive on the one hand; overly negative on the other), and a competitive relationship with my siblings. You might already be able to guess what difficulties I might find myself encountering in the church.

My father stopped drinking when I was seven and my relationship with him began to improve very slowly. He died when I was fourteen, well before I had reached a point of being really comfortable with him, and certainly before I could establish an adult-to-adult relationship with him. A couple of years later my nearest sister left home and I had my mother to myself for two years. At one level I reveled in her undivided attention, at another level I began to feel suffocated by the intensity of our relationship. By the time I finished school I was desperate to leave and establish an identity for myself that was completely separate from my family. My mother and I became full-time students at different universities. We both filled our lives with interesting learning and relationships but we both struggled with ambivalence about our need for each other. By that time my older siblings had produced a number of grandchildren for her and some of the intensity of our relationship was redirected towards them. I married at twenty-two and my mother died when I was twenty-six, a year after I entered pastoral ministry.

---

43. It is somewhat unorthodox outside family systems circles to speak of one's own family of origin at an academic conference, but Bowen theorists have discovered that some of our most important research is done within our own families. Murray Bowen shocked the psychiatric community in 1967 when he presented a paper on his own efforts toward differentiation within his family of origin. See Bowen, "On the Differentiation," 467–69.

Before I began to study Bowen's family systems theory I had a rather linear understanding of the relationship between family of origin and church life: since I had been deeply hurt by growing up in a dysfunctional family, I carried the scars into adult life and those scars left me vulnerable to further hurt. People "bump up against each other" all the time in churches, so I am bound to get hurt regularly. If I am to be a mature Christian leader then I must respond to each hurt in a godly way, by being ready to forgive and move on. Of course, I was rarely able to do that as well as I thought I should. I was often hurt. I was often angry; and I was suffering from severe burnout by the time I was twenty-eight.

After studying the family systems theory for a number of years, I no longer see myself as scarred and vulnerable. Rather, I see myself as someone who has developed certain automatic ways of managing relationships that contributed to the survival of a family that was effectively in crisis for the first seven years of my life. Many of those automatic reactions are no longer helpful, and certainly do not contribute to the health of the churches in which I serve. I have learned to focus more on observing my reactions and slowing down my responses to give myself time to think and be less automatic. One of the observations I have made is that in relationship with people in authority I have a tendency to flip from being unrealistically positive to being distant and cut off, at the slightest indication that their attitude to me has begun to cool. That is, I tend to flip from relating to them like my mother to relating to them like my father. Because the church is so much like a family it is perfectly natural and understandable that I should do that. However, it isn't helpful.

Today: Church and Family/Church as Family

So, if I bring together what I know about Jesus's teaching about the church as family and my understanding of the family systems theory and my understanding of my own automatic functioning, what does it mean for me to be a well-functioning member of the church family today?

First, I remind myself of the conclusion I reached earlier: Jesus called his disciples to be prepared to become estranged from their families for his sake, but he did not call them to initiate estrangement. Be willing to be estranged, he says, but make sure it really is your discipleship that causes the estrangement, and not an abrogation of responsibility or a preference for more congenial company.

In other words, hang in there with your family of origin to the fullest extent consistent with your faith in Christ; and a little beyond what is consistent with your courage and inclination. Be present and accounted for in your family system. Turn up at the important events and let your voice be heard even when you know your opinions are not welcome. At the same time, listen to family members, and learn to tolerate the discomfort you feel when you strongly disagree with them.

As Christian people we have two families, and Jesus warns that there might be conflict between them. He calls us to give him our highest loyalty, but he does not call us to abandon our families in order to immerse ourselves in our church family. There is a paradox here. The more we cut ourselves off from our families of origin the more the intensity of our family relationships will turn up in our church family; and the more we will react automatically in ways we learned as we were growing up; and the less we will notice that we are doing that. The more we work at having real relationships within our family of origin, the more freedom we will have to make thoughtful choices about how we act in our church family.

Jesus spoke about the church as a family with God as the only father. Paul and John wrote about the church as the bride of Christ. "Therefore a man leaves his father and his mother and clings to his wife, and they become one flesh" (Gen 2:24). Marriage involves leaving and clinging. The quality of the clinging is proportional to the quality of the leaving. To function well as the bride of Christ, we each need to leave our families well; not cutting off, not running away, and not remaining entangled in their apron strings, but thoughtfully considering what it means to have a responsible, adult relationship with these people upon whom we had once been utterly dependent.

Conclusion

We operate within two family systems, our family of origin and the church family. For the first readers of the Gospels there was a real danger that conversion would lead to estrangement from family and the loss of property and security. Generally speaking, that is not our situation. Today, it is more likely that we will cut ourselves off emotionally from our family of origin and so import all the intensity, anxiety, and dysfunction of our families into the church. Across the centuries Jesus's advice is equally relevant: stand firm in your families and hold onto your Christian convictions whatever their opposition may be, and at the same time fulfill your responsibility to them; be present and accounted for. In that way the church can operate as the family of God; the bride of Christ; a new creation untainted by the anxious relationships that orbit around it.

Bibliography

Aristotle. *The Politics*. London: Penguin, 1992.
Bowen, Murray. "On the Differentiation of Self." In *Family Therapy in Clinical Practice*, edited by Murray Bowen, 467–528. Northvale: Jason Aronson, 1985.
———. "Toward the Differentiation of Self in Administrative Systems." In *Family Therapy in Clinical Practice*, edited by Murray Bowen, 461–66. Northvale: Jason Aronson, 1985.
Burridge, Richard A. *What Are the Gospels? A Comparison with Graeco-Roman Biography*. Grand Rapids: Eerdmans, 2004.
Dixon, Suzanne. *The Roman Family*. Baltimore: Johns Hopkins University Press, 1992.
Duling, Dennis C. "The Matthean Brotherhood and Marginal Scribal Leadership." In *Modelling Early Christianity*, edited by Philip F. Esler, 159–82. London: Routledge, 1995.
Friedman, Edwin H. *Generation to Generation: Family Process in Church and Synagogue*. New York: Guilford, 1985.
Gilbert, Roberta M. *The Eight Concepts of Bowen Theory*. Leading Systems, 2008.
Hanson, K.C. "How Honorable! How Shameful! A Cultural Analysis of Matthew's Makarisms and Reproaches." *Semeia* 68 (1994) 81–111.
Hellerman, Joseph H. *The Ancient Church as Family*. Minneapolis: Fortress, 2001.
Josephus, Flavius. "Josephi Vita." In *Flavii Iosephi Opera*, vol. 4, edited by Immanuele Bekkero, 287–354. Lipsiae: Teubner, 1856.
Levi-Strauss, Claude. *The Elementary Structures of Kinship*. Translated by James Harle Bell, John Richard von Sturmer, and Rodney Needham. Boston: Beacon, 1969.
Moxnes, Halvor. *Putting Jesus in His Place*. Louisville: Westminster John Knox, 2003.
———. "What Is a Family? Problems in Constructing Early Christian Families." In *Constructing Early Christian Families: Family as Social Reality and Metaphor*, edited by Halvor Moxnes, 13–41. London: Routledge, 1997.
Neyrey, Jerome H. "Loss of Wealth, Family and Honor: A Cultural Interpretation of the Original Four Makarisms." In *Modelling Early Christianity*, edited by Philip F. Esler, 139–58. London: Routledge, 1995.
Oakman, Douglas E., and K. C. Hanson. *Palestine in the Time of Jesus*. Minneapolis: Fortress, 1998.
Philo. *The Works of Philo: Complete and Unabridged*. Vol. 4. Edited and translated by C. D. Yonge. Peabody: Hendrickson, 1993.
Pilch, John J., and Bruce J. Malina. *Biblical Social Values and Their Meanings: A Handbook*. Peabody: Hendrickson, 1993.
Richardson, Ronald W. *Creating a Healthier Church: Family Systems Theory, Leadership and Congregational Life*. Creative Pastoral Care and Counseling Series. Minneapolis: Fortress, 1996.
Rohrbaugh, Richard L. "Legitimating Sonship: A Test of Honour." In *Modelling Early Christianity*, edited by Philip F. Esler, 183–97. London: Routledge, 1995.
Taylor, Nicholas H. "The Social Nature of Conversion in the Early Christian World." In *Modelling Early Christianity*, edited by Philip F. Esler, 128–36. London: Routledge, 1995.
Wesley, Margaret L. "Angels and Devils in my Family of Origin." In *Bowen Family Systems Theory in Christian Ministry: Grappling with Theory and its Application*

through a Biblical Lens, edited by Jenny Brown and Lauren Errington. Sydney: Family Systems Practice, 2019.

———. "Family Fractured and Reconfigured at the Cross." In *Loss and Discovery: Responding to Grief with the Compassion of Christ and the Skills of all God's People*, edited by Margaret Wesley. Melbourne: Mosaic, 2013.

———. *Son of Mary: The Family of Jesus and the Community of Faith in the Fourth Gospel*. Australian College of Theology Monograph Series. Eugene: Wipf & Stock, 2015.

5

Leadership in Apostolic Perspective

Acts 20:17–35[1]

Allan Chapple

A GENERATION AGO, PULITZER Prize winner James MacGregor Burns observed, "One of the most universal cravings of our time is a hunger for compelling and creative leadership."[2] If anything, this is even truer now than it was then—and it is just as pressing in the church as it is in the wider society: "It may well be that there is no more urgent challenge facing the church today than identifying, preparing, calling, authorizing, supporting, and encouraging faithful and capable leaders."[3] It has also become obvious that this craving to experience authentic leadership is matched by another: namely, the deep desire on the part of many pastors to exercise such leadership in the local church. We see this reflected in the way leadership textbooks have been pouring off the presses, both secular and Christian, and in the proliferation of leadership seminars and conferences.

These developments have not pleased everyone. Some warning voices are attempting to make themselves heard, and they have serious charges to

---

1. An earlier version of this chapter was published in *Churchman* 129, no. 2 (2015) 115–29. The editor, the Reverend Dr. Gerald Bray, has kindly given permission for it to be used here.

2. Burns, *Leadership*, 1.

3. Robinson and Wall, *Called to Be Church*, 236.

level. Prominent among them is theologian David Wells. Two decades ago he protested at what he called the "professionalization of the ministry"—a trend which he characterized as follows: "The central function of the pastor has changed from that of a truth broker to manager of the small enterprises we call churches."[4] Wells continued this protest in his next book,[5] in which he noted the promotion of a new paradigm of ministry: "The modern pastor . . . must be an efficient manager or, perhaps more to the point, a capable C.E.O." In his most recent book, he sees no reason to diminish his warnings about the dangers of this trend:

> We turn to structures and programs, appearances and management, advertising and marketing. Our preoccupation is with what we *do* and therefore with what we *control* . . . What is of primary interest in a technological world is technique, for that, after all, is how we manage everything else . . . In the kingdom of God, though, things are different . . . Being mastered by God is infinitely more important than having the know-how to manage the church . . . Business savvy, organizational wizardry, cultural relevance are simply no substitute for this.[6]

It is hard to deny that Wells and others like him[7] have a serious point—but equally, it is difficult to dismiss all of the current focus on leadership as simply worldly or irrelevant. In a volume intended to bring the church to the point of "breaking with the idols of our age," Os Guinness addresses this matter with commendable balance:

---

4. Wells, *No Place for Truth*, 13. The relevant section of the book is chapter VI: The New Disablers, 218–57.

5. Wells, *God in the Wasteland*.

6. Wells, *Courage*, 212–13 (original emphasis).

7. One example of many which could be cited is Brian Dodd's *cri de coeur*: "[The] lack of a divine reference point is all too obvious in the burgeoning market of leadership books and seminars. We have hungered after the world's wisdom and stuffed ourselves on secular practices, techniques and buzzwords . . . This trend to rely on secular leadership strategies, to equate ministry with management, has affected and infected the thinking of almost an entire generation of Christian leaders . . . as a pastor, I fell into no shortage of leadership seminars, books and tapes—Christian and otherwise. They dazzled and excited me . . . But many, if not most, Christian leadership books today are hardly Christian apart from proof-texting use of Scripture and application to church life. Distinctively Christian hallmarks of leadership found in the Bible are all but absent most of the time in popular Christian literature: the cross, self-sacrificial servanthood, love and gentleness, Spirit-led and Spirit-powered ministry through weak vessels, prayer, suffering, and the like . . . What was striking about Paul's leadership was not the ways that it reflected the effective leadership style of the people in his day. In fact, what was so impressive was the uniquely Christ-centered and cross-reflecting style of leadership that he exhibited." See, Dodd, *Empowered Church*, 11, 13, 14.

> The managerial revolution . . . could provide the church with a large, varied, and powerful toolbox . . . If Christians would use the best fruits of the managerial revolution constructively and critically, accompanied by a parallel reformation of truth and theology, the potential for the gospel would be incalculable.[8]

This is surely the right approach—but note how it makes everything dependent on whether we are able to sustain the necessary "reformation of truth and theology." How is such ongoing reformation possible? It should be obvious that the only way forward here is a constant return to the Bible, without which we are bound to lose our hold on the truth and to cease reforming our theology and practice. It is the Bible that must shape both our convictions about ministry and our conduct in ministry—for if the Bible doesn't do so, the world around us will. Our boundaries are porous, and we are in constant danger of being infiltrated and polluted by what the world has on offer. But when the Bible gives us so much to choose from, where shall we begin?[9]

To learn about leadership in and of the church, Paul's address to the elders of the church in Ephesus (Acts 20:17-35) is an obvious place to go.[10] This is the only speech in Acts directed at a Christian audience. In it, Paul reflects on his own leadership (vv. 18-27, 33-35) in order to prepare the elders for the new situation in which they will now be exercising theirs (vv. 28-32). The most obvious reason for his detailed review of his ministry is that he regards it as providing the example they should follow.[11] So how

---

8. Guinness, "Sounding Out the Idols," 154.

9. Good examples of how much relevant material there is in Scripture are provided by Laniak, *Shepherds*, and Tidball, *Ministry by the Book*.

10. While many regard this (and the other speeches in Acts) as Luke's own creation, it is very doubtful that this is the case. It would be surprising if Luke's account of the speech showed no signs of his editorial hand, but the many thematic and lexical similarities with Paul's letters show that its contents originated with Paul and not Luke: see especially Walton, *Leadership and Lifestyle*; see also Dupont, *Le Discours de Milet*, 26-30; Porter, *Paul in Acts*, 117; Trebilco, *Early Christians*, 177-96; Witherington, *Acts*, 610-11, 615-16, 627.

11. "[A] key aim of Paul's address is the presentation of a model of leadership for imitation . . ." Walton, *Leadership*, 200; cf. pp. 84-86, 134-136. Although widely held, this view has been challenged by Gaventa, "Miletus Speech," 36-52. She argues that Paul "does not present himself as an independent leader to be emulated" (46) and that "the real actors" responsible for the church are not the elders but "the characters of God, Jesus, and the Holy Spirit" (48). That this involves an unnecessary disjunction can be seen as soon as we ask how God, Jesus, and the Holy Spirit do their church-generating, church-sustaining work. It is clear that they use means, most notably the work Paul has done and now the leadership to be exercised by the elders. It is true that there would be no church without the work of "the real actors"—but it is also true that the church is to

does he characterize his leadership—and in what respects does he expect theirs to match his? With this snapshot to guide us, what is Paul's apostolic perspective on the character of leadership in and of the church?[12]

The Heart of Leadership

Paul's fundamental answer—the one from which all the others spring—is that he was "serving the Lord" (*douleuōn tō kyriō*, v. 19) in Ephesus. In one way, this speaks of his distinctiveness as an apostle: he is Christ's slave (*doulos*),[13] because the Lord (*kyrios*) "arrested" him (Phil 3:12) and commissioned him for service (v. 24). Yet there is a sense in which all believers are Christ's slaves, for he is the *kyrios* to whom all now belong and whom all are to serve.[14] So although there are many ways of serving, no Christian is ever more than a slave—not even an apostle! That is why Paul specifies that he served with humility (v. 19). In setting an example, he was also following an example: that given by the Lord himself.[15] "The mark of the true servant of God is a towel and not a scepter. He serves Christ by serving his people."[16] There is therefore no place in the church for the hubris that turns leadership into an assertion of individual or institutional power. Leadership that is authentically Christian is not first and foremost a display of dominance, for it is not about reaching the top and staying there. Nor is it primarily an exercise of authority, for it begins and always remains under the authority of the only *kyrios* of the church, the Lord Jesus. Rather, the essential character of Christian leadership is humble service. We must never forget that we are servants of the Lord who said, "I am among you as one who serves" (Luke 22:27).

This approach to leadership goes hand in hand with Paul's perception of the church. This becomes evident in verse 28, which constitutes the center

---

be shepherded by the "overseers" (*episkopoi*, v. 28), whose role is clearly secondary but no less real than that of the primary actors. It is a matter of both-and, not either-or as Gaventa implies.

12. Since it is likely that most who read this chapter will do so because they have a leadership role of some kind in their church, I will often refer to "us" and not just to "them" (the Ephesian elders), since, along with the rest of Scripture, this too "was written to teach us" (Rom 15:4).

13. See Rom 1:1; Gal 1:10; Phil 1:1; cf. Titus 1:1.

14. See Rom 14:18; 1 Cor 7:22; Eph 6:6; Col 3:24; cf. Rom 6:16, 22.

15. Note especially Mark 10:42–45; Luke 22:24–27; John 13:1–17. It is clear from Phil 2:5–8 that Paul knew about this example and regarded it as of fundamental importance.

16. Wiersbe and Wiersbe, *Ten Power Principles*, 36.

and crux of his speech.[17] Here we see that the church has Trinitarian roots.[18] First and foremost, it is God's church, the assembly that belongs to him (*tēn ekklēsian tou theou*).[19] He has made it his own at great cost to himself, having secured it by the blood of his very own [Son] (*dia tou haimatos tou*).[20] Its life is shaped by the Spirit, who has appointed them as overseers. Paul does not need to elaborate on any of this, for these are foundational truths that the elders have already learned from him. Yet the implications are profound and far-reaching. One of the most important of these lies in Paul's choice of preposition: the Spirit has made them overseers "in" the flock, not "over" it (*en hō humas to pneuma to hagion etheto episkopous*).[21] Those who are to shepherd the flock are sheep themselves! To use the more common family image, those whom we lead are our brothers and sisters. It is therefore essential that the character of our leadership matches its context—the nature of the church must govern the nature of its leadership. So what kind of leadership should be exercised among us? As we have seen, Paul regards humble service (v. 19) as the only appropriate stance for those whose calling is to lead the God-owned, blood-bought, Spirit-directed community that is the church (v. 28). Bonhoeffer makes the point this way: "Pastoral authority can be attained only by the servant of Jesus who seeks no power of his own, who himself is a brother among brothers submitted to the authority of the Word."[22]

So, no one serves as an owner or ruler; no one stands over and above the church; no one has an intrinsic right to exercise control—for the church

---

17. Numerous proposals have been made about the structure of this speech. The most convincing in my judgment is the chiasmus detected by Bossuyt and Radermakers, *Témoins*, 599–601. Verse 28 is the centre of this chiastic structure, in which verses 18–21 and verses 33–35 are a recall of the past, verses 22–24 and verse 32 deal with the present, and verses 25–27 and verses 29–31 anticipate the future. Although he sees the structure differently, C. K. Barrett also regards verse 28 as "both the practical and the theological centre of the speech" (*Acts*, vol. 2, 974).

18. Bossuyt and Radermakers, *Témoins*, 604, 606–7; Cheng, *Characterisation of God*, 122–23; Dupont, *Discours*, 150–57; Fitzmyer, *Acts*, 680; Schnabel, *Acts*, 865; Zmijewski, *Die Apostelgeschichte*, 749.

19. For this reading, see Metzger, *Textual Commentary*, 425–27.

20. For good discussions of the textual variants and translation options here, with reference to other significant discussions, see Harris, *Jesus as God*, 136–41; Walton, *Leadership*, 95–98. It is difficult to see why I. Howard Marshall has rejected this understanding of the phrase on the grounds that "it uses the adjective as equivalent to a noun, which is grammatically possible but unparalleled" ("Place of Acts," 163). The plural is used this way in Acts 4:23 and 24:23 (and also in John 1:11; 13:1; 1 Tim 5:8), and there is plenty of evidence outside the New Testament for using the term as a noun (Spicq, *Theological Lexicon*, 2:205–11 [especially p. 210]).

21. Zmijewski, *Apostelgeschichte*, 750.

22. Bonhoeffer, *Life Together*, 85.

is not ours to own or rule. Yet there is authority in Christian leadership—but it is the authority of those who live under that of the church's only *kyrios*, the Lord Jesus. It is an authority that is dependent and not inherent; it is exercised in self-giving not in self-assertion; it is aimed at the good of those who are served and not the glory of those who serve. It is seen in humble service, exercised "in" the church, not "over" the church.[23]

The Instrument of Leadership

How has Paul been engaged in this kind of service? Here too he gives one fundamental answer from which all the others spring: he serves—not only in Ephesus but everywhere—by testifying to the gospel of God's grace (v. 24). In this way Paul makes it clear that the gospel—the "word of grace" (v. 32)—is at the center of his ministry and of his entire life. It is by his witness to the gospel that he fulfilled the commission given to him by the Lord Jesus (v. 24). It is by his witness to the gospel that he discharged his responsibility for those to whom he is sent (vv. 26–27). His leadership is that of one who serves the Lord as a servant of his word. The rest of what Paul says about his ministry of the word focuses especially on how comprehensive and also how costly it was, alerting the elders to what their own ministry will and should be like.

He reminds them that his ministry was comprehensive in its *manner*: communicating the word of God involved announcing or declaring (*anangellō*; vv. 20, 27), teaching (*didaskō*; v. 20), testifying (*diamartyromai*; vv. 21, 24), heralding (*kēryssō*; v. 25), and admonishing (*noutheteō*; v. 31). It was also comprehensive in its *focus*: Paul's message concerned God's grace (vv. 24, 32),[24] God's kingdom (v. 25),[25] God's purpose—that is, his salvific plan (v. 27).[26] So it dealt with "the fulfillment of God's kingdom purposes in the person and work of Jesus Christ, which is the biblical-theological framework within which the gospel was preached."[27] And because his message involved the whole of God's purpose (v. 27), his ministry too was comprehensive in its *scope*: it was not only conducted in public places and from house to house (v. 20), but was also directed to both Jews and gentiles (v. 21).[28] It meant caring for all of the flock (v. 28), including the weak (v. 35).

23. Schnabel, *Acts*, 862–64.
24. See Acts 13:43; 14:3; 15:11.
25. See Acts 19:8; 28:23, 31.
26. Barrett, *Acts*, vol. 2, 973; Witherington, *Acts*, 622.
27. Peterson, *Acts*, 567, n. 58.
28. "'The whole purpose of God' is an understanding of God's purpose of salvation

Finally, it was comprehensive in its *objectives*: by evangelistic proclamation Paul aimed to elicit a right response to God and the gospel (namely, repentance toward God and faith in the Lord Jesus: v. 21), and by earnest and untiring pastoral admonition he aimed to ensure that every member of the church remained faithful (v. 31).

All of this has something vital to say about the nature of Christian leadership. Most important of all is the fact that the ministry of the word lies at its heart. The Swiss reformer Heinrich Bullinger saw this very clearly:

> The church truly can by no means spring or be builded by the decrees and doctrines of men . . . Men's doctrines set up men's churches, but Christ's word buildeth the Christian church . . . our Lord God, having given doctors [teachers] unto the church, doth found, build, maintain, and enlarge the church by his word, yea, by his word only.[29]

The ministry of the word upon which the church depends is wide reaching, because God's word is comprehensive in its content and scope. So, in our context, those who make known the whole purpose of God are "those who expound Scripture faithfully, and from it establish the people in faith, in the fear of the Lord, and in all godly practices."[30]

This ministry of the word is also focused, because the word is centered upon God's grace (vv. 24, 32). No leadership is authentically Christian if it does not magnify the grace of God. What does this mean in practice? First and foremost, it is to magnify the Christ of God—and especially to magnify his cross and resurrection as the heart of all true faith and the key to authentic godliness. Christian leadership is always grace-centered—that is, always Christ-centered, cross-and-resurrection-centered, gospel-centered. Magnifying the grace of God means, secondly, maintaining a steadfast reliance upon the grace of God, not only as the key to salvation but also as the key to service. It means recognizing and rejoicing in the sufficiency of God's grace rather than in my competence as a leader. This means leadership that rests on grace rather than power, that comes not out of personal strength but out of weakness-made-strong.[31] Such leadership is not only based on grace; it also expresses grace. We see this in Paul's tears (v. 31)—tears which

---

that recognizes its world-embracing dimensions." Tannehill, *Narrative Unity*, 257.

29. Bullinger, "Holy Catholic Church," 26, 28.

30. Calvin, *Acts*, 181.

31. Note how Paul urges Timothy to find his strength in God's grace (2 Tim 2:1). This reflects the surprising lesson Paul himself had to learn: that weakness does not disqualify us from ministry if we rely on the sufficiency and power of that grace (2 Cor 12:7–10).

speak of his deep commitment to the believers in Ephesus,[32] and thus of his love for them.[33] We also see it in his hard physical work (*kopiaō*, v. 35), which not only funded his ministry but also gave him the resources to help the "weak."[34] (We should note here that while the ministry of the word was the heart of Paul's ministry, it was clearly not the whole of it.) With this conduct he cut across one of that society's basic patterns: the principle of reciprocity, in which each benefit entailed an obligation. The support he gave the weak would have been regarded as obligating them to give him loyalty and service as their patron or benefactor.[35] But in keeping with the teaching of Jesus, Paul gave this support freely, with no thought of receiving anything in return (v. 35).[36] In both his tears and his hard work, then, we see that the grace which is his message also shapes and fills his ministry. In this, too, his ministry was a model for that of the elders.

The Cost of Leadership

In addition to reminding the elders how comprehensive it was, Paul also indicates that his ministry of the word was costly. There were two senses in which this was true: it meant enduring opposition and it involved swimming against the cultural stream. Paul's witness to the gospel generated strenuous opposition, strong enough to bring him to tears (v. 19).[37] But these trials have not silenced him—and even though their intensity is about to increase (v. 23), he has set himself to continue bearing witness to the

---

32. Schille, *Die Apostelgeschichte*, 745.

33. His tears signify his "careful and compassionate concern." See Bruce, *Book of Acts*, 393; cf. Peterson, *Acts*, 571; Walton, *Leadership*, 132; Witherington, *Acts*, 624.

34. In other Pauline contexts, this term refers to those who do not have a robust grasp of the implications of the gospel (Rom 14:1–2; 1 Cor 8:9–13), but the context here points to members of the church who lacked the needed resources (health or employment?) to provide adequately for themselves.

35. On the principle of reciprocity, see Joubert, *Paul as Benefactor*, 69–72. On the debate as to whether patronage or benefaction is the better understanding of the cultural background, see Lowe, "Paul, Patronage and Benefaction," 57–84.

36. Capper, "Reciprocity," 518; Schnabel, *Acts*, 852; Witherington, *Acts*, 626. Paul's stance here is decidedly countercultural: "Greco-Roman benefactors generally used their benefactions to increase their own honour, and not so much to alleviate the wants of others" (Joubert, *Benefactor*, 217). His conduct was part of what amounted to a "revolution of social values" (Judge, "Cultural Conformity," 173), in which he subverted the system of patronage and its *quid pro quo* character (Winter, *After Paul*, 184–205).

37. Although some believe that these tears, like those referred to in verse 31, were to do with his care for the believers, the wording of verse 19 most naturally links them with the opposition Paul faced (Walton, *Leadership*, 76).

gospel of grace regardless of the cost (v. 24). Although opposition has come and will continue to come, Paul is resolved to be steadfast and persevering. He is willing to pay the price of leadership, to serve under the banner of the cross. And the same should also be true of these elders.[38]

The countercultural dimensions of his leadership would also have proved costly for Paul. His commitment to the work of the gospel meant being countercultural in three ways in particular—in his humble demeanor and his manual labor, as well as his support of the weak. As to the former: because he was the Lord's slave, Paul served with humility (*tapeinophrosynē*, v. 19). Although believers were taught to see this as a mark of godliness,[39] the Greco-Roman world, shaped by a culture of self-promotion and the pursuit of honor, generally regarded it as an expression of weakness and of low or servile origins.[40] Yet for Paul, such humility is a necessary mark of leadership that is authentically Christian. By serving in this way, however, he risked the disfavor of those who looked for a more assertive and self-confident style of leadership. One notable way in which he expressed humility (and thus risked this disfavor) was in his manual labor, the hard work with which he supported himself and members of his mission team (v. 34). Here too Paul was swimming against the cultural stream, as there was a marked tendency in Greco-Roman society to regard manual labor as demeaning, especially for those who were or wanted to be somebody.[41] Ironically, it seems that it was in the church—and especially the church at Corinth—that Paul paid the highest price for his countercultural approach to ministry.[42] We too might have to say "No" to the church and not just to the world in order to offer leadership that is properly Christian.

It is clear that Paul took great care to see that his conduct in ministry conformed to his message. He was obviously willing to face the risk of being

---

38. Cunningham, *Many Tribulations*, 270; Mittelstadt, *Spirit and Suffering*, 126-27, 129.

39. See Eph 4:2; Phil 2:3; Col 3:12; 1 Pet 5:5; cf. 1 Pet 3:8.

40. Dickson, *Humilitas*, 85-95; Hellerman, *Reconstructing Honor*, 34-63.

41. Note especially the way Paul refers to manual labor as one of the signs of apostolic lowliness (1 Cor 4:9-13). On this see Witherington, *Conflict and Community*, 142-44; cf. Witherington, *Acts*, 625-26.

42. As we discover in 2 Cor 10:1—13:10, many of the Corinthians much preferred the leadership of the "super-apostles" to that of Paul. His stance on these two issues—and the opposite approach seen in these other leaders: boasting rather than humility, and expecting financial support rather than working to pay their own way—was one of the principal reasons for this preference (2 Cor 11:7-11, 18-23; 12:13-15). While there is no direct evidence that Paul faced these problems in Ephesus, it is worth noting that these are the two matters with which his speech begins and ends. Is the emphasis they thus receive a sign that these were issues for at least some in the church in Ephesus?

misunderstood or marginalized because of the ways this put him out of step with the world around him. If there was a price to pay for faithfulness, he was willing to pay it, for he was serving the Lord who held nothing back, paying for the church with his blood (v. 28). What we learn from Paul here is that Christian leadership does not mean prestige and privilege but service and sacrifice. It is not an exaggeration to say that our leadership is authentic only when it is cruciform. As Calvin observes, Paul's reflections on his time in Ephesus were a reminder that "he had been among them under the contemptible form of the cross . . . because he gladly submitted himself to endure the ignominy of the cross of Christ."[43]

Christian leadership is not an exercise in triumphalism; it is not about being on top or in control. Instead, it means following Jesus in the way of the cross: "The race is not to the top, where the power and prestige are. The race, for followers of Jesus, is to the bottom where humility, surrender and service are to be found."[44] There is legitimate power in this leadership—but it is safe only in the hands of those who are growing down in humility. Only such a leader can be relied upon to use power as a resource for service rather than as a route to greatness.

Confidence in Leadership

Perhaps the most striking feature of Paul's ministry of the word is the conviction that obviously lay at the heart of it: namely, the sufficiency and power of the word of God. We see this as Paul looks back on his ministry in Ephesus. He had not held back from declaring anything that was for their benefit (v. 20). This is not Paul's way of saying that he gave them other useful material along with the word of God! Rather, it is an indication of how wide and comprehensive the gospel message is. Everything that is truly profitable for them—everything that concerns their eternal salvation—is given to them in Paul's message.[45] We see this again in verse 26 when Paul declares himself to be like a faithful sentry, clear of responsibility for their "blood."[46] How did he fulfill this solemn responsibility for the church? He gives the answer in verse 27: he kept watch over their eternal well-being by declaring and teaching the gospel in which God reveals his *boulē*, his whole saving

---

43. Calvin, *Acts*, 173.

44. Dodd, *Empowered Church*, 142.

45. Calvin, *Acts*, 174; Dupont, *Discours*, 79–80; Haenchen, *Acts*, 591.

46. On the meaning of this idiom and its biblical background (especially Ezek 3:16–21; 33:1–9), see Bossuyt and Radermakers, *Témoins*, 603; Dupont, *Discours*, 129–32; Witherington, *Acts*, 622.

purpose. Paul is clearly confident that the word of God is sufficient to do the work of God in the lives of his people.

The same conviction is evident as Paul looks ahead, as he considers the threats that will come from both inside and outside the church. He knows that "fierce wolves" will take advantage of his absence to attack the flock (v. 29) and that some of the elders would prove to be unfaithful, distorting the truth to secure a following for themselves (v. 30). What leadership strategy does he offer in the face of these twin perils? How are the elders to shepherd the flock when these dangers threaten? He has nothing to point to except his own example of earnest pastoral admonition (v. 31). The elders will guard the flock in the same way he discharged his responsibility for it: namely, by means of a constant presentation of the gospel, which both reveals (vv. 26–27) and advances (v. 32) God's saving purpose. Like Paul, they must place their confidence in the word of God:

> To show oneself fainthearted in the face of the demands of pastoral ministry is to show little trust in the divine word whose servants and witnesses we are. It is from the power with which the word is endowed that the elders must expect the fruits of their labors . . .[47]

As Paul indicates (v. 32), this confidence in the gospel also means confidence in the God whose word it is.

And what about Paul himself? Does he have no strategy of his own for combating the twin perils of external attack and internal apostasy? How will he respond to the fact that all of his hard work risks being undermined and overturned? We find the answer in verse 32, where he entrusts the elders to God and the gospel. This is an especially striking indication of his convictions, in three ways. First, by entrusting them to God, Paul shows that he regards God as the ultimate leader of the church.[48] As God's work undergirds Paul's own ministry, the elders should be confident that he will also be at work in and through their shepherding of the flock. Because the church belongs to him (v. 28), they can trust him to care for it—and also for them (v. 32). Second, one source of the trouble that Paul can see coming is some of the elders themselves—and it is by perverting the gospel (v. 30) that they will cause the problems he foresees. Yet he does not seek to introduce some other defense or remedy in addition to the gospel; it remains the gospel upon which he relies. He is obviously convinced that God does all of his saving work in people's lives by and with his word. Third, in this context

---

47. Dupont, *Le Discours*, 284 (author's translation).
48. Jervell, *Die Apostelgeschichte*, 513–14; Salmeier, *Restoring the Kingdom*, 130.

we might have expected him to say something about entrusting the gospel to the elders—but instead, he entrusts the elders to the gospel! He thus expresses his confidence in the power and sufficiency of God's word to build them up in the present and so to bring them to glory at the end, giving them their eternal inheritance. So, in the face of serious threats, what does Paul do? He looks only to God and his word—not because there is nowhere else that he could look, but because he clearly believes that there is nowhere else he should look. And the same goes for these leaders: the future health and security of the church lie not in their personal charisma or their managerial savvy but in their comprehensive and persevering ministry of the word.[49] Again, Bullinger saw this clearly:

> Let us therefore hold that the true church is not built by man's decrees, but that she is founded, planted, gathered together, and builded only by the word of Christ. We do add that it is out of doubt that the church of God is preserved by the same word of God . . . *and that neither can it at any time be preserved by any other means . . .*[50]

This very strong assertion—that there is only ever one means by which God's church is preserved—shows how well Bullinger grasped the point Paul was making here in verse 32.

Conclusion

Paul gives the Ephesian elders a detailed reminder of his ministry among them because he intends it to provide a pattern for theirs as they face leading the church in his absence. This means that his leadership can also serve as a model for ours. In so doing, it provides us with a template by which to assess the validity of contemporary views of leadership. While there will undoubtedly be much that we can learn from these views, we should not overlook the importance of our discovery that authentic Christian leadership is in many ways radical and countercultural. This means that in order to prove faithful, we may well need to imitate Paul in swimming against powerful social and cultural currents. That is because there are nonnegotiables in Scripture without which our leadership will simply echo what the world desires and approves.

Paul's address alerts us to at least some of these nonnegotiables. We have learned that church leaders are to be servants of the Lord and shepherds

---

49. Krodel, *Acts*, 390–91.
50. Bullinger, "Holy Catholic Church," 27 (emphasis added).

of his flock. Authentic Christian leadership is not primarily the exercise of power and authority, but humble service under the authority of the church's only *kyrios*. It is not mostly about organizational effectiveness or personal strength and charisma; fundamentally, it is a matter of faithful testimony to, reliance on, and exhibition of the grace of God. Its foundation is the work by which Father, Son, and Spirit create and care for the church. Its chief instrument is the powerful and comprehensive gospel, the word of God. Its most important distinctive is that in and through it all we see the pattern of the Servant-Lord, whose service was both lowly and costly.[51]

This is by no means all that Paul—or the rest of the New Testament, or the Bible as a whole—has to teach us about Christian leadership. Yet none of what there is still to learn overshadows or undermines the fundamentals Paul sets out in this speech—which may well be why Luke apparently saw no need to include any other reports of apostolic instruction for church leaders: this speech gives us everything essential.

Bibliography

Barrett, Charles K. *The Acts of the Apostles*. 2 vols. International Critical Commentary. Edinburgh: T. & T. Clark, 1994–98.
Bonhoeffer, Dietrich. *Life Together*. London: SCM, 1954.
Bossuyt, Philippe, and Jean Radermakers. *Témoins de la Parole de la Grâce: Lecture des Actes des Apôtres, 2. Lecture continue*. Brussels: IET, 1995.
Bruce, F. F. *The Book of the Acts*. Rev. ed. New International Commentary on the New Testament. Grand Rapids: Eerdmans, 1988.
Bullinger, Heinrich. "Of the Holy Catholic Church." In *The Decades of Henry Bullinger, Minister of the Church of Zurich. The Fifth Decade*. The Parker Society, 3–48. Cambridge: The University Press, 1852.
Burns, James MacGregor. *Leadership*. New York: HarperPerennial, 2010.
Calvin, John. *The Acts of the Apostles 14–28*. Calvin's New Testament Commentaries, 7. Grand Rapids: Eerdmans, 1966.
Capper, Brian. "Reciprocity and the Ethic of Acts." In *Witness to the Gospel: The Theology of Acts*, edited by I. Howard Marshall and David Peterson, 499–518. Grand Rapids: Eerdmans, 1998.
Chapple, Allan. "Leadership in Apostolic Perspective: Acts 20:18–35." *Churchman* 129, no. 2 (2015) 115–29.
Cheng, Ling. *The Characterisation of God in Acts: The Indirect Portrayal of an Invisible Character*. Paternoster Biblical Monographs. Milton Keynes: Paternoster, 2011.
Cunningham, Scott. *"Through Many Tribulations": The Theology of Persecution in Luke-Acts*. Journal for the Study of the New Testament Supplement Series 142. Sheffield: Sheffield Academic, 1997.
Dickson, John. *Humilitas*. Grand Rapids: Zondervan, 2011.

---

51. Pesch, *Die Apostelgeschichte*, 208; Tannehill, *Narrative Unity*, vol. 2, 259–60; Walton, *Leadership*, 134–36.

Dodd, Brian J. *Empowered Church Leadership: Ministry in the Spirit according to Paul.* Downers Grove: IVP, 2003.

Dupont, Jacques. *Le Discours de Milet: Testament Pastoral de Saint Paul (Actes 20, 18-36).* Lectio Divina 32. Paris: Cerf, 1962.

Fitzmyer, Joseph A. *The Acts of the Apostles.* Anchor Bible. New York: Doubleday, 1998.

Gaventa, Beverley Roberts. "Theology and Ecclesiology in the Miletus Speech: Reflections on Content and Context." *New Testament Studies* 50, no. 1 (2004) 36–52.

Guinness, Os. "Sounding Out the Idols of Church Growth." In *No God But God: Breaking with the Idols of Our Age*, edited by Os Guinness and John Seel, 151–74. Chicago: Moody, 1992.

Haenchen, Ernst. *The Acts of the Apostles: A Commentary.* Oxford: Basil Blackwell, 1971.

Harris, Murray J. *Jesus as God: The New Testament Use of Theos in Reference to Jesus.* Grand Rapids: Baker, 1992.

Hellerman, Joseph H. *Reconstructing Honor in Roman Philippi: Carmen Christi as Cursus Pudorum.* Society for New Testament Studies Monograph Series 132. Cambridge: CUP, 2005.

Jervell, Jacob. *Die Apostelgeschichte.* Kritisch-exegetischer Kommentar über das Neue Testament. Göttingen: Vandenhoeck and Ruprecht, 1998.

Joubert, Stephan. *Paul as Benefactor: Reciprocity, Strategy and Theological Reflection in Paul's Collection.* Wissenschaftliche Untersuchungen zum Neuen Testament 2.124. Tübingen: Mohr Siebeck, 2000.

Judge, E. A. "Cultural Conformity and Innovation in Paul: Some Clues from Contemporary Documents." In *Social Distinctives of the Christians in the First Century: Pivotal Essays by E. A. Judge*, edited by David M. Scholer, 157–74. Peabody: Hendrickson, 2008.

Laniak, Timothy S. *Shepherds after My Own Heart: Pastoral Traditions and Leadership in the Bible.* New Studies in Biblical Theology 20. Leicester: Apollos, 2006.

Lowe, Bruce A. "Paul, Patronage and Benefaction: A 'Semiotic' Reconsideration." In *Paul and his Social Relations*, edited by Stanley E. Porter and Christopher D. Land, 57–84. Pauline Studies 7. Leiden: Brill, 2013.

Marshall, I. Howard. "The Place of Acts 20.28 in Luke's Theology of the Cross." In *Reading Acts Today: Essays in Honour of Loveday C. A. Alexander*, edited by Steve Walton, Thomas E. Philips, Lloyd K. Pietersen, and F. Scott Spencer, 155–70. Library of New Testament Studies 427. London: T. & T. Clark International, 2011.

Metzger, Bruce M. *A Textual Commentary on the Greek New Testament.* 2nd ed. Stuttgart: Deutsche Bibelgesellschaft, 1994.

Mittelstadt, Martin William. *The Spirit and Suffering in Luke-Acts: Implications for a Pentecostal Pneumatology.* Journal of Pentecostal Theology Supplement Series 26. London: T. & T. Clark International, 2004.

Pesch, Rudolf. *Die Apostelgeschichte (Apg 13–28).* Evangelisch-Katholischer Kommentar. Zürich: Benziger, 1986.

Peterson, David G. *The Acts of the Apostles.* Pillar New Testament Commentary. Grand Rapids: Eerdmans, 2009.

Porter, Stanley E. *Paul in Acts.* Peabody: Hendrickson, 2001.

Robinson, Anthony B., and Robert W. Wall. *Called to Be Church: The Book of Acts for a New Day.* Grand Rapids: Eerdmans, 2006.

Roloff, Jürgen. *Die Apostelgeschichte*. Das Neue Testament Deutsch. Göttingen: Vandenhoeck and Ruprecht, 1981.

Salmeier, Michael A. *Restoring the Kingdom: The Role of God as the "Ordainer of Times and Seasons" in the Acts of the Apostles*. Princeton Theological Monograph Series. Preston: Mosaic, 2011.

Schille, Gottfried. *Die Apostelgeschichte des Lukas*. 3rd ed. Theologischer Handkommentar zum Neuen Testament. Berlin: Evangelische, 1989.

Schnabel, Eckhard J. *Acts*. Zondervan Exegetical Commentary on the New Testament. Grand Rapids: Zondervan, 2012.

Spicq, Ceslas. *Theological Lexicon of the New Testament*. 3 vols. Peabody: Hendrickson, 1994.

Tannehill, Robert C. *The Narrative Unity of Luke-Acts: A Literary Interpretation*. 2 vols. Minneapolis: Fortress, 1990.

Tidball, Derek. *Ministry by the Book: New Testament Patterns for Pastoral Leadership*. Nottingham: Apollos, 2008.

Trebilco, Paul. *The Early Christians in Ephesus from Paul to Ignatius*. Grand Rapids: Eerdmans, 2007.

Walton, Steve. *Leadership and Lifestyle: The Portrait of Paul in the Miletus Speech and 1 Thessalonians*. Society for New Testament Studies Monograph Series 108. Cambridge: Cambridge University Press, 2000.

Wells, David. *The Courage to be Protestant: Reformation Faith in Today's World*. 2nd ed. Grand Rapids: Eerdmans, 2017.

———. *God in the Wasteland: The Reality of Truth in a World of Fading Dreams*. Grand Rapids: Eerdmans, 1994.

———. *No Place for Truth, or, Whatever Happened to Evangelical Theology?* Grand Rapids: Eerdmans, 1993.

Wiersbe, Warren W., and David W. Wiersbe. *Ten Power Principles for Christian Service*. Grand Rapids: Baker, 1997.

Winter, Bruce W. *After Paul Left Corinth: The Influence of Secular Ethics and Social Change*. Grand Rapids: Eerdmans, 2001.

Witherington III, Ben. *The Acts of the Apostles: A Socio-Rhetorical Commentary*. Grand Rapids: Eerdmans, 1998.

———. *Conflict and Community in Corinth: A Socio-Rhetorical Commentary on 1 and 2 Corinthians*. Grand Rapids: Eerdmans, 1995.

Zmijewski, Josef. *Die Apostelgeschichte*, Regensburger Neues Testament. Regensburg: Friedrich Pustet, 1994.

6

The Pastor–Teacher and the Church

Scot McKnight

I'VE BEEN A PROFESSOR for twenty-seven years, and I've been attached to an academic institution as a student or professor since I was five years old, which means I've spent more than fifty years in school. I've done a few other things part-time, like coaching basketball and running a baseball camp, but mine has been an academic life. The life of a professor is a good life and a good calling, and I'll omit the grunts and groans of committee work, marking papers, administrators, colleagues, and especially those students who are full of it. The life of a professor in fact is a privileged and a protected life. We spend much of our time figuring out how to find time to do what we do best and what we want to do most: be left alone to read, think, and write. I am trying to make it clear that I'm not a pastor, since this chapter will be devoted to the pastor and the church!

The life of a pastor, on the other hand, and I say this as an outsider, is a noble calling and a privileged calling, but I have to admit that I have no envy to leave the ivory tower and enter into the fray of the church. Students are bad enough, but if you wait a semester or a year or, at most four years, they'll go away. Parishioners, usually the wrong ones, camp out at a place and instead of leaving often wish and work for the pastor to leave. The pastoral vocation is a noble calling, but it is often a severe challenge, and I want to keep that attitude in front of us as I sort through the one thing that unites pastors with professors: *we teach*. Yes, we teach in a different context: one academic and one in the context of a local church; we teach with different goals and aims, or "outcomes": one gives assignments and tests students and passes or fails, while one teaches and preaches and often wonders what is sinking in, but there are no tests and no grades and no failures and no one passes and moves on. And we teach in yet a different context: professors often teach by way of provocation, challenge, and deconstruction, while pastors, unless they are on the fast track to their next church, can't simply provoke and deconstruct. The pastor teaches pastorally while the professor teaches—well, what's the best word here? How about "objectively"? More often than not, though perhaps this is also a simplification, the difference can be boiled down to this: pastors teach in order to form a person, while a professor teaches in order to fill a mind.

That *personal* dimension of teaching, and by this I mean the full scope of instruction and admonition and accountability, marks the life of the pastor-teacher, and so I want to devote this chapter to the teaching life of the pastor. It should be now clear that I will make observations about the pastor-teacher from the angle of a professor who has some "pastoral" responsibilities and who speaks in churches and who believes the church is the irreducible core of what God's mission in this world is all about. But I don't want to pretend that I'm a pastor speaking to pastors.

Distinguishing professors from pastors draws our attention to the discussion among theologians about the "marks" of the church.[1] One of the marks of the church, especially in the Protestant tradition, is preaching the word. I shall participate in some ways in that "mark" in this chapter. When attended by other marks, which many Protestants would say includes the Eucharist and discipline, and which Catholics would say means one, holy, catholic and apostolic, and which charismatics might say involves the gifts of the Spirit, and which others might say means whenever someone is doing justice or kingdom work; . . . well, we don't all agree here, but when preaching is attended by the other marks, we have a church. Perhaps it is this that distinguishes the pastor from the professor. The professor participates in only one mark while the pastor participates in church because all the marks are present.

To focus our attention on the pastor and the church, I'm going to ask you to open your Bible to James 3:1—4:12, which I think is the earliest pastoral letter in the entire New Testament. I'm pressing accuracy here by calling this a "letter," because I don't mean that James 3:1—4:12 was a separable letter in the way some think 2 Corinthians 2:14—7:4 or chapters 8–9 were separable letters. (I learned 2 Corinthians at the feet of someone, Murray

---

1. See Jenson and Wilhite, *Church*, 58–101.

Harris, from this "neck of the woods"—though there are still some who think New Zealand and Australia are not part of the same country! From our neck of the woods it's all "down under.")

Back now to James 3:1—4:12.[2] I want to begin by repeating a widely-held theory that James 3:1 to 4:12 is one section in James, and that it is addressed to leaders, and that those leaders are designated "teachers." The upshot, then, is that we have a section addressed exclusively to teachers about how to govern themselves in the context of the messianic community, whether you prefer the term synagogue (2:2) or church (5:14). I'm not sure I'd say the teachers are the same as "elders" of 5:14, but those sorts of issues can be shelved until clearer light can be shed on them.

Not all are as convinced as I am of this arrangement, so permit me to offer a brief defense. I begin with a general observation about how James is organized. James is not organized like a Pauline or Petrine Epistle, which follow a more linear, logical line of thinking. Nor is James like 1 John with its rondo-like features. Instead, James is organized by topics that, while they are related to what precedes and unfold with a variety of rhetorical features, are not logical inferences or ordered progressions. James 3:1-12 is the first of four themes that may, or may not be, connected to speech in the messianic community. I say "may not be" because it is not clear that either 3:13-18 or 4:1-10 is centrally focused on speech patterns, though each can be interpreted in that way. (And we would do well to remind ourselves that how we put a few paragraphs together might make sense to us and to our friends, but it might not make sense to others or, and this matters most, to the original author.) The four themes, taken at face value for what they say in and of themselves, can be ordered like this:

1. Teachers and the Tongue (3:1–12)
2. Wisdom (3:13–18)
3. Dissensions (4:1–10)
4. Community and the Tongue (4:11–12).

If 3:1–12 is about teaching and the tongue, and if 3:13 is still addressed to teachers, then it makes sense that the whole of chapter three is shaped toward addressing teachers. Furthermore, 4:1–10 carries forward an implicit theme of 3:13–18, namely, dissension just as it carries forward a theme about the tongue.

---

2. My discussion in the rest of this section is drawn from my commentary on James. See McKnight, *Letter of James*, 265–67.

Still, it should be observed that the word "teacher" occurs only in 3:1 and never again. So, when James turns in 4:11 to "brothers," we can either assume the brother is the teacher (as in 3:1) or we can conclude that he has expanded his audience from teachers to all males or, more generically, to anyone in the community, which is how both the NRSV and the TNIV render 3:13. In which case, then, James 3:1—4:12 would not be entirely directed toward the teachers of the messianic community. Had James intended to speak exclusively to the teachers for the entire section, he could have made that more clear.

That fault line now exposed, I still think the balance of the evidence, especially inasmuch as 3:13 seems still concerned with teachers, suggests that the entirety of 3:1—4:12 is addressed to the teachers of the messianic community. What the fault line does not prevent is the use of this entire text to speak to us as pastor-teachers, whether or not it was originally directed exclusively to the pastor-teachers of the messianic community. With that preface now in place, let's make some observations about teaching and the church. I've read James long enough to warn us that it is now time to duck, because James is about to come after us, and although I am the one who delivers his words, this won't keep me from ducking too!

First, Wise Pastor-Teachers are Tongue-Biters

I don't know about you, but something James says strikes me as eminently unfair. But it's not and that's why James said it. Our section begins with a warning: "Not many of you should become teachers" (3:1a). On face value, this looks like James is seeking to restrict the *number* of teachers but the flow of the text in 3:1–12 and beyond is not on number but on *impact*. James is concerned with the "the impact of too many talking and teaching in irresponsible, unloving ways."[3] So, rather than lowering the number who are admitted to our seminaries or the number who can speak from the pulpit or behind the lectern, James points right at us and says the issue is our *impact*.

His concern is the discordance between what we say and what we teach and how we live, and the discordance between what we teach or say, and what God requires of us. It is true that the fathers of the church, like Chrysostom and Oecumenius and the Venerable Bede, find in James 3:1 a warning about *doing* what we teach, which is exactly what Jesus criticized the Pharisees for in Matthew 23:2 and 23:6–8, but a closer reading of this text does not reveal so much a contrast between what we teach and how

3. McKnight, *Letter of James*, 269.

we live. Instead, the focus here is on *the inflammatory impact of our words disguised as true teaching*.

I want to develop this idea. Notice what James says in 3:3–12 because in reading this text we are captured by his concrete images and we hear his major concern, which never says anything about the contradiction of teaching and praxis. Instead, the focus is on impact.

> If we put bits into the mouths of horses to make them obey us, we guide their whole bodies. Or look at ships: though they are so large that it takes strong winds to drive them, yet they are guided by a very small rudder wherever the will of the pilot directs. So also the tongue is a small member, yet it boasts of great exploits.
>
> How great a forest is set ablaze by a small fire! And the tongue is a fire. The tongue is placed among our members as a world of iniquity; it stains the whole body, sets on fire the cycle of nature, and is itself set on fire by hell. For every species of beast and bird, of reptile and sea creature, can be tamed and has been tamed by the human species, but no one can tame the tongue—a restless evil, full of deadly poison. With it we bless the Lord and Father, and with it we curse those who are made in the likeness of God. From the same mouth come blessing and cursing. My brothers and sisters, this ought not to be so. Does a spring pour forth from the same opening both fresh and brackish water? Can a fig tree, my brothers and sisters, yield olives, or a grapevine figs? No more can salt water yield fresh.

The tongue's impact is like that of a bit that guides large animals, a rudder that governs a ship, a fire that burns down forests, and the capacity of humans to tame wild animals. The tongue, James opines, is a "world of iniquity" and it "stains the whole body" and is "set on fire by hell" and, if that's not enough, it is a "restless evil, full of deadly poison." His concern is the impact of the tongue of the pastor-teacher who disguises his or her poison as pastoral work!

We've all been taught this; we've all read it; we've all had reminders; some of us have learned from this and have either learned to keep our mouth shut or we have really grown to where our tongue is rarely the problem. But there are times when we are reminded once again that what James says is profoundly important. For example, I've been blogging for many years averaging more than three posts a day with the result that there are now thousands of posts on my blog. Bloggers have a platform and sometimes we weigh in on matters outside our expertise, which I do sometimes on politics but that's all good fun (except for those who disagree with me). One time, after reading a news report about a well-known pastor/preacher in the US who, along with uber-made-up wife, got into a fight with an airline attendant, I wrote a post opining about the pastor. I was irritated and so I gave him a nickname, "the blinker and his wife." Well, that post lasted less than an hour because I had some heavy-hitting criticism about living up to the *Jesus Creed* and about the level of civility I claim for the blog. In the end I took the post down and got to thinking about the power of words. It didn't help that I was working on James at that time.

It was wrong, and I confessed it and I moved on, but this is what went through my mind: What if "the blinker" catches on? What if others begin to use that term for others? Will nicknaming people become a trend? In other words, I got to thinking about impact. A social-media-expert friend of mine told me over coffee one day that the secret to my blog was "perspective" and that I kept myself above the fray, and when I didn't it was obvious and ugly, and he urged me to learn that my blog made it because of that perspective. Recently I wrote a post about the nonsense being created by a particular group, and I sent it to a colleague to get feedback because I knew it was too hot and I wanted him to offer advice. He did, and he said it sounded like a "rant." Kris, my wife, said to me later, "Don't forget what Bob said. Perspective. Stay above the fray." I wonder if learning to stay above the fray is what James wants us all to have in mind when it comes to the tongue. Perspective on things prevents us from having negative impact.

James's impact concerns are devastatingly severe in this text, and a little context in the Letter of James might make this take on some new clarity. The bindings that held together the Jewish culture at the time of Jesus were being snapped, torn, and cut to pieces by violent groups like the Zealots, by Romans who had power, and by Pharisees who couldn't make up their minds on how best to bring about God's promised kingdom of peace, justice, and salvation. From the opening pages of the Gospels to the end of Revelation, that very kingdom is the fundamental hope and the emotive promise that sustained everything. But our world knows about things like peace and international treaties, and our way of settling difficulties is to hold a summit, gather the principal leaders to get our heads around problems, and seek solutions. That is our culture, but it was not James's culture.

There are lines in James that we either ignore or spiritualize, and these lines are at work in everything that emerges in 3:1—4:12. The lines include these:

> You must understand this, my beloved: let everyone be quick to listen, slow to speak, slow to anger; for your anger does not produce God's righteousness. (1:19–20)

> Those conflicts and disputes among you, where do they come from? Do they not come from your cravings that are at war within you? You want something and do not have it; so you commit murder. And you covet something and cannot obtain it; so you engage in disputes and conflicts. (4:1–2)

We are prone to ignore what these words say: my own reading of these texts is that violence is breaking out as a way of accomplishing God's will, and that violence includes physical fights and extends even into murder. It is of course possible James only means this stuff metaphorically, but anyone who knows the hot-headedness of first-century life, anyone who knows how this language is at times used of the Zealots, anyone who has read the War Scrolls from the first cave at Qumran, knows that some Jews thought the way to accomplish God's will—justice—was to use violence. Jesus and James were against it, but they only needed to be against it because there were some who were for it.

The warnings about teachers using their tongues, then, I am suggesting were designed to thwart outbreaks of violence and to reverse the thunder of language that did nothing but divide, conquer, and demean.

That's the realism of our churches, too. Maybe folks are not thinking of picking up knives or guns and "wimping" on one another, but when verbal wars are present, they divide the church. And leaders, including pastor-teachers, are sometimes in the middle of it, because they lose perspective on what is going on.

Before we move on, I want to "apply" this message about the *impact* of the tongue, and I want to apply it to what is often called the "put-down." The British are particularly gifted in the direction of put-down and in the clever art of settling scores without getting in another's face. Once George Bernard Shaw sent two tickets for the opening night to one of his plays to none other than Winston Churchill and added to the invitation, "Bring a friend—if you have one." Now that's a British put-down if I've ever seen one, but it is perhaps only outdone by Churchill's response: that he was engaged that night and that he'd come for the second performance, "if there is one." This sort of banter is fun to read but, knowing that red-blooded males and females sometimes mean more than fun in their put-down, I am forced to ask if we are engaging in the same kind of put-downs in our churches with folks in the church. At times we might say of some well-known preacher that his sermons are better than they sounded or that "there's nothing new in what he says," and what we are saying is that we are envious or jealous or just plain worried about our own status.

The tragic irony of the entire mess of verbal assault is that it springs from a person, a pastor-teacher, a Christian, someone who follows Jesus, who is being transformed by God to bring forth sweet words and not bitter words, who is designed as an olive tree to produce olives, who is designed as a grapevine to produce grapes, but instead is producing bitter, salt water (3:9–12). These are James's metaphors, living and real in the Holy Land, for humans have been given a tongue to bless other humans and not curse them.

It's time to move on. James frames this tongue-trashing in 3:1–12 with two ideas: we will be judged more severely, and perfection. To the first I say only this: we as teachers will be judged more severely because our words have more potency, because we stand in the front in positions of authority, and because our words dig deeper and travel further and potentially do more damage and wreck more lives. To the second I say this: the word "perfection" is a bit tricky in James, but in my estimation it is best to understand it not as sinlessness but as love, as a life shaped by the perfect law that brings liberty (1:25), by the "Jesus Creed" in 2:8, and by mercy (2:12–13). A perfect teacher, then, is one who embodies grace, love, and freedom in ways that lead the community into the paths of peace and wisdom (3:13–18). These two categories, then (that we will stand before a judge and that we are called to a mature, loving life), reframe how the tongue is to be used by the pastor-teacher. The questions we are then to ask are fourfold: Is what I am saying the wise thing to say? Is what I am saying the loving thing to say? Is what I am saying something that will survive God's scrutiny? Is what I am saying a blessing to others?

These words about words are most important when our situations are heated and heady as they were in James's day. May God give us the wisdom to appropriate them as James did in his day.

Second, Wise Pastor-Teachers are Peacemakers

We inhabit a youth culture and a newness culture; the world of Jesus and James was a wisdom culture. Wisdom is the skill of learning to live in God's world in God's way, and in light of Jesus Christ, "God's way" is the way exemplified in the life, death, burial, resurrection, and exaltation of Jesus Christ. For wisdom to take root in us as pastor-teachers requires what I call "receptive reverence" (from Proverbs 1:3–4).[4] We professors and pastors

---

4. I develop this point in McKnight, "James' Secret: Wisdom in James in the Mode of Receptive Reverence," 201–16.

have to become wise in order to develop a receptive reverence toward wisdom, and toward the wise.

James is pulling the wisdom card as well as the peace card in 3:13–18 as the way for the pastor-teacher, as the way for the hotheaded teachers who thought violence could bring God's justice, and for teachers who thought verbal fisticuffs could accomplish God's designs. Again, let's read these verses because they say so much on their own:

> Who is wise and understanding among you? Show by your good life that your works are done with gentleness born of wisdom. But if you have bitter envy and selfish ambition in your hearts, do not be boastful and false to the truth. Such wisdom does not come down from above, but is earthly, unspiritual, devilish. For where there is envy and selfish ambition, there will also be disorder and wickedness of every kind. But the wisdom from above is first pure, then peaceable, gentle, willing to yield, full of mercy and good fruits, without a trace of partiality or hypocrisy. And a harvest of righteousness is sown in peace for those who make peace.

In 3:13 it sounds like James is once again appealing to the significance of works for genuine believers (1:22–27; 2:14–26).[5] But, in this context, what he says varies from what he says in those other two passages. It is not so much that a person's faith must reveal works, but more that a genuinely wise teacher is a person whose works are enveloped in a "gentleness born of wisdom." Notice that the structure of James's words is not that a wise person does works but that the godly teacher does his or her works in ways that manifest meekness and wisdom. (It is perhaps easy to think of the reverse: of doing good deeds in ways that are unwise, foolish, violent, or hotheaded.)

The wise teacher, or sage, will "show" "works" in his or her "good life." James no doubt has in mind good human behavior, but in James's context one cannot fail to observe that it involves compassion on the poor (1:9–11, 26–27; 2:2–4; 5:1–6) and loving speech patterns (1:19–21; 3:1–12; 4:1–12). James's language here is somewhat redundant, and I translate literally to make the point clearer: let him show "out of the good life" and then adds immediately "his good works." Works flow from "the good life," or the pattern of one's life, a term (*anastrophe*) common in Paul (Gal 1:13; Eph 4:22; 1 Tim 4:12) and 1 Peter (1:15; 2:12; 3:1–2, 16; 2 Pet 2:7; 3:11) but not found elsewhere in James. James's concern here is a pattern of life that routinely and habitually manifests good works. The pastor-teacher is to be marked by

---

5. This discussion of James 3:13 draws on McKnight, *Letter of James*, 301–3.

a life of good works done wisely. Maybe a "mark" of the church is not just "pastor" but "wise pastor."

The topic of wisdom leads James to the topic of humility. The oddity of humility as a virtue among early Christians in the context of the Roman world, especially emphatic in Paul's letters, has been observed by many. But, *anavah*, the Hebrew term for this moral virtue, was also important to the rabbis. It goes back to the classic line about Moses, who when being criticized, was described in these words: "Now the man Moses was very humble, more so than anyone else on the face of the earth" (Num 12:3). And Jesus too was humble (Matt 11:29; 21:5; 2 Cor 10:1). The implication of this evidence is that humility or gentleness is non-retaliation in the face of criticism. Wise teachers are non-retaliatory, and teachers know full well the temptation to respond with harshness. Wisdom, then, for James has to do with both a grasp of God's will and a life that conforms to that will, indicated by the virtues we are about to read of in 3:14–18. And it is there that we will be able to find a full understanding of what James means by "wisdom." But, for now we need to observe that wisdom, as can be seen in Proverbs 1:1–7, produces in sages and leaders the following attributes: a receptivity toward instruction, the moral virtues of righteousness, justice, and equity, a cognitive prudence and instruction, and as well what can best be translated with the word "skill" (*tahbulot*; 1:5; see also 9:7–12). A life skilled in wisdom and humility: that's what James wants for his pastor-teachers.

According to verse eighteen, the pastor-teacher who does good works in the context of wisdom pursues *peace*. In the heat of battle in a local church, when the steam is bursting from the tops of folks in the church, some of whom have the funds to keep the place afloat, the aim of the pastor-teacher is a community marked by peace. The only way to accomplish *shalom* in the messianic community is for leaders to sow peace, which means practicing concrete deeds of peace, peacefully. Put slightly differently, our habit is to be one of doing peaceful acts in peaceful ways to bring about justice in our community.

It begins with you and it begins with me. It begins today and it begins with our next action. And it not only begins now, it needs to continue as a pattern of life. Peaceful communities will stand up and witness to a local history of peace-acting pastor-teachers.

Third, Wise Pastor-Teachers Understand the Power of Desires

If we are right that James 3:1—4:12 is shaped for pastor-teachers, James lays great responsibility for peaceful communities on those leaders. If we are wrong, no text speaks more directly toward warmongering between leaders or between leaders and congregations than James 4:1–10. Either way, we can move forward, and to do that we will focus on James 4:1 and then offer a few observations on the difficult to interpret 4:4–6.

The question James asks is about origins: "Those conflicts and disputes among you, where do they come from?" The Old English "Whence," if it weren't so old, is the best word. The words James uses are graphic and could be rendered "Where does all this warring and swording come from?" It's too easy for Western (and Southern) democrat-oriented citizens to make these terms metaphorical, so I suggest we think in this case about the Saul, who became Paul. His approach to religious problems was the approach of violence: he got the messianists killed (Acts 8:3; 9:1–2, 21; 22:4, 19; 26:10–11; Gal 1:23). Ralph Martin joins other James scholars in thinking we are not to exclude out and out physical violence here.[6] Be that as it may, the question James asks the pastor-teachers is the question of origins. Where does this kind of stuff come from?

James answers the question with a question that assumes the answer: "Do they not come from your cravings that are at war within you?" He locates the problem in their desires, their cravings, a similar word to what he will use in 4:2. Careful readers of James recall 1:14–15, where James probes the soul of sin in the fashion both of Augustine's *Confessions* and of C. S. Lewis's *Screwtape Letters*: "But one is tempted by one's own desire, being lured and enticed by it; then, when that desire has conceived, it gives birth to sin, and that sin, when it is fully grown, gives birth to death."

"Go ahead," James is saying to us, "go ahead and think about it. Every time there are skirmishes in your congregation it begins with desires." But the desires James has in mind are the desires for power and control, the desires for authority, for violence, to fight back, and get back. The tongue is unleashed by desire, wisdom is thwarted by desire, and internal conflicts among the messianists emerge out of desire.

In the United States there is a development among pastors to reaffirm pastoral authority, and a pastor-friend told me he was at an installation of a pastor when the preacher stated in no uncertain terms that leadership was about "imposing your will on a group." It really is simpler if one person makes all the decisions, especially if that person is a male. But such an ordered simplicity is not usually observed by pastors who know the strange concoctions that congregationalism and the so-called priesthood of all believers as well as democratic votes put into play in local churches. So some want to centralize power. They find support in the Bible. Anyone who

---

6. Martin, *James*, 144.

reads the Pastoral Epistles, or even how things seemed to have worked in Acts or between the lines in the other Pauline letters, knows that some kind of authority was connected to the pastor-teacher because he/she was the pastor-teacher. Historically, too, elders ran the scene in the Jewish world, and elders were elders because they were older than anyone else. So we've got a brouhaha in the United States on pastoral authority. What bothers me most is *the sorts of people who are staking a claim for pastoral authority are authoritarian people who want to be in control.* When one local church voted not to be agglomerated into a growing empire of another church led by an authoritarian pastor who was gobbling up one church after another, that pastor wrote a strong post on his site that congregationalism was from Satan. Again, to be sure, congregationalism has its downsides, but it is the authoritarian air of those opining about pastoral authority that concerns me. When John Stott talks about such a topic I listen. Some more recent voices concern me because I have read James on "desire."

Pastor-teachers who want to control are the problem because control comes from desires that are at war. There is no simple fix here, for the tension between good, solid, biblical leadership, and control hums loudly and harmoniously enough that we cannot always tell the difference between control and leadership. The posture I believe every pastor-teacher must take is that he or she is first and foremost a follower of Jesus and not a leader of others. Good followers are better leaders than leaders are good followers. The problem here in James's messianic community is *not* that there are, to use an old American expression, too many chiefs and not enough Indians. The issue, as I said at 3:1, is not numbers. The issue with the leaders is the same as with the tongue: it's about impact as a result of how the leadership is exercised. The problem is desire.

This is why I appreciated so much Andrew Purvis's book *The Crucifixion of Ministry*.[7] He argued front to back that the pastoral task is to discern the present ministry of the present Christ in the present situation, and not to see what "I" the pastor-teacher can contribute or offer or do. Pastor-teachers who see they are called to make room for Christ have subdued the desire to control. Mark Allan Powell, in a most interesting book called *What Do They Hear?* revealed that when pastor-teachers (and professor-teachers) read the Bible, in particular the Gospel passages, they identify with Jesus while lay folks identify with the other persons in the narrative—and almost never Jesus.[8] To be sure, we are mediators of Jesus to other folks, but do we mediate from *his* side or from the side of the characters in the stories?

---

7. Purvis, *Crucifixion of Ministry*.
8. Powell, *What Do They Hear?*

Maybe the fact that we identify with Jesus is a sign that we want to control the context and that our desires are in control. The best leaders are the best followers of Jesus.

Years ago, when I was a young professor and when I was using highlighters to mark books, I read John Stott's *The Preacher's Portrait*, a book in which Stott was doing what Stott does so well, that is, examine biblical passages with expositional nuance.[9] That book explores what a pastor is in five categories: steward, herald, witness, father, and servant. That book was followed up two decades later with *Between Two Worlds*, and Stott added a new category: the pastor-teacher is a *bridge-builder*.[10] Without ever mincing words and without diminishing the significance of the pastor-teacher, Stott never thought of suggesting the pastor was someone who controlled the church or who dominated, or who set off battles. Christ may have been the controversialist, but the pastor was not.

One more. Tom Wright's little book on Scripture, first called *The Last Word* and now called *Scripture and the Authority of God* touches a chord that so resonates with me that I feel compelled to apply it in this context.[11] Some folks confess the authority of the Bible, but Tom is not quite happy with that because he thinks it wiser to speak of the authority of *God* speaking to us through Scripture. I agree with him here, as I often do. But there's something powerfully pastoral here. Perhaps those who most want to defend the authority of *Scripture* line up with those who think leadership is imposing one's will on a group, while those who speak of the authority of God think leadership is guiding others to live under God by following Jesus. Perhaps.

Well, I promised I'd say something about 4:4–6 before we left this third point, and I fear that I've about run out of space and time. What concerns James here is the choice between friendship with God or friendship with the world. The "world" can be expanded by pastor-teachers to mean most anything, including watching Australian Rules Football or drinking Australian wine. I would suggest to you that in James, in the context of 3:1—4:12, we are talking about the tongue's destructive power, bad works that produce demonic-shaped communities, and most especially about warring and swording in the messianic communities. In the wider context of James, it refers to lack of compassion (1:26–27) and to the rich abusing their power (2:5). Friendship with God, on the other hand, is to use the tongue properly, to do good works in the context of wisdom, to be a pastor-teacher whose desires are subdued by God's desires, and to be a person who submits to

---

9. Stott, *Preacher's Portrait*.
10. Stott, *Between Two Worlds*.
11. Wright, *Scripture*.

God and humbles himself or herself before God. One more attempt to put this into a bundle: friendship with the world is about lording over others; friendship with God is about letting God alone be Lord. The wise pastor-teacher is first and foremost in submission to God.

What can't be ignored is that this is an either-or for James: either you love lording over others, or you love God being Lord. You can't have both, and every time we feel the desires creeping to the surface and every time we are tempted to use the tongue to put someone in place, and every time we are tempted to tear a group apart, we have aligned ourselves with the enemy's forces, the enemy's desires, and the enemy's designs.

Fourth, Wise Pastor-Teachers Know They Are Not God

A warning about lording it over others is good advice, and we can all benefit from it. A warning about the desire to control is needful. What James does next perhaps surprises, but it should not. James doesn't mess around: he sees all of this as the attempt to take the place of God and to sit on the judgment seat. We need to read verses 11–12:

> Do not speak evil against one another, brothers and sisters. Whoever speaks evil against another or judges another, speaks evil against the law and judges the law; but if you judge the law, you are not a doer of the law but a judge. There is one lawgiver and judge who is able to save and to destroy. So who, then, are you to judge your neighbor?

All of a sudden we're talking about sitting in the judgment seat and James connects words of "slander" with being God. The logic is a bit hard to follow but it works like this: God is the lawgiver, therefore God is the judge over the laws. When humans begin to judge—and here he doesn't mean "discern" but to "sit in condemnation, offer a damning eternal verdict"—they have usurped God's place, who alone is the Judge.

This leads us back to what I said about Tom Wright's book on Scripture. The Bible isn't a rule book but is instead God's revelatory word to us, and the minute we turn it into a constitution or a lawbook we lose contact with the *person who is speaking*, and it quickly becomes the book we have mastered and which we are using to master others. What has happened to the pastor-teachers in James's community is not how they understand Scripture. What has happened is that they have an inflated view of themselves, though surely they think they are speaking on God's behalf. James's concern, once again, is the tongue, the false wisdom, the desires that lead to warring and swording, and what he wants is humility, wisdom, and submission to God. The pastor-teacher who feels it is his or her responsibility to offer evaluations of everyone, to comment on someone's status before God or their theology or their spirituality, is a usurper.

Discernment can exist without it becoming judgment. But there is again a tension that hums loud enough that we are driven, if we are wise, to become humble about our evaluations of others. The tension is found in James: these words are found in a passage about the tongue and about how pastor-teachers are to speak, and in the midst of these words James bluntly calls his audience "Adulterers!" For James there is no problem between control of the tongue, the sign of perfection for the truly loving person, and discerning that someone is out of line. So, let's toss into the rubbish bin the all-too-common evasive technique of saying "It's not mine to judge." Well, yes, it's not yours to "judge" but it is yours to discern.

James, though, is not worried about discerners. He's worried about those who think they are discerning but have instead usurped the place of God. They have assumed the judgment seat, a seat very common to anyone who was in a first-century synagogue, but instead of seeing themselves as guides who lead others to follow Jesus and submit to God, they see themselves in control and the judge.

Conclusion

I close by going back to James 3:2, that the pastor-teacher who can control her or his tongue is nothing short of perfect. Surely one of the more interesting words in James is "perfection," which in Greek is *teleios*. Doug Moo's second commentary on James is shaped by this term, which he translates as "spiritual wholeness."[12] Moo is a Lutheran-nurtured evangelical while Patrick Hartin is a Catholic, but Hartin's book on the Christian life according to James is entitled *A Spirituality of Perfection*.[13] For him perfection refers to wholeheartedness in dedication to God, wholehearted in that faith leads to works, wholehearted in that the follower of Jesus is characterized by integrity, and wholehearted in showing compassion for the poor. Getting evangelicals and Catholics to agree on "perfection" is not an easy task, so let's take their agreement seriously. First, a brief sketch of the term in James:

> Let endurance have its *full effect*, so that you may be *mature* and complete, lacking in nothing. (James 1:4)

12. Moo, *Letter of James*.
13. Hartin, *Spirituality of Perfection*.

> Every generous act of giving, with every *perfect* gift, is from above, coming down from the Father of lights, with whom there is no variation or shadow due to change. (James 1:17)

> But those who look into the *perfect* law, the law of liberty, and persevere, being not hearers who forget but doers who act— they will be blessed in their doing. (James 1:25)

> You see that faith was active along with his works, and faith was *brought to completion* by the works. (James 2:22)

> For all of us make many mistakes. Anyone who makes no mistakes in speaking is *perfect*, able to keep the whole body in check with a bridle. (James 3:2)

The apostle Paul uses this term in significant places, as well. For instance, "Yet among the *mature* [or perfect] we do speak wisdom" (1 Cor 2:6), and he has an eschatological perfection when love wins: "but when *the complete* [perfection] comes, the partial will come to an end" (13:10; see Eph 4:13; Col 1:28; 4:12), and he urges his followers to become "mature" (or perfect) in 1 Corinthians 14:20 (see also Phil 3:15). Paul's emphasis is eschatological. But Paul's focus is not James's, and it leads us to ask if James's understanding of "perfection" is to be connected to Jesus's own teachings.

Once again, we are back to Matthew, and Matthew alone. Twice Jesus uses this term in the First Gospel. I quote both.

> Be *perfect*, therefore, as your heavenly Father is perfect. (Matt 5:48)

> Jesus said to him, "If you wish to be *perfect*, go, sell your possessions, and give the money to the poor, and you will have treasure in heaven; then come, follow me." (Matt 19:21)

God is perfect, and the followers are to be perfect. Too many moral theories have been spun from this term, not the least of which was Wesley's, though we can leave those to some other discussion for now. Closer inspection of Matthew reveals that perfection means *a life of loving others by extending compassion to the poor*. The most accurate way to read "perfection" in Matthew 5:48 has a noble history. What view might that be? Many scholars have understood "perfection" in 5:48 as nothing more than a summary term for enemy love in the verses preceding it, namely 5:43–47. Fittingly enough, this is more or less the way Luke saw it when he either edited or translated the original into the word "merciful" at Luke 6:36. He said, "Be merciful as your heavenly Father is merciful." Merciful and enemy love are two clear indications of what "perfection" means for Jesus. It is not without importance that the rich young ruler was told to be perfect and the very thing he was told to do was to *love the poor by selling what he had to help them*. It's not quite enemy love, but it is love, the concrete love of helping others, that Jesus had in mind.

As Hartin observes, James breathes the same air that Jesus breathes—*Jewish* air. To be "perfect" means to be whole or complete, and that means to be all you were designed to be; it connotes giving oneself to God and to others; and it implies obedience to God. When it comes to perfection in the book of James, then, James is not only Jewish, he sounds like a Jesus-kind of Jewishness. He wants the pastor-teacher to be *perfect*, and perfection means obeying the Torah, now understood to be the "law of liberty" and the "royal law" of love of neighbor, and it means especially using one's tongue properly, for that is the instrument with which one often treats one's neighbor. The connection is not without importance for history. Like brother, like brother. Perfection and love of neighbor are one and the same for both the Jesus of Matthew's Gospel and for his brother, James.

The pastor-teacher is called to perfection in the tongue, and that means you and I are to weigh what we say so that our words make love grow in our family, in our neighborhood, and in our church. If we season our words with love, we will be wise and we will not be warring and swording, but we will see our place under God, and not as little gods and goddesses. For James, it all comes down to the tongue. You and I may think this is some kind of weird reductionism, and we'd be flat-out wrong. Take that from someone who lives off words, spoken and written.

Bibliography

Hartin, P. J. *A Spirituality of Perfection: Faith in Action in the Letter of James*. Collegeville, Minnesota: Liturgical, 1999.
Jenson, Matt, and David E. Wilhite. *The Church: A Guide for the Perplexed*. New York: T. & T. Clark/Continuum, 2010.
R. P. Martin. *James*. Word Biblical Commentary. Waco: Word, 1988.
McKnight, Scot. "James' Secret: Wisdom in James in the Mode of Receptive Reverence." In *Preaching Character: Reclaiming Wisdom's Paradigmatic Imagination for Transformation*, edited by Dave Bland and Dave Fleer, 201–16. Abilene: Abilene Christian University Press, 2010.
———. *The Letter of James*. New International Commentary on the New Testament. Grand Rapids: Eerdmans, 2011.
Moo, D. J. *The Letter of James*. Pillar New Testament Commentaries. Grand Rapids: Eerdmans, 2000.
Powell, Mark Allen. *What Do They Hear? Bridging the Gap between Pulpit and Pew*. Nashville: Abingdon, 2007.

Purvis, Andrew. *The Crucifixion of Ministry: Surrendering Our Ambitions to the Service of Christ.* Downers Grove: IVP, 2007.

Stott, John R.W. *The Preacher's Portrait: Some Classic New Testament Word Studies.* Grand Rapids: Eerdmans, 1988.

Stott, John. *Between Two Worlds: The Challenge of Preaching Today.* Grand Rapids: Eerdmans, 1994.

Wright, Tom. *Scripture and the Authority of God.* London: SPCK, 2005.

7

I Am A Woman

Please Let Me Be Who I Am In God

Karen Siggins

Perhaps you have heard the story of the trader who searched bazaars in the Middle East for rugs he could then export. He was riding his horse through a bazaar one day when a very large handwoven rug caught his eye and brought him to a sudden halt. He called out to the old lady sitting, head bowed, on a small prayer rug at the front of the stall and asked if the rug was for sale. She told him it was. The trader asked the price and the ensuing conversation went something like this:

> "The rug is one hundred rupees, sir."
>
> "One hundred rupees for that rug!"
>
> "Absolutely, sir, one hundred rupees. Not a single rupee less."
>
> The trader looked from the old lady to the rug and back again. He said, "In all the bazaars, in all the countries, in all the stalls in the Middle East, I have never seen a rug that beautiful." I imagine the old lady, head still lowered, may have rolled her eyes, discreetly of course, as she answered, "Yes I know that sir. That is why I am selling it for one hundred rupees and not one rupee less."

With scant disregard for the bargain of a lifetime the trader replied, "In the name of Allah, if you know how beautiful your rug is, why would you ever sell it for only one hundred rupees?"

The old lady looked at the trader for the first time and he could see she was surprised. She didn't speak for a moment and then said, "Because, sir, I never knew that there were numbers above 100, until this moment. I never knew."

Cynthia Neal Kimball relates this story with reference to Genesis 1:26–31, highlighting the unacceptable cost when the good of the created order, redeemed by the cross of Christ, is not realized. Kimball writes, "There *are* numbers above 100, and there is a terrible cost when people are kept ignorant of their possibilities."[1] Certainly, the story serves this purpose well and reflects the starting premise for this paper: there is no created "God-ordained hierarchy"[2] built upon the given of biological sex or various constructs of gender.[3] Instead, there is the equality of the Bible narrative that Ronald Pierce and Rebecca Merrill Groothuis sketch in the helpful terms of a sequence of equalities:

- equally created in God's image (Gen 1:27)
- equally fallen (Rom 3:23)
- equally redeemable (John 3:16)
- equally participants in new covenant community (Gal 3:28)
- equally heirs (1 Pet 3:7)
- equally filled and empowered by the Holy Spirit for ministry (Acts 2:17–18)[4]

Let's be clear that this is not to claim that biblical equality denies any created differences between women and men. In addition, the biblical story and extra-biblical church history clearly accommodate gender differences across time and cultures. Alan Johnson reminds us that "interchangeability" is not the goal of biblical equality,[5] and this holds true both *within* and *across* gender divides according to the Spirit's distribution of demonstrably

---

1. Kimball, "Gender Complementarity," 464–65.
2. Pierce and Groothuis, "Introduction," 13.
3. Van Leeuwen, a psychologist and philosopher, has authored an interesting article on the concept of "gender" as verb rather than noun and "gendering" as something we are called to *do* rather than something we *are*. See Van Leeuwen, "Opposite Sexes."
4. Pierce and Groothuis, "Introduction," 13.
5. Johnson, "My Journey," 126.

neutral gifts.[6] There is, after all, a lot of truth in Dorothy Sayers's famous declaration, "Women are more like men than anything else."[7]

There *are* numbers above one hundred! This paper, however, is not primarily concerned with debating the theology of biblical equality and it will not address this or historical, philosophical, practical or missional aspects relevant to the debate in contemporary contexts where women are excluded from accredited or ordained ministry by those advocating male leadership.[8] I have never been drawn to enter the arena of this debate publicly, although the fact that I am a woman and the lead pastor of a local Baptist church does mean I am sometimes a point of reference for the discussion. I am very thankful for those who do take up the conversation in the most contentious places and agree with John Stackhouse that God calls us differently to various aspects of activism.[9]

I have largely contented myself with being sure of my call and theological position,[10] occasionally indulging in moments of quiet seething,[11] and celebrating milestones with friends and colleagues. Just recently I celebrated with a friend, mentor, theological educator, and longtime Baptist and Church of Christ pastor, as she accepted an appointment to the board of an international teaching ministry that advocates male leadership.

My own activism has taken a new direction in recent years and it is this emphasis that provides the focus for this paper. I am concerned to address issues related to the practice of biblical equality in the context of twenty-first-century Western Protestant churches that, at least on the paper of Constitutions, Statements of Faith, Best Practice documents, and Ministry Guidelines, give assent to the biblical narrative of equality and the new creation secured by Jesus at the cross and so compellingly described

---

6. Long, "Gifted Bride," 100.

7. Johnson, "My Journey" 126.

8. Pierce and Groothuis, "Introduction," 17. I like the honesty and accessibility of the phrase "male leadership." As synonyms you will find such words as "patriarchalists," "traditionalists," "hierarchicalists," and "complementarians."

9. Stackhouse, *Finally Feminist*, 101.

10. Helpful books that address theological issues of women in ministry include: Husbands and Larsen, *Women, Ministry*; Payne, *Man and Woman*; Pierce and Groothuis, *Biblical Equality*; and Storkey, *Created or Constructed*.

11. Marshall, "Call to Ministry," 126–27. Although seething is not recommended as a long-term response, let me indulge in one funny incident from just such a moment. It was 1984 and Molly Marshall had been appointed as the first woman in the School of Theology at Southern Seminary in Kentucky. Hostile letters were received, and one man wrote to the dean asking, "Have you run out of intelligent men to teach our preacher boys?" Molly says, "Were I not such a sweet Christian, I would have responded to the letter with a couple of simple words—'Years ago.'"

in Galatians 3:26–29.[12] My concern is that these claims notwithstanding, there remains a significantly small number of women in ordained or accredited ministry roles at any level and most particularly in senior roles.[13] A brief survey within my own context of the Australian Baptist denomination shows that of the 744 Baptist churches and fellowships listed, six have women as their lead pastor. The numbers of associate pastors are considerably higher at about one hundred but still statistically incongruent with the numbers of churches and the numbers of women within these churches.[14]

I am not advocating functional equality for the sake of more balanced statistics and I agree with those who warn against addressing the equality issue with a focus on rights rather than gifting.[15] I contend, however, that the numbers tell us we are still too busy drawing lines that divide rather than embracing the unity effected by Jesus and embodied in his followers through the Spirit.

Recently, when preaching from Joshua 22, I was struck by what this episode in the life of the Israelites has to say about the practical working out of equality within the contemporary church. The tribes of Gad, Reuben, and the half tribe of Manasseh built a symbolic altar to act as a witness for generations to come that God is the God of all Israel. This action and the resulting interaction between East and West Bank tribes highlights what Robert Hubbard describes as the "little Jordans" that threaten to seep into relationships within the church family and shift the ground on which we are standing.[16] As twenty-first-century Christians we acknowledge the unity won for us in Jesus Christ; we claim our place as God's people bound together in Jesus and through the Spirit but our now-and-not-yet experience of God's kingdom means we daily face the challenges of the "little Jordans" such as:

- relational distance (Josh 22:1–9)
- forgetting to talk with each other (Josh 22:11–14)
- assuming the worst of each other's motives even when experience gives us every reason to trust each other (Josh 22:15–18)

---

12. Fee, "Male and Female," 172–85.
13. Catford, "Third Wave," 14.
14. This information was gathered in July 2011 via email from the Baptist Unions of Western Australia, South Australia, Queensland, New South Wales, and the Australian Capital Territory. No statistics were made available from the Northern Territory or Tasmania.
15. For example, Willard, "Foreword," 9–10.
16. Hubbard, *Joshua*, 503.

- exaggerated or even invented differences (Josh 22:19–20)
- the fear that results from not being sure of ourselves, of each other and of God (Josh 22:21–34)

With the Joshua 22 lesson in mind the remainder of this "paper will address the issue of the gap between the biblical equality many Protestant denominations assent to, and the actual experience in our churches, particularly, although not exclusively, with reference to ordained or accredited ministers. The topic will be explored under four headings acknowledging in turn that there are still women and men within denominations advocating biblical equality who do not know that there are numbers above one hundred; that young women and men from Generation Y and the emerging Gen Z do not even think to question the existence of numbers above one hundred; that there is the need to redefine ministry in the numbers above one hundred for women and men in the twenty-first century; and finally, that church and denominational leaders will need to be visibly and intentionally engaged in this conversation.

"I never knew that there were numbers above 100, until this moment. I never knew."

The old woman selling rugs is not alone. Mary Hannah Rowe, an ordained Baptist pastor for over thirty years heard God call her to ministry at ten years of age and at first assumed it was a call to overseas mission because she had no other framework to use.[17] Similarly, Ruby Welsh Wilkins knew she was called by God to pastor in the church twenty-two years before it became a possibility. Ruby says "I was amazed. It was part disbelief. I couldn't understand because of my Baptist upbringing."[18]

It would be nice to think that stories like these from the mid-twentieth century are simply amusing anecdotes from a time long past. Aside from the danger of disrespecting the stories of others, it is unfortunately premature to dismiss them just yet and will remain so until we first of all recognize the sin that prompts the theological and social constraints we operate within.[19] Joan Burgess Winfrey draws on Mary Van Leeuwen's *Gender and Grace: Love, Work and Parenting in a Changing World* to suggest that just as human beings are made in God's image for leadership and for community, we fail

---

17. Rowe, "30 Years," 209.
18. Pierce, "I Am Female," 143.
19. Spencer, "Pulpit," 4–8. This article offers the real-life experiences of theological and social constraints from the perspective of ten women currently in ministry.

God's image when we respectively abuse power and/or capitulate responsibility in relationships (Gen 3:16). The former is a sin most often identified with men and particularly patriarchal oppression,[20] while the latter is seen particularly as the sin of women.[21] Joy Ann McDougall helpfully describes women's sin as the underside of pride; a self-silencing and subjugation that reflects the little Jordan of fear where we do not trust self, others, and God.[22]

We may want to debate the concept of gendered sin, the reasons for this state of affairs if we accept it, and issues related to degrees of culpability.[23] Likewise, we need to acknowledge exceptions to the rule. However, the claim for gender-based sin has some credit. In broad terms its credibility is testified to by the gap between the *actual* involvement of women in the New Testament church, the church throughout history, and specifically the history of evangelical women in public ministry since the 1730s, and our *corporate recollection* of this history.[24] Though, as Timothy Larsen highlights, anyone observing the evangelical scene in the last sixty years could be forgiven for not seeing that there are numbers above one hundred for women![25] This is, in part at least, a reflection of sinful patterns of male dominance and female acquiescence. We would do well to address the issue in our churches with a new look at the theology of personal worth in God's economy.[26]

John Stackhouse speaks of God accommodating the weaknesses of his Old Testament people and the church since the time of Jesus, as we struggle with our redemptive experience of the "already but not yet."[27] Clearly this is the case and yet I am wary of the descriptive truth of this becoming a prescriptive excuse for the way things are and perhaps most particularly where we claim to have "settled" the women in ministry issue. There are still too many who will say "I never knew" when we tell them about the numbers above one hundred. We have a responsibility to these people, and we will do well to face the challenge of Stuart Briscoe's question, "What does the Master think of those who bury the gifts of others?"[28]

---

20. Stackhouse, *Finally Feminist*, 57.
21. Winfrey, "Holy Joy," 435–36. See also Matthews, "How I Changed," 154–63.
22. McDougall, "Weaving Garments," 149–65.
23. McDougall, "Weaving Garments," 156.
24. Durso and Durso, "Baptist Women Ministers," 1-7; Husbands, "Reconciliation," 129.
25. Larsen, "Public Ministry," 231.
26. Hybels, "Gender Equality," 107–20.
27. Stackhouse, *Finally Feminist*, 92.
28. Briscoe, "Buried Talents," 63.

Of Course There are Numbers Above One Hundred! Where's My Space?

The generations we often refer to as Y and Z have grown up or are currently growing up in a culture that is difficult to define concisely. This difficulty arises because these generations have cut their teeth on individualism and personal fulfillment fueled by a global and social awareness and a technological revolution[29] unthinkable only two generations ago. This makes them difficult to nail down both figuratively and literally! The twenty-somethings we find in our churches (when we can find them there!) have had their faith shaped by this culture and it quite simply does not occur to most of them to question the access of women to ordained, accredited, or in fact, any ministry roles. If this generation sees an issue at all it belongs in the context of the developing world, or the minds of equally distant "pushy" and "strident" older women.[30]

Imagine then the surprise and dismay of this new generation of Christian women when they find there is no place for their particular experience of God's call on their lives and that they are cut off from ministry by the little Jordan of exaggerated or invented differences.[31]

These women are our sisters and daughters and nieces and sooner than we think, our granddaughters. I am deeply concerned when I look at them and see young women seriously committed to being all that God calls them to, whether homemaking, or ordained ministry, or volunteer work, or business development. What will they do with the blank looks and deafening silence when they step up to serve in the churches where we claim biblical equality? What will they do with the theological debate they have no need of or interest in?

Clearly it is not all doom and gloom and some of these young women have and will find opportunities to serve as they understand they are called to do. Yet even here I find myself uneasy. I wonder if the opportunities for women are too often limited to the areas of children's, youth, or family work. I wonder if the doors to school and hospital chaplaincy and administrative pastoral roles instead of senior ministerial teaching and preaching roles are just a little too wide. I wonder about the cost of the present portrayal of women in ministry as "god-chicks, princesses, and powerful people who can make a difference."[32] The latter has occurred mostly in the context of

---

29. Catford, "Third Wave," 12.
30. Catford, "Third Wave," 16.
31. Catford, "Third Wave," 16.
32. Catford, "Third Wave," 16.

the larger and livelier Pentecostal and charismatic churches where congregations have conceded it is no longer acceptable to practice a two-for-one clergy arrangement whereby the pastor's wife acted as a second unpaid minister. Theological revolution and a new understanding of biblical equality is most often cited as the causative factor. Cheryl Catford suggests that in fact there is more at play and particularly an admirable desire to accommodate cultural norms. Unfortunately, the ensuing changes are not necessarily built on a new understanding of biblical equality. Instead they seem to be modifications around the edges of historical patterns of male domination and female subjugation of responsibility, and in fact fall back on the tried and tested images of women as pretty and fragile; beautiful and strong or in some cases as earthy and maternal.[33] We must not replace one stereotype with another and avoid the much harder work of reimagining biblical leadership for both women and men. This will be the topic of the next section of this paper.

If young women do not resonate with the imagery of god-chick or earth mother; if they are met with a debate that holds no relevance, or a "stained glass ceiling"[34] they thought did not exist, they may leave the church. They *are* leaving mainstream Protestant churches, although they remain in higher than average percentages in the active Pentecostal and charismatic churches.[35] It's not that we are losing them. We are dismissing them.[36] We are dismissing the called and the equipped and often the very people who exhibit the academic standards, the biblical knowledge and theological understanding, and the "pastoral imagination" that theological seminaries and churches are crying out for.[37]

If promoting the gospel is the chief mission of the church, then we must make space for called and equipped women to minister in the church. As I. Howard Marshall writes, "the vast contribution that women can make and feel called to make to it [the cause of the gospel] could make a tremendous difference to our effectiveness in evangelism and building up the church."[38] Others go further and say not only can the mainstream church ill-afford to dismiss gifted women in the face of the decline in congregational numbers;

---

33. Catford, "Third Wave," 17; Daniel, "Pastor's Husband," 29; Sanders, "Holy Boldness," 201–9; Van Leeuwen, "Opposite Sexes," 187–88.

34. McDougall, "Weaving Garments," 153–54.

35. Plantinga, "How I Changed," 195; Sanders, "Holy Boldness," 200.

36. Fitzgerald, "Call," 57.

37. McDougall, "Weaving Garments," 150.

38. Marshall, "Women in Ministry," 63.

to do so is to set the church up for future embarrassment equivalent to the church's shame over slavery.[39]

Redefining Ministry in the Numbers Above One Hundred

In redefining ministry so as to make places for women and men to respond to God's call to ministry we will be attending to the little Jordans of perspective and to exaggerated or invented differences that can draw divisive lines between people in the church. To that end, a number of paradigms have been offered by theologians, educators, psychologists, and others. In this section of the paper I offer a broad overview of these paradigms and a list of some of the essential characteristics of an acceptable model.

Henri Blocher represents one end of the spectrum, and what I shall call the "exceptional women" paradigm. Blocher argues that an ordinary/extraordinary distinction reconciles conflicting New Testament passages and allows for "modern extraordinary Priscillas" to minister particularly in preaching and teaching roles in the church.[40] Certainly there is wisdom in the advice given to many women who have pioneered in pastoral leadership roles, and which in turn they have passed onto other women: the advice of quietly doing what God has called you to and letting the "results" speak for themselves. I believe, however, that the cost of this approach as a mainstay position is no longer acceptable and the risks are too high. The costs are to the women who *do* excel, acknowledged by Blocher with a quote from Charlotte Whitton: "Whatever she does, a woman must do it twice better than a man to get equal recognition. Fortunately, it's not difficult."[41] Joking aside, it *is* difficult, costly and exhausting for body, mind, soul, and relationships, and there is every indication that the next generation of women are less prepared to pay this price. This brings us to the risks which I have captured in two questions. Are there enough exceptional women in enough churches modelling leadership options for young women? Who will replace the current exceptional women when they tire of being exceptional or when their ministry time comes to an end?

Moving on from Blocher, other paradigms offer a more middle ground perspective and suggest various ways of reframing the debate on common

---

39. Campolo, "Is Evangelicalism Sexist?" 77–78; Gundry, "Bobbed Hair," 104; Matthews, "How I Changed," 158; Plantinga, "How I Changed," 192.
40. Blocher, "Women, Ministry," 239–49.
41. Blocher, "Women, Ministry," 249.

ground.[42] The necessary conversation and thrust of these approaches goes some way towards addressing the little Jordans of forgetting to talk and assuming the worst of each other.

Finally, there are the paradigms that embrace a broad hermeneutic position usually with reference to the redemptive or reconciliatory story of the Bible.[43] These paradigms locate ministry in the relational context of grace, and as such hold the most promise. Their proponents are concerned to make sense of the biblical meta-narrative, and while acknowledging various perspectives do not shy away from clear statements of theological conviction.

The best paradigm in which to redefine ministry, then, is one which allows at least the following:

- A redemptive framework that acknowledges mutual gifting and advocates the ministry of the sexes alongside rather than opposite each other,[44] as the good expression of God's creation within the body of Christ.[45]

- An understanding of ministry as obedient human response to Jesus and the priority of that call for both women and men over other holy responsibilities, just as the hospitable Martha and the respectful man who wanted leave to bury his father learned (Luke 9 and 10).[46]

- The identification of characteristics which we define socially as feminine and masculine as *together* describing biblical leadership.[47]

- A voice for men in the role of the pastor's husband. Lillian Daniel quite rightly points out that the pastor's husband is not constrained by traditional role expectations and has the unique opportunity to help rewrite expectations both for pastors and their spouses.[48]

---

42. George, "Egalitarians and Complementarians," 266–88. Sumner, "Middle Way," 250–65.

43. See Pierce and Groothuis, *Biblical Equality*, Part IV, 355–428; Hancock, *Christian Perspectives*; Husbands, "Reconciliation," 127–47.

44. Leeuwen, "Opposite Sexes?," 181; Webb, "Redemptive-Movement," 382–400.

45. Cohick, "Prophecy," 96–97.

46. Peterson, "Identity and Ministry," 165.

47. Ward, "Not So Different?," 10–12.

48. Daniel, "Pastor's Husband," 28.

Engaging in the Conversation—The Responsibility of Rug Trader and Rug Seller Alike!

The rug trader brought the numbers above one hundred to the attention of the old woman. I hope she recovered quickly from her surprise and reentered the conversation with an appropriately recalculated price tag for her rug! This would make a satisfactory conclusion to the story and would serve to highlight the contemporary responsibility of both men and women to cross the little Jordan of relational distance that can result from our different perspectives. In the final section of the paper I will suggest some practical action towards women and men taking responsibility for liberating all of God's children to the ministry they are called to and equipped for.

As a very first step we can create opportunities within mainstream Protestant churches to tell the stories of women in ministry. A number of the books and journals referred to in this paper do exactly this but they only scratch the surface of a rich deposit of historical and contemporary stories waiting to be told.[49] While it is right to be cautious about practices that may be either patronizing or strident we do need to tell women's stories regularly at our pastors' conferences, in our denominational magazines, and via our electronic communication. Within my own context of Baptists in Western Australia there are a number of as yet unrecorded stories of women who have trained for ministry at the Baptist Theological College (now Vose Seminary) who are now in ministry in other denominations or ministries other than that which they trained for. These are stories about who we are as Baptists in Western Australia and we need to hear and consider and respond to them, along with the stories of women currently serving in accredited ministry roles.

Second, it will serve the gospel well to revisit the dominant imagery of the stories that are told about experiences of call to ministry.[50] Just as the paradigms that work best for redefining ministry are those of redemption and reconciliation so the most eloquent and engaging stories of call are those that are told in terms of "new creation."[51] It may be that the language of new creation and community will resonate well with women, and with both younger men and women.

A third step towards the shared responsibility of liberating all those called by Christ and empowered by the Spirit to serve in ministry is the preparedness of church leaders and denominational leaders to do more than

---

49. Robins and Fowler, "Married with Children," 321–26.
50. McDougall, "Weaving Garments," 158.
51. McDougall, "Weaving Garments," 159.

sympathetically pass on the bad news to women that there are no places to serve.[52] Tony Campolo calls for leaders to "zealously affirm" the rights of women to assume leadership roles in the church;[53] Molly Marshall writes of male ministers and denominational leaders as necessary gatekeepers tasked with holding the door wide open for women called to lead;[54] and Joy Ann McDougall claims, quite rightly, that a neutral stance is insufficient.[55]

Men do continue to exercise more power than women in our churches and responsible stewardship of that resource includes advocacy and education of congregations on behalf of women.[56] Advocacy will need to extend to proactive promotion of women into leadership teams and positions. This ought not to occur without relevant gifting but will from time to time demand the choice for a gifted and called woman over a more experienced man simply to give women the opportunities to experience and model ministry possibilities.[57]

Fourth, women called to lead must prepare well and take the ordination or accreditation practices of their denominations seriously. It serves only to reinforce systemic issues and a "second-class ministry" culture if women content themselves with ministering outside of the accepted and normative protocols.[58]

Finally, women and men will be liberated to God's call on their lives more and more if we accept Ann Svennungsen's assertion that gender isn't always *the* issue but that it is *always* an issue where women are in pioneer roles. It remains for women and men in leadership to navigate the fine line between raising the gender issue too often and not raising it often enough.[59]

Conclusion

Beyond the four walls of the church in the Western world there lies the increasing expectation that there will be equal opportunity for women and men to work and live according to the skills and interests they have.

52. Durso and Durso, "Cherish the Dream," 21.
53. Campolo, "Is Evangelicalism Sexist?," 77–78.
54. Marshall, "Call to Ministry," 130–31.
55. McDougall, "Weaving Garments," 161.
56. Stackhouse, *Finally Feminist*, 96; Sanders, "Holy Boldness," 211.
57. Armstrong, "Lessons," 33; Barton, "How I Changed," 35; Hybels, "Gender Equality," 116.
58. Bellinger, "I Listened," 38; Durso, "My Journey," 137; McDougall, "Weaving Garments," 152; Pierce, "I Am Female," 148; Svennungsen, "Lead the Flock," 23.
59. Svennungsen, "Lead the Flock," 24.

Statistically there is still a gap between this expectation and reality, yet women do work at high levels in government departments, in the private business sector, in the academic world, and in the arts and sciences. This same expectation is increasingly evident in the church in the ministry hopes and aspirations of the young women and men of Generations Y and Z. This is as it should be, not because culture dictates, not because the younger generations have it all sorted, but because Jesus has made the way for every human being to be liberated to whatever he or she is called to be and do for the sake of the gospel.

The issue of women in leadership, however, is currently active even in churches and denominations where we claim to have settled the matter. Contributing factors are the little Jordans of differing perspectives, insufficient conversation, distrust, exaggerated and inaccurate understanding of differences, and the fear that results when we are unsure of our worth in God's eyes. In this paper I have outlined some of the contemporary expressions of the issue and offered some practical suggestions for a future we can be optimistic about if together we do the hard work of discovering who God is "for us *today*."[60]

I started with a story and will end with a prayer, from Christina Rossetti cited by Timothy George:[61]

> Jesus who didst touch the leper, deliver us from antipathies; who didst eat with them who washed not before meat, deliver us from fastidiousness; who didst condone inhospitality, deliver us from affront-taking; who didst not promise the right or the left, deliver us from favouritism; who, having called didst recall Peter, deliver us from soreness; who didst love active Martha and contemplative Mary, deliver us from respect of persons. Deliver us while it is called today. Thou who givest today, and promisest not tomorrow.

Bibliography

Armstrong, John. "Lessons My Mother Taught Me Without Trying." In *How I Changed My Mind About Women in Leadership: Compelling Stories from Prominent Evangelicals*, edited by Alan F. Johnson, 21–34. Grand Rapids: Zondervan, 2010.

Barton, Ruth Haley. "How I Changed My Mind about Women in Leadership." In *How I Changed My Mind about Women in Leadership: Compelling Stories from Prominent Evangelicals*, edited by Alan F. Johnson, 35–48. Grand Rapids: Zondervan, 2010.

---

60. Husbands, "Reconciliation," 128.
61. George, "Egalitarians and Complementarians," 288.

Bellinger, Elizabeth Smith. "I Listened to the Story and I Believed." In *Courage and Hope: The Stories of Ten Baptist Women Ministers*, edited by Pamela R. Durso and Keith E. Durso, 31–42. Macon, GA: Mercer University Press, 2005.

Blocher, Henri. "Women, Ministry and the Gospel: Hints for a New Paradigm?" In *Women, Ministry and the Gospel*, edited by Mark Husband and Timothy Larson, 239–49. Downers Grove: InterVarsity, 2007.

Briscoe, Stuart. "Buried Talents." In *How I Changed My Mind about Women in Leadership: Compelling Stories from Prominent Evangelicals*, edited by Alan F. Johnson, 61–66. Grand Rapids: Zondervan, 2010.

Catford, Cheryl. "Riding the Third Wave: Biblical Equality in the 21st Century." *Zadok* 109 (2010) 11–18.

Campolo, Tony. "Is Evangelicalism Sexist?" In *How I Changed My Mind about Women in Leadership: Compelling Stories from Prominent Evangelicals*, edited by Alan F. Johnson, 67–80. Grand Rapids: Zondervan, 2010.

Cohick, Lynn H. "Prophecy, Women in Leadership and the Body of Christ." In *Women, Ministry and the Gospel*, edited by Mark Husband and Timothy Larson, 81–97. Downers Grove: InterVarsity, 2007.

Daniel, Lillian. "The Pastor's Husband." *The Christian Century* 126, no. 14 (2009) 28–31.

Durso, Keith E. "I Wouldn't Take Nothing for My Journey: The Story of Ella Pearson Mitchell." In *Courage and Hope: The Stories of Ten Baptist Women Ministers*, edited by Pamela R. Durso and Keith E. Durso, 132–41. Macon, GA: Mercer University Press, 2005.

Durso, Keith E., and Pamela R. Durso. "'Cherish the Dream God Has Given You': The Story of Addie Davis." In *Courage and Hope: The Stories of Ten Baptist Women Ministers*, edited by Pamela R. Durso and Keith E. Durso, 18–30. Macon, GA: Mercer University Press, 2005.

Durso, Pamela R., and Keith E. Durso. "Baptist Women Ministers: Called and Gifted by God." In *Courage and Hope: The Stories of Ten Baptist Women Ministers*, edited by Pamela R. Durso and Keith E. Durso, 1–17. Macon, GA: Mercer University Press, 2005.

Fee, Gordon. "Male and Female in the New Creation." In *Discovering Biblical Equality: Complementarity without Hierarchy*, edited by Ronald W. Pierce and Rebecca Merrill Groothuis, 172–85. Leicester: InterVarsity, 2004.

Fitzgerald, Sue. "The Call Does Not Stop, For New Avenues of Ministry Keep Opening Up." In *Courage and Hope: The Stories of Ten Baptist Women Ministers*, edited by Pamela R. Durso and Keith E. Durso, 58–75. Macon, GA: Mercer University Press, 2005.

George, Timothy. "Egalitarians and Complementarians Together? A Modest Proposal." In *Women, Ministry and the Gospel*, edited by Mark Husband and Timothy Larson, 266–87. Downers Grove: InterVarsity, 2007.

Gundry, Stanley N. "From Bobbed Hair, Bossy Wives and Women Preachers to Women Be Free: My Story." In *How I Changed My Mind about Women in Leadership: Compelling Stories from Prominent Evangelicals*, edited by Alan F. Johnson, 93–106. Grand Rapids: Zondervan, 2010.

Hancock, Maxine, ed. *Christian Perspectives on Gender, Sexuality and Community*. Vancouver: Regent, 2003.

Hubbard, Robert L. Jr. *Joshua*. The NIV Application Commentary. Grand Rapids: Zondervan, 2009.

Husbands, Mark. "Reconciliation as the Dogmatic Location of Humanity: Your Life is Hidden with Christ in God." In *Women, Ministry and the Gospel*, edited by Mark Husband and Timothy Larson, 127–47. Downers Grove: InterVarsity, 2007.

Hybels, Bill and Lynne. "Evangelicals and Gender Equality." In *How I Changed My Mind about Women in Leadership: Compelling Stories from Prominent Evangelicals*, edited by Alan F. Johnson, 107–20. Grand Rapids: Zondervan, 2010.

Johnson, Alan F. "My Journey from 'Male Only Leadership' to 'Biblical Gender Equality.'" In *How I Changed My Mind about Women in Leadership: Compelling Stories from Prominent Evangelicals*, edited by Alan F. Johnson, 121–30. Grand Rapids: Zondervan, 2010.

Kimball, Cynthia Neal. "Nature, Culture and Gender Complementarity." In *Discovering Biblical Equality: Complementarity without Hierarchy*, edited by Ronald W. Pierce and Rebecca Merrill Groothuis, 464–80. Leicester: InterVarsity, 2004.

Larsen, Timothy. "Women in Public Ministry: A Historic Evangelical Distinctive." In *Women, Ministry and the Gospel*, edited by Mark Husband and Timothy Larson, 213–38. Downers Grove: InterVarsity, 2007.

Long, Fredrick J. "Christ's Gifted Bride: Gendered Members in Ministry in Acts and Paul." In *Women, Ministry and the Gospel*, edited by Mark Husband and Timothy Larson, 98–126. Downers Grove: InterVarsity, 2007.

Marshall, I. Howard. "Women in Ministry: A Further Look at 1 Timothy 2." In *Women, Ministry and the Gospel*, edited by Mark Husband and Timothy Larson, 53–79. Downers Grove: InterVarsity, 2007.

Marshall, Molly T. "God Does Indeed Call to Ministry Whom God Will, Gender Notwithstanding." In *Courage and Hope: The Stories of Ten Baptist Women Ministers*, edited by Pamela R. Durso and Keith E. Durso, 120–31. Macon, GA: Mercer University Press, 2005.

Matthews, Alice. "How I Changed My Mind about Women in Leadership." In *How I Changed My Mind about Women in Leadership: Compelling Stories from Prominent Evangelicals*, edited by Alan F. Johnson, 154–63. Grand Rapids: Zondervan, 2010.

McDougall, Joy Ann. "Weaving Garments of Grace: En-gendering a Theology of the Call to Ordained Ministry for Women Today." *Theological Education* 39, no. 2 (2003) 149–65.

Payne, Philip B. *Man and Woman, One in Christ: An Exegetical and Theological Study of Paul's Letters*. Grand Rapids: Zondervan, 2009.

Peterson, Margaret Kim. "Identity and Ministry in the Light of the Gospel: A View from the Kitchen." In *Women, Ministry and the Gospel*, edited by Mark Husband and Timothy Larson, 148–68. Downers Grove: InterVarsity, 2007.

Pierce, John. "I Am Female, But God Knew That Before He Called Me: The Story of Ruby Welsh Wilkins." In *Courage and Hope: The Stories of Ten Baptist Women Ministers*, edited by Pamela R. Durso and Keith E. Durso, 142–49. Macon, GA: Mercer University Press, 2005.

Pierce, Ronald W., and Rebecca Merrill Groothuis. "Introduction." In *Discovering Biblical Equality: Complementarity without Hierarchy*, edited by Ronald W. Pierce and Rebecca Merrill Groothuis, 13–19. Leicester: InterVarsity, 2004.

Plantinga, Cornelius Jr. "How I Changed My Mind About Women in Church Leadership." In *How I Changed My Mind about Women in Leadership: Compelling Stories from Prominent Evangelicals*, edited by Alan F. Johnson, 185–96. Grand Rapids: Zondervan, 2010.

Robins, Mandy, and Christine Fowler. "Married with Children: The Experience of Women Ministers of Word and Sacrament in the United Reformed Church." *Journal of Beliefs and Values* 29, no. 3 (2008) 321–26.

Rowe, Mary Hannah. "30 Years of Women's Ordination." *Dialog: A Journal of Theology* 39, no. 3 (2000) 206–13.

Sanders, Cheryl L. "Holy Boldness, Holy Women: Agents of the Gospel." In *Women, Ministry and the Gospel*, edited by Mark Husband and Timothy Larson, 200–12. Downers Grove: InterVarsity, 2007.

Stackhouse, John G. Jr. *Finally Feminist: A Pragmatic Christian Understanding of Gender*. Grand Rapids: Baker, 2005.

Storkey, Elaine. *Created or Constructed: The Great Gender Debate*. Carlisle: Paternoster, 2000.

Svennungsen, Ann. "When Women Lead the Flock." *Congregations* 30, no. 3 (2004) 21–24.

Spencer, Aída Besançon. "The View from the Pulpit: Honest Advice for Women in Ministry." *Mutuality* 16, no. 4 (2009) 4–8.

Sumner, Sarah. "Forging a Middle Way between Complementarians and Egalitarians." In *Women, Ministry and the Gospel*, edited by Mark Husband and Timothy Larson, 250–65. Downers Grove: InterVarsity, 2007.

Van Leeuwen, Mary Stewart. "Opposite Sexes or Neighboring Sexes? What Do the Social Sciences Really Tell Us?" In *Women, Ministry and the Gospel*, edited by Mark Husband and Timothy Larson, 171–99. Downers Grove: InterVarsity, 2007.

Ward, Rosie. "Not So Different? Gender, Communication, and Leadership Style." *Mutuality* 16, no. 4 (2009) 10–12.

Webb, William J. "A Redemptive-Movement Hermeneutic: The Slavery Analogy." In *Discovering Biblical Equality: Complementarity without Hierarchy*, edited by Ronald W. Pierce and Rebecca Merrill Groothuis, 382–400. Leicester: InterVarsity, 2004.

Willard, Dallas. "Foreword." In *Women, Ministry and the Gospel*, edited by Mark Husband and Timothy Larson, 9–10. Downers Grove: InterVarsity, 2007.

Winfrey, Joan Burgess. "In Search of Holy Joy: Women and Self-Esteem." In *Discovering Biblical Equality: Complementarity without Hierarchy*, edited by Ronald W. Pierce and Rebecca Merrill Groothuis, 431–47. Leicester: InterVarsity, 2004.

8

Living in God's Mission

Theses for a Systematic Ecclesiology

JOHN MCCLEAN

Introduction

> I am writing these instructions to you so that, if I am delayed, you may know how one ought to behave in the household of God, which is the church of the living God, the pillar and bulwark of the truth. Without any doubt, the mystery of our religion is great: He was revealed in flesh, vindicated in spirit, seen by angels, proclaimed among Gentiles, believed in throughout the world, taken up in glory. (1 Tim 3:14b–16)

PAUL'S WORDS TO TIMOTHY are a biblical precedent for a systematic ecclesiology which aims to help the church understand itself and discern how it should live.[1] The apostle reflects on his letter to his protégé and says that it offers instructions on how to "behave," instructions grounded in the identity of the church of God. He moves directly from this statement to declare the "mystery" of piety (*eusebia*) which is the story of Christ. That

---

1. This chapter assumes Pauline authorship of the Pastoral Epistles. For a discussion of the issues involved, see Towner, *Letters*, 8–26, 83–88. Towner concludes that although the question of authorship remains open, it is quite permissible to consider Paul the primary author "however much or little others contributed to their material and composition" (88).

is, the existence of the church is to correspond to Christ's work. Within Christ's work Paul's instructions have an immediate context. He is aware that some needs in the church have been exacerbated by his absence from them. He also writes for the church as it will exist in "later times" (1 Tim 4:1). Together, these elements set the direction for a systematic ecclesiology which seeks to describe the identity of the church as based on the work of God in Christ, and to do so in a way which helps the church to live in its context. This chapter provides a series of theses based on these ideas to help the church reflect on its own life and mission.

Before beginning this task, however, it will be helpful to deal with some preliminary matters. First, why is consideration of context important? The primary reason is that it is inevitable. We always think from our own context, and theology is better to make this explicit and view it as a virtue to be developed rather than a vice to be suppressed.[2] It is impossible to bracket out considerations of context and although it may seem counter-intuitive, including a concern for context in ecclesiological reflection may actually help the study avoid being overwhelmed by its context.[3]

Second, my proposal for systematic ecclesiology is one which reads Scripture as a normative account, but it does so in self-conscious awareness of its own context. Asserting that Scripture is normative is not sufficient, certainly not for ecclesiology. How is Scripture normative? I suggest that a systematic ecclesiology must seek to understand the biblical presentation of the church in the light of the identity of God and his mission. Biblical descriptions of church, and instructions for the church are largely "paradigmatic." They are neither to be replicated (in a new context "replication" is impossible), nor are they to be discarded. Rather, they show us the kind of way in which the church lives.[4] As we see the life of the church in the light of mission of God, the Spirit may lead us into expressions of the same life in our own context.[5] With these considerations now in place, let us proceed.

---

2. For reflection on how ecclesial context has shaped various proposals see, Healy, *Church, World*, 40–43.

3. Context is not included in this account of ecclesiology in order to produce a correlationist theological method. As Healy says, "Practical-prophetic ecclesiology" must deny . . . any proposal to change the concrete church made merely in order that it may better fit the norms of a non-Christian worldview or social context." Healy, *Church, World*, 50.

4. Marshall, *Fresh Look*, 76, suggests that Acts "does not . . . present a detailed paradigm for the ongoing life of the church," but does show several important features of the emerging Christian church.

5. See Runia, "God-Given Ministry."

The Nature and Mission of the Church: Thirteen Theses

1. *The Church Is the Result of God's Mission*

To situate ecclesiology in the mission of God is to assert the priority of God's work for the identity of the church. "Gospel and church exist in a strict and irreversible order, one in which the gospel precedes and the church follows."[6]

God's mission has a long history, reaching back at least to Abraham. Its center, both historically and conceptually, is the coming of Christ who brings God's kingdom. Jesus Christ is the sent one—the emissary (John 3:34; 4:34; 17:18; 20:21). The divine mission is executed in the person and work of Christ who comes in the Spirit, and then by the Spirit who comes from Christ and in whom Christ is present. The mission is announced and progresses by the proclamation of the person and work of Christ in the apostolic gospel by the power of the Spirit. To speak of God's mission is to speak of the whole of salvation—the electing purposes of God, the reconciling work of the Son in the world, and the vivifying presence of the Spirit. This is a Trinitarian summary of the mission which is presented in historical narrative in the Bible.[7]

Shenk begins his account with the sending of the church and concludes that there is no primal form prescribed for the church drawing the conclusion that "the church is infinitely translatable and adaptable."[8] In contrast, I would assert that the foundation in God's mission sets constraints on such translation. The church is thus warned against becoming obsessed with the new and experimental, particularly where this is motivated by desire for greater consumer appeal.[9] At the same time, understanding church in the light of God's mission provides a critical tool for the assessment of tradition.[10]

---

6. Webster, "Evangelical Ecclesiology," 10; cf. his further discussion, 17–19. Cf. Shenk, "New Wineskins," 73.

7. Thompson, *Trinitarian Perspectives*, 69–72.

8. Shenk, "New Wineskins," 74.

9. Mannion, "Postmodern Ecclesiologies," 129.

10. What does not flow authentically from the mission of God has no place in the church of God. A missional stance grounded in God's mission should open us to learn critically from other church traditions. It is important that elements from other traditions are adopted with integrity, understanding how they flow from the mission of God and being alert to where they fail to do so. This should raise an interest in comparative ecclesiology not as a way of abandoning one's own tradition but as a way of testing and understanding them. See, for example, Haight, *Christian Community*, vol. 2.

Beginning ecclesiology with the mission of God determines a stance with respect to the world.[11] God's mission springs from his love and cannot be thought of as set against the world. Yet the very notion of redemption shows that God's mission will not simply affirm the world or leave it as it is. Further, classic Christology recognizes that the mission of God is not a matter of realizing latent capacities in creation nor assisting lost humanity to find its own path back to God. The kingdom of God requires that the sent one should be God, the Word becomes flesh. The incarnation affirms the value of the created order, but also highlights the need for God to act. So the church, as it embodies God's mission in the world, recognizes the value of culture and human society. Yet it refuses to identify itself with human cultures. The church must understand itself as a counterculture, and as such neither as the institution of a "Christian nation," nor as a mirror of the culture.

2. The Church Participates in Trinitarian Fellowship

The goal of mission, from the point of view of the church, is that God brings his people into fellowship with himself.[12] This goal is set in the larger cosmic purpose of God bringing the creation to share in God's glory under Christ's rule (Rom 8:19–21; Eph 1:10, 20–23; Col 1:15–20).[13]

Knox highlights this goal with his description of the heavenly gathering of the people of God in Christ. "The assembly, or church, which Christ is building now is primarily a supernal heavenly assembly."[14] The writer to the Hebrews tells the readers that they now participate in a heavenly assembly, based on Christ's entry into the heavenly temple on their behalf (Heb 1:3; 8:1–2; 9:11–12, 24).

This gathering in Christ exhibits an important biblical pattern. One prophetic promise is that God will gather his scattered people, and the nations, to Jerusalem. This is the "centripetal" movement of the Old Testament, in which people move toward Jerusalem.[15] Often missiology moves directly

---

11. Allen, "Church," 115.

12. That the triune existence of God provides the space in which the church may exist as a sanctified creature is beyond the scope of this chapter. See Allen, "Church," 114–15.

13. The cosmic goal of God's mission is closely related to the redemption of God's people. It is in the restoration of God's image bearers in communion with God that the creation itself comes to share in God's glory (Rom 8:21). See Watts, "New Exodus," 18–22.

14. Knox, "Denominations," 44. Cf. Hebrews 12:20–24.

15. Scobie, *Ways of Our God*, 516–17. "Just as the Jews of the Dispersion come in

to the centrifugal New Testament movement of the church going out, and in so doing misses the christological key to the shift. There is a New Testament ingathering to the ascended Christ and so to the heavenly assembly. On this basis, as the result of God's mission, the church is sent out into the world.

The theme of the people of God gathered to God in Christ and by the Spirit aligns with the theme of the "invisible church" in Reformed ecclesiology.[16] The Reformed approach to start ecclesiology with the invisible church (e.g. Westminster Confession 25:1–2) expresses a key theological insight: the church is God's people in fellowship with God grounded in our union with the ascended Christ.

3. In the Mission of God His Church is Gathered to Meet Together By the Spirit

The invisible is expressed in the visible: God's people *meet*.[17] In Acts the life of the church is characterized by meetings (Acts 1:14; 2:46; 4:24, 31; 6:5–6; 11:26; 12:12; 14:27; 15:6; 16:40; 20:7). In the Epistles as well, there is a constant (and obvious) assumption that the church meets (1 Cor 5:4; 11:34; 14:26–40; Eph 5:19; Col 3:16; 4:16; 1 Thess 5:27; 1 Tim 4:13) as well as instruction to meet (Heb 10:25). God's gathered people are gathered to God and one another by the Spirit. This gathering is concrete and physical in meeting face-to-face with each other. The divine-human relationship is given central expression in meeting to hear God's word, to praise him, and to share the Lord's Supper.

Knox insists on the importance of "local, physical, geographic assemblies" yet gives primacy to the "heavenly assembly."[18] Knox develops his po-

---

pilgrimage to Zion, so in the new age shall all nations participate in that pilgrimage." The prophets foretold that the nations come to learn from God and his law (Isa 2:2–4; Mic 4:1–4), join in worship (Isa 19:19–22; 56:6–7; 60:7; Jer 3:17; 16:19; Ps 86:9; Zech 14:16), and share in the Lord's salvation (Isa 45:22–23; 51:5; Zech 2:11; Ps 99:10).

16. Allen, "Church," 24–25.

17. According to Webster, "Election generates a polity, a common life"; Webster, "Ecclesiology," 19.

18. Knox, "Church"; "Demythologising," 48–55; "Churches," 15–25. These, and other more popular presentations on the doctrine of the church, can be found in Knox, *Selected Works*, vol. II, 9–98. "The Church and the Denominations" is not included in *Church and Ministry*. In explaining this claim he makes some perplexing statements, such as that Paul was persecuting the heavenly church (Acts 9:1) and that apostles, prophets, and teachers were appointed to this church (Eph 4:11). See, Knox, "Denominations," 46. At least as perplexing is his argument that New Testament exhortations for Christians to continue to meet demonstrate that New Testament believers thought of themselves primarily as members of the heavenly church (47).

sition christologically, but not pneumatologically, which may help explain why his position tends to hold the heavenly assembly in some contrast to the visible church.[19] If the gathering of God's people is both a christological heavenly assembly and a pneumatological earthly assembly, and if those two actions of God are carefully coordinated, then we have a conception of church which holds the invisible and the visible together.

The importance of physical gathering suggests that a "virtual church" is theologically dubious. The importance of physical presence for Christian fellowship is reflected in Paul's desire to see the churches in Rome and Corinth and to see Timothy (Rom 1:11–12; 15:22–23; 1 Cor 4:19; 11:34; 2 Tim 1:4; 4:9, 21).

4. Churches are Meeting-Communities

The church meets and is a community—an ongoing complex network of interpersonal relationships in which people know and relate to each other in a range of ways within a shared social context. A community has ongoing existence, and distinctive obligations to each other because they share communal life. A church is both meeting and community. It is a community expressed as a meeting, and a meeting which sustains a community.

Webster warns against an occasionalism in which the church is thought to exist only in moments when the Spirit "seizes dead forms and gives them temporary animation."[20] His warning applies to the implicit occasionalism in Knox's view. Knox argues that "Church . . . in the Greek New Testament always refers to an actual assembling" and "fellowship . . . only exists when it is experienced" for it "consists of a word spoken and responded to in the context of receiving one another and appreciating one another."[21] It is not clear that Knox intends his statements to be taken in an occasionalist sense to imply that the church and fellowship have only a heavenly existence apart from when they have concrete expression in Christian assembly. However, his stress so falls on the assembly that he makes no acknowledgment of the ongoing relationships which exist because of the meeting.[22]

---

19. I can find only one reference to the work of the Spirit in Knox's *Church and Ministry*. Cole has raised the question of how "heavenly" descriptions should be understood. See Cole "Doctrine," 3–17. See also Giles, "Where on Earth?," 17–19; and, Giles, *What on Earth?* My criticisms are not identical to those of Cole or Giles.

20. Webster, "Ecclesiology," 27. Perhaps he is thinking of Barth's comments that the church is visible only in the way the lettering of an electric sign is visible when the current passes through it. Cf. Barth, *Church Dogmatics*, IV/2, 619.

21. Knox, "Demythologising," 54.

22. His concession that "it is possible to speak of elders of a gathering . . . when

The implication of this perspective is that meeting-communities are the base form of church. A ministry which encompasses multiple congregations should be viewed as a grouping of churches, rather than as a single church. Alternately, if several congregations wish to identify as a church, then they should strive to create a genuine meeting-community; simply sharing the use of a building and ministry personnel does not create a meeting-community.

Another implication may be that we should favor multiple smaller congregations, rather than megachurches, since the possibility for genuine community is far greater in the smaller congregations. (There is no need to be overly doctrinaire about the size of "smaller," since the ability to have genuine community is as much determined by the culture and structure of the congregation as it is by the absolute size.)

The central place of meeting-communities in God's mission underlines the importance of church planting.[23] Peter Wagner famously declared that "the single most effective evangelistic methodology under heaven is planting new churches."[24] Yet, as Wagner recognized, it is not merely that starting new churches gives effective penetration of the gospel into unreached groups. The gospel creates churches, they are the goal of the mission.

According to this thesis "churchless faith" cannot be accepted as fully formed Christian practice.[25] We must allow that believers who have left "church" may in fact still be part of a Christian meeting-community.[26] How is such a community identified as a church, rather than "post-church"? A missional perspective will bring us back to the classic "marks of the church" identified by the Reformers.[27] It is in the gospel declared and demonstrated in the sacraments that God executes his mission and gathers his community and these mark a community as the church of God.

---

there is no gathering going on at the moment," seems to lean strongly toward occasionalism. Knox, "Demythologising," 54.

23. Hibbert, "Place of Church," 330–31.

24. Wagner, *Church Planting*, 11.

25. See Jamieson, "Churchless Faith."

26. Jamieson notes that 65 percent of the church leavers he interviewed were involved in groups made up of people on "a similar faith path." Some of the groups Jamieson describes have self-consciously abandoned identification with the church and do not see themselves as God's people assembled in Christ. On the other hand, some of the groups have taken on many of the functions of church and are seen by participants as churches ("Churchless Faith," 221–22).

27. Avis, *Theology of the Reformers*, 13–77.

5. The Meeting-Community is an Anticipation of the Eschatological Outcome of God's Mission

The mission of God forms his meeting-community in Christ and by the Spirit, but the outcome of the mission is only fully realized in the new creation. Then God's people will see him face-to-face.[28] All present expressions of gathering in the Spirit anticipate the eschaton.[29]

The reason why the invisible church should be allowed some primacy in ecclesiology is not because invisible is better than visible or because the heavenly is real and the earthly is shadow. Rather it is because the heavenly is eschatological—"invisibility marks the life of the Church due to her eschatological placement."[30] Our life is now hidden with Christ in God and we await the appearing of Christ when the church will appear with him in glory (Col 3:3–4).

Church is not an interim arrangement to be superseded but is already the firstfruits of the coming harvest (2 Thess 2:13; James 1:18; Rev 14:4). It is the glimmer of dawn, the sign that there is more to come because it is part of that which is to come. It is in the church that a new humanity appears (Col 3:9–11).

Hope for the future must mark the life of the church. This is not a mere sunny optimism, nor a general cheerfulness. Rather it consists of a determined readiness to face this "present evil age" and still to live in hope. In a society which is increasingly marked by fear of the future, the church can live distinctively as a community of hope: raising families, caring for the creation, serving the poor, and participating in the society. The church does not create the future, it is a witness to God's future.

Claims about the authority of the church, one of the traditional themes of ecclesiology, can only be understood as the church is seen as existing because of God's work. The mission of God calls the church to recognize now the rule of God which all will recognize in the fullness of the kingdom. Christ rules the church, in and through his gospel and by his Spirit, and so by his inscripturated revelation.[31] God's people will rule with him (Dan

---

28. Scobie, *Ways of Our God*, 143, 396, 735–36.
29. Mostert, "Kingdom Anticipated," 25–37. Cf. Healy, *Church, World*, 10.
30. Allen, "Churches," 116.
31. See Pannenberg, *Systematic Theology*, vol. 2, 459. Pannenberg offers a doctrine of Scripture which affirms its inspiration and authority but offers little adumbration of this and is explicitly critical of the Reformation "scripture principle." However, his eschatological understanding of revelation offers a perspective which can be filled out into a more satisfying doctrine of Scripture. See Grenz, *Reason for Hope*, 47–49, 182; and Gutenson, *Doctrine of God*, 47–50.

7:27; Matt 19:28; Rom 5:17; Rev 20:4; 22:5) and share in his authority. Thus, the authority of the church itself is entirely derivative from its participation in Christ and by the Spirit in the rule of God. Postmodernity is highly critical of claims to authority. The church is in a position to show a very different form of authority to that of hypermodernity: a derived, ministerial, anticipatory authority which is used in service of God and others.

6. The Meeting-Community is a Broken Anticipation of the Eschatological Outcome of God's Mission

The meeting-community always reflects the "not yet" even as it bears witness to the presence of eschatological life; it is a broken anticipation of God's future.[32] As a result the New Testament epistles are replete with rebukes, warnings, and even threats. Paul tells the Corinthians that they are people of the Spirit who participate in eschatological wisdom, but he had to speak to them "as people of the flesh, as infants in Christ" (1 Cor 2:6—3:1).

The notion of anticipation asserts that the church cannot claim to have arrived, but that it must always be a pilgrim church and stand under judgment as well as grace. The church must retain a stance of humble confession in all it does. In practice this should be expressed in serious and thoughtful confession of sin, individual, and corporate, as the church meets. Such confession should not be perfunctory, nor should it focus solely on the individual sins of those present, as if individuals have come to church to confess. The church sins.[33]

Aware of its brokenness, the church must be ever on guard against the abuse of its authority and must keep it within the bounds allowed by participation in Christ and the Spirit. It must not "go beyond what is written" though it will be prone to do so (1 Cor 4:6). Constrained, self-critical use of authority will look very different to authoritarianism and to poll-driven politics.

---

32. The term comes from Pannenberg's description of church in which he says that "the mystery of salvation achieves only broken anticipation in the church's historical form." Pannenberg, *Systematic Theology*, vol. 3, 43.

33. Healy, *Church, World*, 8–9, highlights the failure of the Roman church to confess its own sin, but it is not clear that Protestant churches are much more consistent in expressing their awareness of sin.

7. Christian Identity and Experience is Realized In and Through Participation in the Meeting-Community[34]

Modern evangelicalism constantly reinforces the message that the Christian life is the life of the individual, with some support from the church.[35] This inverts the relationship of the church and individual; for believers—who we are alone rests on who we are together.[36] If Christian identity is granted by God through the church then it is odd to claim that the church does not worship or is not called to mission or has no "face to the world." Worship, mission, and involvement in the world must be corporate if they are to be Christian.

This thesis also underlines the impact of church discipline. For the church to call a member to account or even to expel them is an act directed to the Christian identity of the person. Such an act may not be as empty as we often suspect.

8. The Meeting-Community is To Be Shaped by the Mission of God and By its Goal

Church exists because of God's work and it exists in anticipation of the eschatological gathering. So its life, in all aspects, should be characterized by the mission of God. Pragmatism in church life must be questioned. Strategies drawn from management, marketing, and even community development require interrogation and challenge.[37]

Whatever structure a church has should express and support its life as a meeting-community. Sometimes structure is viewed as the antithesis to the freedom and spontaneity of authentic spiritual life. Structures can become an obstacle to genuine community, but they are also necessary for such a life. We need to have a time and space to meet, shared practices when we meet, and leadership in our communities.

Are there structural elements in Scripture which are paradigmatic for Christian churches? Although there are, they are very simple in comparison to the complex structures of most contemporary churches. In the

---

34. See Kenneson, "Gathering," 54–67.

35. Spiritual growth, evangelism, ethical reflection, and a host of other concerns are viewed as primarily the task of individuals.

36. According to Bannerman, "the Christian is more of a Christian in society than alone, and more in the enjoyment of privileges of a spiritual kind when he shares them with others, than when he possesses them apart." See Bannerman, *Church of Christ*, 91.

37. Thompson, *Trinitarian Perspectives*, 77.

New Testament church members entered the community by baptism (Matt 28:19; Acts 2:38; Rom 6:3–4; Eph 5:4). The church met together for worship on the Lord's Day (Heb 10:24–25; 1 Cor 16:1; Acts 20:7) which consisted of prayer (Rom 15:30; 1 Cor 11:4–5; 2 Thess 3:1; 1 Tim 2:1), song (Rom 15:11; 1 Cor 14:15; Eph 5:19; Col 3:16; Heb 2:12; James 5:13), reading of Scripture and proclamation of apostolic doctrine (Acts 2:42; Eph 4:11–12; Col 3:16; 1 Thess 5:12; 2 Tim 1:13; 4:1–2, 13), and eating together, including sharing the Lord's Supper (Matt 26:17–29; Mark 14:12–25; Luke 22:7–22; 1 Cor 10:21–22; 11:18–34). Each of these flows directly from the identity of the church in the mission of God and are paradigmatic practices for the church. There is another set of practices in the New Testament which provide much of the content of the church's life together: greeting one another (1 Cor 16:20; 2 Cor 13:12; 1 Thess 5:26; 1 Pet 5:14), showing hospitality (Rom 12:13; 16:23; 1 Tim 5:10; Heb 13:2; 1 Pet 4:9; 3 John 8), prayer for each other (Heb 13:18), sharing with each other (John 17:9; Col 4:3; 1Thess 5:25; 2 Thess 1:11; 3:1) and care for the poor (James 1:27; Gal 2:10).

What key features might be reflected in the patterns of the church's life? First, the church is a *community which listens to the gospel*. The church exists because of the mission of God and is sustained as it continues to attend to the announcement of that mission.[38] Next, the church is a *community of witness*. Following Barth, Webster suggests that witness to the words and actions of God is the principal activity of the church. He describes witness as "astonished indication."[39] The church must live displaying and declaring its wonder at God and his mission. Third, it is a *community of worship and holiness*. The eschatological church worships God (Rev 7:9–15; 21:21–26; 22:3). So the call to the church now must be to worship God both in adoration and in action.[40] Such worship spills over into the church's life, in accordance with the divine call to "Be holy because I am holy" (Lev 11:44–45; 1 Pet 1:16; 1 Thess 4:7). The community is to reflect the character of God and his pattern in their lives.

In addition, the church is a *community of love*. The church is called to be an inclusive community. The vision of God's people gathered includes those "from every nation, from all tribes and peoples and languages" (Rev 7:9). In Christ the divisions of humanity are overcome and there is "the possibility of unity without the dissolution of plurality, via friendly reciprocity between different groups of natural affinity" (Rom 10:12; 1 Cor 7:19; 12:13;

---

38. Webster, "Ecclesiology," 30–34.
39. Webster, "Ecclesiology," 29.
40. Volf, "Worship," 203–11. Contra Woodhouse, "Church Music," 17–18.

Gal 3:28; 5:6).[41] If church is an anticipation of this eschatological gathering, significant questions can be raised about strategies which rely heavily on the "homogenous unit principle." In a multicultural and multilingual society, it is inevitable and desirable that different churches will engage different areas of society. However, to aim at one social group in analogy to a "market segment" with the result that a church has little apparent interest in other groups in society raises serious questions about how such a church anticipates the eschaton.

Finally, the church as a meeting-community *is polycentric*. The relationships in a meeting-community are in Christ with God, and with one another. These relationships are not mediated by a leader or priest, but rather, in its human relations, the church is "polycentric community."[42] This is reflected in the New Testament "one another" instructions. In the Christian community the primary relationship between believers is mutual fellowship, service, and submission; the primary relationship is not to a leader. Believers are members of the same body (Rom 12:5; Eph 4:25) and must love one another (John 13:34–35; 15:12, 17; Rom 12:10; 13:8; 1 Thess 3:12; 4:9; 2 Thess 1:3; Heb 13:15; 1 Pet 1:22; 4:8; 1 John 3:11, 23; 4:7, 11–12; 2 John 1:5). This love is shown in mutual honor (Rom 12:10; Phil 2:3; 1 Pet 5:5), acceptance (Rom 15:7), and edification (Rom 14:19). Volf offers further theological reasons for understanding the church as a polycentric community. The church is not a single subject or agent but "a communion of interdependent subjects." This communion is constituted by the Spirit through the communal confession in which Christians speak the word of God to "one another" and salvation is mediated through "one another" rather than through the officeholders.[43]

Catholic ecclesiology has distinguished between the teaching church (the hierarchy) and the listening church (the people) and in its traditional form has held that the teaching church is basic. This thesis protests such conceptions. The church has leadership, but the leadership does not constitute the church. Evangelical ministries can be prone to elevating leadership and treating it as the *sine qua non* of church life. Complex leadership structures with carefully graded levels of authority and responsibility can subvert the church's true character as a polycentric community. This tendency can express itself in almost any system of polity and must be guarded against.

This thesis offers encouragement to churches which have small numbers, limited resources, and little formal leadership, whether rural churches

---

41. Cameron et al., "Christian Understanding," 28.
42. Volf, *Our Likeness*, 224.
43. Volf, *Our Likeness*, 222.

or small urban groups. Their life is no less the life of the church in the Spirit than a large suburban church.

9. The Leadership of the Meeting-Community is Conditioned by the Ministry of the Meeting-Community as a Whole

It is clear that there were people who held particular offices or positions of ministry in the New Testament church.[44] The office of elder/overseer is a paradigm for contemporary church leadership. However, theology has a long record of locating the "ministry" of the church in the offices, or at least giving them the primary role in ministry.[45] This order needs to be reversed (and has been in the majority of recent ecclesiology). It is the church which receives a ministry. The base form of ministry is mutual ministry through the use of gifts. For the good of the community God gives people particular positions (offices), but never as an alternative to mutual ministry among the people of God. Those in leadership receive their ministry in and through the ministry of the church and are called to assist and support the ministry of the whole church.[46]

---

44. The most prominent were the "apostles" (Matt 10:2; Mark 3:16–19; Luke 6:13; Acts 1:13, 23–26). There are also elder/overseers (Acts 11:30; 15:4; 20:28; Phil 1:1; 1 Tim 3:1; 4:14; 5:17; Titus 1:5, 7; James 5:14; 1 Pet 5:1–5) and deacons (Rom 16:1; Phil 1:1; 1 Tim 3:8–13). Fung, "Ministry," 175, concludes that "there is ample evidence which more than suffices to show that the early Christian communities were not amorphous associations run on haphazard lines; on the contrary, most if not all of them had at least a rudimentary . . . form of church organization . . . There is no intrinsic incompatibility between spiritual gifts and an organized ministry involving ecclesiastical office and official authority . . . function, gift and office are perfectly fused into a united whole [and] several of the charismata mentioned by Paul significantly find their counterparts in the qualifications laid down for presbytery-bishops and deacons in the Pastorals." See also Merkle, *Elder and Overseer*, 67–119.

45. Smith, *All God's People*, 354, briefly traces the shift from the New Testament view that all are Christ's servants to a "distinction . . . between the common people, the laity, and those in leadership, (the clergy)" in which the "later group became professional ministers, and the former group were largely excluded from God's service." He claims that "it was not until the second half of the twentieth century that a strong movement toward ministry of all God's people took place . . . It is now generally accepted that all of God's people are to be His ministers." See also Bulley, *Priesthood*, and Faivre, *Emergence*.

46. "The various offices or ministries of the church have as their presupposition and basis the one common office of ministry of the church. This common calling is to continue the mission of Jesus Christ in witness to the lordship of God . . . All are called and sent to give prophetic witness to the gospel of Jesus Christ, to engage together in worship of God, and to serve others." Pannenberg, *Systematic Theology* 3:373.

One of the contemporary trends which this thesis warns against is the focus on celebrity Christians. Although churches have largely laicized their view of ministry, our cultural emphasis on expertise and professionalization threatens this. Churches and leaders should encourage and celebrate the ministry of all.

10. The Meeting-Community Should Have a Leadership Structure Which Reflects Its Existence as the Meeting-Community Produced by the Mission of God

The leadership structures of the church have the goal of enabling the church to live its life effectively. The church is formed and guided by the gospel and the leaders of the church teach and apply the gospel for the building of the church (Eph 4:11–12; Gal 6:6; Heb 13:13). The Pastoral Epistles assert that sound apostolic doctrine promotes godliness and that the elders of the church must know and teach this doctrine and be examples of godliness. These connections underline how leadership is to enable the church to be what it is called to be.

Church leaders are to reflect the existence of the church in servant leadership. The community is called to serve one another for the sake of Christ. So leaders are to reflect Christ's humble service (Mark 10:42–45). Although they should receive respect and submission (1 Cor 16:16; 1 Thess 5:12; 1 Tim 3:8, 11; Heb 3:17), Christian leaders do not lord it over the meeting-community, but serve (2 Cor 1:24; 4:5; 1 Cor 9:19; 1 Pet 5:4; 1 Tim 3:3).

Just as the structures of church leadership should reflect the community, they also should be polycentric. The New Testament church under the instruction of the apostles developed a pattern of plural elders in each church.[47] Such a pattern has a theological rationale in the nature of the meeting-community which the mission of God creates. As such, plural eldership is a feature of the New Testament which is paradigmatic for contemporary churches. Such a pattern can be reflected in a range of ways in the life of a meeting-community.

---

47. Merkle, *Elder*, 134, 143–60.

11. A Meeting-Community Denies Its Identity If It Seeks to Exist in Isolation from Other Churches

The relationship of Christ with his people finds primary expression in the meeting-community, yet no single church is church alone. Each church anticipates the eschatological gathering of the people of God and so is properly termed a "catholic" church. On this basis it seeks fellowship with other churches.[48] This fellowship is grounded in those spiritual realities which have called each church into existence and makes it a church; each church has the gospel in common (Col 1:5–6), they share in apostolic fellowship with the Father and the Son (1 John 1:3–4), they have the one Spirit, Lord, and God, and are one body with a common hope, faith, and baptism (Eph 4:4–6). In the New Testament unity was expressed in apostolic oversight (Acts 14:23; 15:22; 2 Cor 11:28; Col 1:24—2:3; 1 Pet 1:1), greetings (Rom 16:5–16; Col 4:15), the exchange of writings (Col 4:16) and personnel (Col 4:12; Rom 16:1, 3; Acts 18:2), financial support (Rom 15:25–28; 2 Cor 8:19), and maintaining common practices (1 Cor 4:17; 7:17; 11:16; 13:33–34; 16:1).

Within the limits of what is feasible for a meeting-community, opportunities to fellowship with other churches should be embraced as fully as possible. This can be expressed in a wide range of forms. From this point of view denominations, while not primary to the identity of a meeting-community, have a proper place. The fellowship between churches implies mutual accountability. With the repeated shattering of unity between churches over the generations, real ecumenical accountability is not possible. Yet churches can and should have real accountability to one another.

This is an urgent question for many churches. Denominational churches face a decline of denominational discipline, so there is little or no real accountability. Independent congregations are flourishing in church planting movements, emerging churches, and house churches. How are they to make themselves genuinely accountable?

---

48. "A church cannot reflect the eschatological catholicity of the entire people of God and at the same time isolate itself from other churches . . . The church that refuses to do this would not be a catholic church and thus would be no church at all. Openness to other churches should lead to a free networking with those churches and . . . these mutual relations should be expressed in corresponding ecclesial institutions" (Volf, *Our Likeness*, 267, 275).

12. Churches Deny Their Identity If They Fail to Participate in the Mission of God in Fellowship with Other Churches

Perhaps surprisingly some evangelicals have held that the church, as church, does not have a mission.[49] However, since the church is itself created by the mission of God and exists because of the gospel which declares God's salvation and kingdom, it seems obvious that the church has a place in this mission.[50] Because the church is formed by the mission of God and formed around the gospel then all aspects of church life will have a mission dimension. The doxological call of the church is itself a perspective on mission.

As a catholic church each individual congregation has a global responsibility for mission; however, the meeting-communities take responsibility, first of all, for their own location and work in fellowship with other congregations. That there is an incompleteness about this mission, and even conflicts between churches within it, reflects the anticipatory nature of church.

13. The Meeting-Community Participates in the Mission of God by Living as the Church in the World

The concluding thesis returns to the mission of the church in the light of the mission of God. The mission of the church has a clear focus and center, which is to bear witness to God and his mission in word and deed through its own ongoing life as the people of God. To borrow from Newbigin, the relationship of the church to the kingdom can be described as sign, foretaste, and instrument.[51] The church enjoys the kingdom already in fellowship with the triune God and so stands as a sign of the kingdom in the world. It is only as the church is sustained in its life as the foretaste and sign of the kingdom that it can also be an instrument for the continued growth of the kingdom. It does so by its words and deeds in the world, which will aim first and foremost at the inclusion of others into God's meeting-communities. There is, then, a proper tension in our conception of the mission of the church. Churches do not exist for themselves, but for God and for the world, yet they serve God in the world and participate in his mission as they continue to exist and reflect on their own life and witness.

---

49. Thompson, "Local Church," 4, mentions Robinson, Cole and Bowers.

50. Köstenberger and O'Brien, *Ends of the Earth*, 191. Thompson, "Local Church," 20, concludes that "The God of mission gathers a missionary people to form a missionary church."

51. E.g. Newbigin, *Household of God*, 168–70; Newbigin, "Church," 6; and Newbigin, *Word in Season*, 33. See also Goheen, "As the Father," 359.

> Precisely because the Church is here and now a real foretaste of heaven, she can be the witness and instrument of the kingdom of heaven. It is precisely because she is not merely instrumental that she can be instrumental.[52]

Newbigin's own thought demonstrates two important implications of such a view of the mission of the church. One is that Christian discipleship must be based in participation in a church which lives its calling. He warns of "a kind of missionary zeal which is forever seeking to win more proselytes but which does not spring from and lead back into a quality of life which seems intrinsically worth having in itself."[53] Evangelicalism, with its often under-developed ecclesiology and lack of attention to thoughtful worship can be prone to this failing.

Newbigin also opposed views of mission which effectively dilute the church into the world. For example, Raiser argues that the classical Christocentric view of church must be replaced with a pneumatological view in which the church is merely one part of the global community with the task to discern the Spirit's work in the world and throw itself into that, whatever form it takes. The church's task is to "cooperate with others in rebuilding the moral fabric that sustains life in community."[54] Newbigin was critical of this view and insisted that the mission of God established the church with its communal life based in fellowship with Christ by the Spirit.

Conclusion

The challenges facing the church in Australia are well known. The number of professing Christians has declined rapidly over the last few decades, indicative of the loss of social status of the church. Australians have a growing suspicion of the institutional churches and are less and less informed about them. Young people are especially disconnected from churches yet are the age group most likely to have conversations about spirituality. The proportion of Australians who attend church has remained relatively stable, but the regularity of attendance has declined. The cultural and ethnic makeup of Australian society and Australian churches is changing rapidly.[55]

In response to such challenges churches in Australia have begun to change their forms, structures, and ministry patterns. No doubt the context

52. Newbigin, *Household of God*, 169.
53. Newbigin, *Household of God*, 169.
54. Raiser, *Church*, 39.
55. For an overview of some of these developments see McCrindle, *Faith and Belief*.

will continue to demand more imaginative and courageous changes. While much will and must change, churches must be defined by God's mission, not by the context. A church which knows that it exists in fellowship with God because of the work of Christ proclaimed by the gospel in the power of the Spirit will seek to express the biblical paradigm faithfully in a changing context. The paradigmatic elements are not complicated—meeting communities which continue to hear the gospel and in response witness, worship, and love, with servant leaders and a connection with God's wider church and his ongoing mission. As these elements are understood in light of the work of God, there is great flexibility in how they can be expressed. I consider that the theses set out above summarize what should be central and constitutional for the church; and provide a basis for ongoing missional experimentation. May the Lord be glorified in and by his churches in our nation, and around the world.

Bibliography

Allen, R. Michael. "The Church and the Churches: A Dogmatic Essay on Ecclesial Invisibility." *European Journal of Theology* 16, no. 2 (2007) 113–19.

Avis, Paul D. *The Church in the Theology of the Reformers*. Atlanta: John Knox, 1981.

Bannerman, James. *The Church of Christ*. Edinburgh: Banner of Truth, 1960.

Barth, Karl. *Church Dogmatics*. IV/2. Edited by Geoffrey W. Bromiley and Thomas. F. Torrance. Edinburgh: T. & T. Clark, 1958.

Bulley, Colin. *The Priesthood of Some Believers*. Milton Keynes: Paternoster, 2000.

Cameron, Andrew J. B., Michael P. Jensen, and Greg J. Clarke. "Towards a Christian Understanding of the Concept of Human 'Community' with Special Reference to the Praxis of a Non-Government Human Services Delivery Organisation." *Evangelical Review of Society and Politics* 3, no. 2 (2009) 22–40.

Cole, Graham. "The Doctrine of the Church: Towards Conceptual Clarification." In *Church, Worship and the Local Congregation*, edited by Barry G. Webb, 3–17. Explorations 2. Homebush, NSW: Lancer, 1987.

Faivre, Alexander. *The Emergence of the Laity in the Early Church*. Mahwah, NJ: Paulist, 1990.

Fung, Richard Y. K. "Ministry in the New Testament." In *The Church in the Bible and the World*, edited by Donald A. Carson, 154–212. Carlisle: Paternoster, 1987.

Giles, Kevin. *What on Earth is the Church?* London: SPCK, 1995.

———. "Where on Earth is the Church? A Critique of Sydney Congregationalism." *Church Scene* 678 (1992) 17–19.

Goheen, Michael W. "'As the Father Has Sent Me, I Am Sending You': Lesslie Newbigin's Missionary Ecclesiology." *International Review of Mission* 91, no. 362 (July 2002) 354–69.

Grenz, Stanley, J. *Reason for Hope: The Systematic Theology of Wolfhart Pannenberg*. 2nd ed. Grand Rapids: Eerdmans, 2005.

Gutenson, Charles E. *Reconsidering the Doctrine of God*. Edinburgh: T. & T. Clark, 2005.

Haight, Roger. *Christian Community in History*, vol. 2, *Comparative Ecclesiology*. New York: Continuum, 2005.

Healy, Nicholas M. *Church, World and the Christian Life: Practical-Prophetic Ecclesiology*. Cambridge: Cambridge University Press, 2000.

Hibbert, Richard Y. "The Place of Church Planting in Mission: Towards a Theological Framework." *Evangelical Review of Theology* 33, no. 4 (2009) 316–31.

Jamieson, Alan. "Churchless Faith: Trajectories of Faith Beyond the Church from Evangelical, Pentecostal and Charismatic Churches to Post-Church Groups." *International Review of Mission* 92, no. 365 (2003) 217–26.

Kenneson, Phillip. "Gathering: Worship, Imagination, and Formation." In *The Blackwell Companion to Christian Ethics*, edited by Stanley Hauerwas and Samuel Wells, 54–67. Blackwell Companions to Religion. Malden: Blackwell, 2004.

Köstenberger, Andreas J., and Peter T. O'Brien. *Salvation to the Ends of the Earth: A Biblical Theology of Mission*. New Studies in Biblical Theology 11. Leicester: Apollos, 2001.

Knox, David B. "The Church and the Denominations." *Reformed Theological Review* 23, no. 2 (1964) 44–53.

———. "The Church and the People of God in the Old Testament." *Reformed Theological Review* 10, no. 1 (1951) 12–20.

———. "The Church, the Churches and the Denominations." *Reformed Theological Review* 48, no. 1 (1989) 15–25.

———. "Demythologising the Church." *Reformed Theological Review* 32, no. 2 (1973) 48–55.

———. *Selected Works, vol. II, Church and Ministry*. Edited by K. Birkett. Kingsford, NSW: Matthias Media, 2003.

Mannion, Gerard. "Postmodern Ecclesiologies." In *The Routledge Companion to the Christian Church*, edited by Gerard Mannion and Lewis S. Mudge, 127–52. New York: Routledge, 2008.

Marshall, I. Howard. *A Fresh Look at the Acts of the Apostles*. Homebush, NSW: Lancer, 1992.

McCrindle, Mark. *Faith and Belief in Australia*. Baulkham Hills, NSW: McCrindle Research, 2017.

Merkle, Benjamin L. *The Elder and Overseer: One Office in the Early Church*. Studies in Biblical Literature 57. New York: Peter Lang, 2003.

Mostert, Christiaan. "The Kingdom Anticipated: The Church and Eschatology." *International Journal of Systematic Theology* 13, no. 1 (2011) 25–37.

Newbigin, Lesslie. "The Church—'A Bunch of Escaped Convicts.'" *Reform* (June 1990) 6.

———. *The Household of God: Lectures on the Nature of the Church*. New York: Friendship, 1954.

———. *A Word in Season: Perspectives on Christian World Missions*. Grand Rapids: Eerdmans, 1994.

Pannenberg, Wolfhart. *Systematic Theology*. Vol. 2. Translated by G. W. Bromiley. Grand Rapids: Eerdmans, 1994.

———. *Systematic Theology*. Vol. 3. Translated by G. W. Bromiley. Grand Rapids: Eerdmans, 1997.

Raiser, Konrad. *Ecumenism in Transition: A Paradigm Shift in the Ecumenical Movement*. Geneva: WCC Publications, 1991.

———. *To Be the Church: Challenges and Hopes for a New Millennium.* Geneva: WCC Publications, 1997.

Runia, Klaus. "The God-Given Ministry between Spirit and Situation." In *God Who is Rich in Mercy*, edited by Peter T. O'Brien and David G. Peterson. Homebush, NSW: Lancer, 1986.

Scobie, Charles H. H. *The Ways of Our God: An Approach to Biblical Theology.* Grand Rapids: Eerdmans, 2003.

Shenk, Wilbert R. "New Wineskins for New Wine: Toward a Post-Christendom Ecclesiology." *International Bulletin of Missionary Research* 29, no. 2 (2005) 73–76.

Smith, David L. *All God's People.* Wheaton: Victor, 1999.

Thompson, John. *Modern Trinitarian Perspectives.* New York: Oxford University Press, 1994.

Thompson, Mark A. "Does the Local Church Have a Mission?" In *Exploring the Missionary Church*, edited by Barry G. Webb, 1–25. Homebush, NSW: Lancer, 1993.

Towner, Philip H. *The Letters to Timothy and Titus.* Grand Rapids: Eerdmans, 2006.

Volf, Miroslav. *After Our Likeness: The Church as the Image of the Trinity.* Grand Rapids: Eerdmans, 1998.

———. "Worship as Adoration and Action: Reflections on a Christian Way of Being-in-the World." In *Worship: Adoration and Action*, edited by Donald A. Carson, 203–11. Grand Rapids: Baker/Paternoster, 1993.

Wagner, C. Peter. *Church Planting for a Greater Harvest: A Comprehensive Guide.* Ventura: Regal, 1990.

Watts, Rikk E. "The New Exodus/New Creational Restoration of the Image of God." In *What Does It Mean To Be Saved?*, edited by John G. Stackhouse, 15–41. Grand Rapids: Baker Books, 2002.

Webster, John. "On Evangelical Ecclesiology." *Ecclesiology* 1, no. 1 (2004) 9–35.

Woodhouse, John. "The Key to Church Music." In *Church Musicians' Handbook*, edited by Sally McCall and Rosalie Milne. Kingsford, NSW: Matthias Media, 1994.

9

Trinitarian Apologetics

Participating in Communities of Surprise, Embrace, and Witness

Brian Harris

Whatever theologians do or do not remember of Karl Rahner's theology, they usually recollect "Rahner's Rule," that the economic Trinity is the immanent Trinity and the immanent Trinity is the economic Trinity.[1] Put differently, God is not other than the God who has been revealed to us, or as the other great Karl of the twentieth century, Karl Barth puts it, "The reality of God which meets us in revelation is His reality in all the depths of eternity."[2] In short, the God revealed in three persons as Father, Son, and Spirit, is the God we can speak of with confidence without thinking that there is some profoundly different Other who has escaped our attention.

If the God whose image we are made in comes to us as Father, Son, and Spirit, what will it mean to be image bearers of such a God, and what should the faith communities we form look like, given that such communities would presumably be profoundly impacted by the nature and being of this God?

The thesis of this paper is simple. The best apologetic for the truth and reality of the gospel is when the church *is* the church, and we are most

---

1. Rahner, *Trinity*, 22.
2. Barth, *Church Dogmatics*, I/1, 548.

truly church when we discover what it is to participate in the rich Trinitarian life of God. *We need an adequate image of God to guide and direct our ecclesiological quest*, and this quest will only have an appropriate apologetic outcome if it is rooted in what has been revealed of the triune life of God. The one God has acted in the world as Father, Son, and Spirit. As we reflect on some key characteristics of the three who are one, and explore what they reveal about God's own self, we are in a position to shape our ecclesiology accordingly. This paper suggests that such modelling would lead to the formation of communities of surprise, embrace, and witness, communities of gentle persuasion, communities that are inviting and winsome, indeed communities that quickly break down the wall between church and world, for the revealed God is assuredly not trapped within the four walls of any particular version of the church, past, present, or future.

A quick example will serve to highlight what I am talking about, and thereafter I will develop the implications for the church of serving a God of surprise, embrace, and witness.

The revealed God is triune. The mathematical complexity of demonstrating that "one plus one plus one equals one" has proved a theological red herring. The only God we can know is the God who is revealed, and traditionally described in terms of one essence in three persons. The revealed God is never an isolated, lonely God, but comes to us in the rich relational life of Father, Son, and Spirit. To image such a God would therefore presumably require a comparably rich communal life in the church. At its very least, the triune God would be a rebuke to any excessive stress on individuality that comes at the expense of the life of the community. Such a stress might be understandable in a world impacted by Adam's fall, but is incomprehensible if parroted in the theology and lifestyle of the church. The strong stress on the individual—often at the expense of the communal—in many of our churches, should be of concern to those who identify as evangelical.[3] This stress starts with an emphasis on individual salvation which is pivotal to the evangelical movement.[4] It continues in the music of the movement:

---

3. See, for example, Robert Bellah's *Habits of the Heart*. One of the issues highlighted in this book is the link between religion and individualism. The privatization of faith, be it the plea from evangelicals to come into a personal (individual) relationship with God, or the more liberal invitation to worship God in whatever shape or form the individual chooses to conceive the divine, tends to see the emphasis fall back to individual response rather than to community mediation. While individualism might lead to ownership of decisions taken, it can also lead to a sense of isolation and alienation. See Bellah, *Habits of the Heart*.

4. Conversionism is one of the four distinctives cited by Bebbington as forming a quadrilateral of priorities for evangelicalism. The others are activism, biblicism, and crucicentrism. See Bebbington, *Evangelicalism*, 2–3.

"My Jesus, I love you, I know Thou art mine" is not really in accord with the prayer Jesus taught his followers, which begins not with "my" but with "our"—"Our Father in heaven" (Matt 6:9). Now a warm intimate relationship with our Father is entirely appropriate, but when it is emphasized at the expense of our communal life, something is amiss.

In Ephesians 3 Paul reminds us of two conditions that help the church partially to comprehend the width, length, height, and depth of Christ's love for us. The first is that "Christ may dwell in your hearts through faith" so that we would be "rooted and established in love" which naturally leads to the second, which is of us being "together with all the saints" in the communal quest to discover the love that "surpasses knowledge" (Eph 3:17–19). All this is a world away from the drift towards what Alan Jamieson calls "churchless faith."[5] The problem with churchless faith is that "together with all the saints" simply disappears. The lonely self, embarked on the "me, myself and I" quest to discover God, is pulled up quickly when the realization that this God is triune, dawns. The self cannot enter into a one-on-one relationship with God, for the One it attempts to relate to, is three persons. The self is thrust immediately into community.

This is not to suggest that the self disappears in community. Again, the triune nature of God helps us avoid this potential trap. The Father is not the Son, the Son is not the Spirit, and the Spirit is not the Father. Colin Gunton titled his 1992 Bampton Lectures "The One, the Three and the Many" which is richly suggestive of the paradox into which we enter.[6] Rather than the disappearance of the self, the self is most truly a self-in-relationship, a self, in community. Outside of community, the self cannot image the God whose likeness it is invited to reflect.

Let us explore some key ways in which the revelation of God should shape our expectation of the life of the church. I suggest that our communal experience of each of the three persons of the triune God should lead us to expect a church of surprise, embrace, and witness. I will work through each in turn.

A Community of Surprise

The church of the living God will always be a community that surprises. The God who is Father and Creator is never dull.

Our very existence starts with surprise. At its most basic level it is the surprise that we are here, that we live, and that we are in a world of

---

5. See Jamieson, *Churchless Faith*.
6. See Gunton, *One, the Three*.

substance rather than nothingness. We intuitively reason that nothingness would be more logical. It would make sense if an implied, but nonexistent creed proclaimed to the nothingness, "In the beginning was nothing, its absence unknown and unlamented, a nothingness with neither form nor force to shape it, world without beginning, and therefore without end." Instead we are born into a clearly existent order filled with others with whom we are invited to interact and participate in the mystery of existence that we can only ascribe to the surprise of a God who is there. Our amazement that we exist is logically linked to an awareness of the wonder of a God who simply must be.[7]

By contrast, picture your average church service. Your thoughts probably go straight to Sunday. There are the rows of people. Depending on the church community you imagine, there may be many significant gaps in each line, or perhaps not many present at all. The heads are probably all oriented in the same direction. The short-range view is of the rear hairstyles of those immediately ahead. The long-range view can be of anything from a pipe organ to a drum kit and keyboard. For a while the people stand and sit at the behest of a group of musicians who may, or may not, be especially talented. These musicians may, or may not, persuade the people in the straight lines to join them in their singing. At some point someone will inform the people in the rows what the church will be doing in the coming weeks and will then take up an offering to support its work. Some will give generously, others will pop in a fiver, yet others will ignore the quest for funds. Soon after, a talking-head will pontificate on some aspect of Christian faith, reflecting views which might be considered orthodox, or not. Depending on the skill of the speaker, after what seems like a brief or interminably long period, the community will sing again and then be dismissed. Some may remain behind for a coffee. Better communities of faith will serve a quality brew, but that assuredly cannot be taken for granted.

The obvious question to ask is what this portrait of church has to do with the portrait of the God of surprises who has been revealed to us. It is all so tamely predictable. The Ian Anderson lyrics of *My God*, made famous by Jethro Tull's rendition of them, laments the church's lameness with the biting words, "And the bloody Church of England, in chains of history, requests your earthly presence at the vicarage for tea." The song begins, "People—what have you done—locked Him in His golden cage. Made Him bend to your religion—Him resurrected from the grave."[8] More than a generation

---

7. Aquinas's first mover argument is well known. For a contemporary elaboration of the argument by a currently popular apologist, see the various works of John Lennox.

8. Song lyrics by Ian Anderson, copyright Chrysalis Music Group Inc.

has passed since those lines were first sung, but little has changed. The talking head of the preacher at the front may assure us that the God of the Bible is, like Lewis's Aslan, not a tame lion, but the version we actually experience seems pretty domesticated. Undoubtedly the church has made many errors in its two-thousand-year existence, but its attempt to trivialize God has been one of the more outrageous.

By contrast, the revealed God is unpredictable and exciting. Adrio König rightly points out that the self-revealed name of God, *I am who I am*, is in essence a promise that God will continue to be who God has always been.[9] The promise "to be" should not be understood in terms of some immovable inner essence, or in terms of ontological being, but rather as faithful continuity to the revealed mission of God. God will continue to *do* what God has always *done*. Rather than a *Deus Absconditus* we are to expect a perpetually involved God, a God whose activity in our midst ensures that we never doubt the divine existence.

This is the God of 1 Samuel 5. The local wisdom was that when nations went into battle, those fighting were simply vehicles in the hands of their gods, and that victory came not to the people who were stronger but to the god or gods who were stronger. This was the Philistines' day, with Yahweh supposedly defeated by Dagon. The ark of the covenant is captured by the Philistines and placed in submission to their god Dagon in his temple in Ashdod. Dagon is left to gloat over this presumably lesser and clearly defeated deity. Instead Dagon falls off his stand, desperately scampering for the exit to the temple, losing his head and hands in the process. Clearly Dagon is under no illusion as to who the more powerful deity is. Shortly after, tumors break out amongst the people of Ashdod, and in the end, they beg to have the ark of the covenant returned. The surprising discovery is that even when God's people seem to be defeated, Yahweh still reigns. Victory comes with or without the aid of the people of God. This God is no tame lion. This God surprises. The question is, what is the relationship of this God to the God experienced in churches Sunday by Sunday?

There have been many times in the history of the church when the God of surprises has empowered the church to be a community of surprise. The early church was often, though not always, such a community. Luke's summary of their early life together found in Acts 2:44–47 and 4:32–37 gives a feel for the new way of life adopted by this fledgling community. Those who observed it found it compelling. There were many converts.

The God who is not a tame lion can clearly not be forced to dance to any tune that the church cares to announce. The church cannot set the

---

9. König, *Here I Am!*, 78–79.

agenda for God. But the church can pray. Indeed, we can pray the opening petition of the Lord's Prayer a little more urgently. "Our Father, who art in heaven, hallowed be Thy name." That little request, "may your name be considered holy," or "may your name be held high," or "may your name be venerated" should be prayed with passion and urgency. It should also be prayed with expectancy. The revealed God is more than capable of ensuring the hallowing of the divine name. While willing to participate in bringing this petition to fruition, the church's primary responsibility is to observe the signs of its fulfillment. As we spot the *missio Dei* within and beyond the four walls of the church we should find a new sprightliness within our step, and the courage to embrace the surprising, delightful, new works of God.

A Community of Embrace

In Jesus, God comes to us as Emmanuel, the God who is with us, the God of embrace. Indeed, if the actions of the Father surprise, the embrace of the Son is just as remarkable. In selecting Bethlehem rather than Rome as birthplace, in appearing to be more at ease with tax collectors, prostitutes, and sinners than with religious leaders, and in choosing not to throw the first stone at the unaccompanied, adulterous woman, the God who comes to us as the Son indicates an embrace that has a particular empathy and focus, and it is not a focus that sits easily with the average religious institution. Indeed, on the basis of his track record, one could easily conclude that Jesus is an unlikely patron for the organization founded to further his mission. But we would make that mistake because, to use Stanley Hauerwas's memorable insight, we forget that we should not be looking "only for the church that does exist but for the church that should exist."[10]

Often our communal life falls short of what it should be. Some years ago Michael Griffiths wrote a book about the church which he called *Cinderella with Amnesia*.[11] When we forget who we are, we are often content to settle to become far less than we are meant to be, and might need to repent of too small a vision for the church.

There are times when the church is a pale version of a community of surprise and embrace. It often bears many similarities to the water polo club my family were part of when we lived in Auckland, a respectable little group committed to ensuring our children had a great experience with water polo. At times we could be quite generous. We were welcoming to new families, especially those whose children showed some natural aptitude for

---

10. Hauerwas, *Community*, 6.
11. See Griffiths, *Cinderella*.

the game. If they were willing to provide transport to away games, umpire, or better still, help to raise funds, they were doubly welcome. We would chat pleasantly about the game as we sat in the stands together, and try to remember to make favorable comments about the performance of the child of the parents we were talking to. When that was impossible, we would retreat to a diplomatic silence. Other than that, the conversation reverted to water polo more frequently than in other contexts, the chit chat we engaged in was much the same as in the school parking lot, the workplace, and the local church. Nothing wrong with that, but it left me wondering in what way the local church was really any different. While we never had any major crisis during those years, I do not doubt that if we had, someone from the club would have phoned to find out how we were and to offer their assistance. Certainly, when we were stuck for transport, others quickly came to our aid, as we did to theirs in comparable situations. So, in what ways is the church different to the water polo club we were part of? True, we did not sing at the water polo club (mercifully we had no karaoke evenings!), and it was a lot less expensive, but in so many ways there was not much difference.

Surely one of the great differences between the water polo club and the church should be the latter's willingness to reach out unconditionally, to welcome and embrace, and to affirm that others belong, *before* they have met a multitude of preconditions.[12] To get into the water polo club there were a fair number of water-polo-related hurdles that one had to cross. While not insurmountable, this was not a club that anyone could get into. Not so the church. Christ's incarnation was not delayed until such time as the planet engaged in impeccable behavior. Both Bethlehem's cradle and Calvary's cross speak of the divine "yes" to humanity in spite of its indifference, cruelty, and fallenness. Tax collector Zacchaeus, the five-time-married and now cohabiting woman at the well, and the Christ-denying Peter, have life narratives where the journey of faith is characterized by welcome rather than a promising behavioral record. This openness to the other is part of what it means to participate in Christ's movement into the world.

Our practice should be shaped by our theology. At times there is a significant gap. Our theological vision is often more compelling, it being a lot easier to talk about loving and accepting people than it actually is to do so in practice. But our only credible apologetic defense can be our practice, the matching of theological convictions with what we actually do. Facing up to any deficit is a helpful place to begin.

While in the past atheists were usually content to justify their lack of belief in God's existence on the basis of *intellectual* objections, it is now

---

12. See Harris, "Behave, Believe, Belong."

increasingly common for that justification to be based on *moral* objections.[13] To quote from the title of Christopher Hitchen's bestselling book, it is alleged that *God is not great* and that *religion poisons everything*.[14] Some would have us believe that religious faith is an evil akin to greed, poverty, and disease, and that it is a significant social problem to be obliterated if we are to attain a better existence. While the famous G. K. Chesterton paradox claims "The Christian ideal has not been tried and found wanting. It has been found difficult; and left untried," a growing tide impatiently dismisses the sentiment as escapist and is unwilling to endure what they claim is the poisonous harvest of religious faith.[15]

That harvest is described in different ways, but ten common components include (in no particular order):

1. Religious warfare
2. Colonial exploitation
3. Racial bigotry
4. The oppression of women
5. Homophobia
6. The exploitation of the environment
7. Retarding the progress of science, especially medical science
8. Academic censorship with a resultant intellectual dishonesty
9. Intolerance of anything new
10. Hypocrisy

Clearly there is nothing attractive about this list, and if it is seen to be the normative result of religious faith, evangelists should expect audiences who are increasingly hostile to their message—presupposing they can find any audience at all. David Kinnaman's study of the attitude of sixteen-to-twenty-nine-year-old Americans towards Christians saw six recurring images.[16] They considered Christians to be:

1. Hypocritical
2. Interested in "saving" people rather than in relating to them

---

13. The remainder of this section is a modified form of part of a paper I presented at the Baptist World Alliance Gathering. Harris, "Faithful Thinking."
14. Hitchens, *God Is Not Great*.
15. Chesterton, *What's Wrong*; see, especially, chapter 5.
16. See Kinnaman and Lyons, *Unchristian*.

3. Anti-homosexual
4. Sheltered
5. Too political
6. Judgmental

Again, the list is far from winsome, and represents a significant barrier to the reception of messages about the love and mercy of God. It is also far removed from the way in which Jesus's ministry was experienced by his peers.

We could argue that these negative images are the fruit of the Christendom era, when membership of the Christian faith was assumed for almost all who lived in the Western world. Christendom was often more about sanctioning the status quo than following Jesus, and we could be hopeful that its demise might free the church to find more authentic expressions of faith in this "after Christendom" era.[17] If the harvest of Christendom was our poisonous list of ten (and I acknowledge that it is excessively one-sided to suggest that the list is fair),[18] is it possible that in the post-Christian era a Christianity that more closely represents and reflects the life of Jesus might emerge?

For this to occur, it is important that we recognize and renounce those elements of religious belief that leave us vulnerable to developing a toxic faith.

To be fair, not all the fruit of Christendom was negative. Christians can claim credit for many of the positive social advances made in the last two thousand years. While multiple social factors are invariably at work in societal evolution, it is not fair to explore the abolition of slavery, the protection of the rights of women and children, the development of the welfare state, or the shift in focus from retributive to restorative justice, without repeatedly referring to the Christian faith that motivated and inspired most of those who championed these causes. And these represent just a small selection of an impressive array of humanitarian achievements.[19]

Sadly, there is also a shadow side. There have been many times in the history of the church when it has been supportive of an oppressive agenda, which on occasion has revealed itself in racism, sexism, homophobia,

---

17. For a discussion of and rationale for the conclusion that we live in a "post-Christendom" era, see Murray, *Post-Christendom* and Murray, *Church after Christendom*.

18. For a very different (and far more positive) interpretation of the church's contribution to society, see Schmidt, *Under the Influence*.

19. A simple but thought-provoking introduction to the topic is found in Andrews, *People of Compassion*.

militarism, ecological and economic exploitation, cultural insensitivity, and more beside.[20] Even if not actively supporting exploitation, faith can easily wear unattractive masks.[21] Let us explore three masks that disappear when the revelation of the incarnated Jesus serves as our ecclesiological model.

First to go is faith as escapism. While it is perhaps understandable that African-American slaves longed for the day when the sweet chariot would swing low to carry them home, it is more difficult to understand why those whose lives are saturated with material abundance are sometimes so heavenly-minded that they are of little use to those on the fringes of life, indeed those who are specially dear to the heart of God. An incarnated Christian faith will ensure that eschatology is used not as a crutch justifying escapism, but as a motivator of daring obedience. As people who have been privileged to see the end of the story, we know that ultimate victory belongs to the people of God. This should give us the courage to live in the light of God's coming kingdom in the present. Baptist theologian Stanley Grenz suggests, importantly, that all theological construction should be eschatologically oriented.[22] Allowing the future to guide the present will see a radically new form of Christianity birthed. Imagine, for example, if we truly lived backwards from the Pauline insight that the ultimate reality is that in Christ "there is neither Jew nor Greek, slave nor free, male nor female, for you are all one in Christ Jesus" (Gal 3:28). This would indeed birth an infectiously different Christianity, one worth following, one with a significant apologetic impact. That this vision flows from good theology must not be overlooked. While many in the pews may be enthralled by the *Left Behind* series, it is possible to extend their eschatological horizon, for in the end, error is best combated with truth.[23] We need to paint a compelling portrait of a thoroughly engaged and incarnated Christian faith, one able to strive in the present because it has had a glimpse of the future.

A second caricature left over from the Christendom era is that faith is often confused with the status quo. This mask bears no resemblance to what is required to be an authentic Christ-follower, but nonetheless for many

---

20. So, for example, Jim Wallis, speaking of the mixed legacy of Evangelicalism, laments, "Evangelicals in this century have a history of going along with the culture on the big issues and taking their stand on the smaller issues. That has been one of the serious problems of evangelical religion. Today, many evangelicals no longer just acquiesce to the culture on the larger economic and political issues, but actively promote the culture's worst values on these matters." Wallis, *Call to Conversion*, 25.

21. The following three paragraphs are a slightly modified form of part of a brief newspaper article I wrote in 2007. See Harris, "When Faith."

22. See, for example, Grenz, *Revisioning*, and Grenz and Franke, *Beyond Foundationalism*.

23. See LaHaye and Jenkins, *Left Behind*.

people things are good provided that they have been around for more than twenty years. Nostalgia, rather than a commitment to a daring faith agenda, is the driver. Onlookers fail to find it inspiring. Perhaps we should stop thinking of ourselves as Christians, but as Christ-followers. This is not a pedantic quibble. To stop viewing ourselves as static nouns and to introduce images of action might help to remind us that the Christian vision is of a daring journey of discipleship. It is a journey that does not bypass the cross and it is one that would never be undertaken without the assurance that resurrection follows crucifixion. If any of this sounds like the status quo, then the status quo is not what it used to be!

A third mask to denounce is faith as smugness and self-righteousness. While most have renounced the wagging finger, the image of Christians as people who see themselves as morally superior to lesser mortals persists. That is not to suggest that we are people without a moral vision. However, a thoughtful Christianity is not proclaimed in "Thou Shalt" terms but is portrayed invitationally. It recognizes that it is one vision amongst other competing visions and that it needs to woo others by the winsomeness of those who have been captured by its contours.

We need to be alert to the potentially abusive nature of faith. While an exhaustive list is beyond the scope of this paper, danger signals that point to toxic faith include an insistence on unquestioning faith, faith as compulsion instead of faith as invitation, the presence of a loveless legalism, or any form of faith that aims for power and control, and attempts to justify the unjustifiable in the name of God. Simply alerting Christ-followers to the possibility of toxic faith makes an important contribution to its destruction.

But this is to focus on the negatives and the risks. In popular expressions of Christian faith it has become common to ask the WWJD question: what would Jesus do? Perhaps in becoming a community of embrace we would supplement this with two additional questions: "what would Jesus think?" and "what would Jesus feel?" Put differently, we need to focus on the trio of orthodoxy, orthopraxy, and orthopathy.

There is another reason to develop a holistic understanding of Jesus and his mission. Theologians routinely note that humans are made in the image of God. It is less common for them to explore the implications of Jesus as the *imago Dei*.[24] We cannot discover what it means to be human unless our quest is rooted in an understanding of the humanity of Jesus. In pondering his humanity, we discover our own.

To be sure, our thinking is likely to be filtered through our preconceived portraits of Jesus, and inevitably these will reflect more than a touch

---

24. See Grenz's discussion of this in Grenz, "*Imago Dei.*"

of contemporary culture. Those who doubt this should study the portrayals of Jesus in art over the last two millennia. We find everything from the all-conquering Christ militant ("Stand up, stand up for Jesus, you soldiers of the Cross") to gentle Jesus meek and mild. Up to a point, we should simply shrug our shoulders and say, "So be it; we can only live in the world in which we find ourselves." But this is a little too defeatist. We can immerse ourselves in the biblical narratives. We can also trust that the Spirit-inspired Scriptures are also the Spirit-illuminated Scriptures. And we can guard against excessively individualistic interpretations of the text by studying it together in community, confident, as I have written elsewhere, "that the Spirit guides the church, and that the community of faith will therefore be pneumatologically guided as it communally attempts to discern truth in a changed context."[25] This brings us to the third person of the Trinity, the Spirit.

A Community of Witness

If God the Father ensures a community of surprise, and God the Son a community of embrace, God the Spirit ensures a community of witness, presence, and power. The apologetic impact of this trio is likely to be profound.

Is aspiring to be a community of witness, presence, and power a hankering back to Christendom? Indeed, is the title of this volume, "Beyond Four Walls," a quest to reclaim the influence and importance the church had in the Christendom era? It depends on how we say it. If the tone is strident and rousing—"Beyond Four Walls, more land to conquer"—then our past has taught us little. If it is a quietly confident, "God's love for the world will always keep flowing outwards, therefore the church will be called always to move Beyond Four Walls," we are on more solid ground.

The revealed God constantly moves out to the world through the Spirit. Rather than creating arrogant, self-sufficient church communities, the Spirit calls us to be communities that readily chant Zechariah 4:6: "Not by strength, nor by might, but by my Spirit, says the Lord." In *A Passage to India* E. M. Forster has his character Mrs. Moore reject "poor little talkative Christianity."[26] Unless the Spirit equips us, "poor little talkative Christianity" is all we are left with.

While the early church paid much attention to the work of the Spirit, in the centuries that followed, pneumatology acted as little more than an afterthought until the second half of the twentieth century. Perhaps in Christendom the church thought the work of the Spirit was superfluous. That risk

---

25. Harris, *Theological Method*, iii.
26. Forster, *Passage to India*, 166.

is long past. In the West the societal move from a soft to a hard secularism is becoming increasingly obvious. "Not by strength, nor by might, but by my Spirit" is our only hope.

What does this mean in practice? It means taking our Zechariah 4:6 chant seriously. We do not have the strength to be the community God has called us to be. It is not that we lack the financial resources; realistically, the church is a wealthy institution. But we lack the moral strength required, we lack the compassion needed, and we lack the wisdom demanded. We cannot rectify these deficits unaided.

We also find ourselves in a deeply compromised position. The church has made so many mistakes. A watching world remembers, and is at best disappointed, sometimes disillusioned, and often angry, and justifiably so. If the Spirit convicts of sin, one of the first places where that conviction must take root is in the church itself. Our abuse of power and privilege, our failure to protect many children entrusted to our care, and our lack of deep compassion, should break our hearts. Repentance begins with the people of God. Only the Spirit can bring this about.

Strangely, it could be from this position of brokenness—knowing our weaknesses, failings, and vulnerability—that the church might again arise. For God often uses broken things. Paul notes in 1 Corinthians 1:27 that God chose the foolish things in the world to shame the wise, and the weak things in the world to shame the strong. Our great need provides an opportunity for the Spirit to move and equip. For indeed, "Not by strength, not by might, but by my Spirit" is our only hope. Perhaps the transformation of the church into a community of genuine compassion and care will be the most significant witness to our age.

Conclusion

For a brief moment forget every image that promptly springs into mind when you hear the word church. Imagine instead the rich Trinitarian life of the God revealed as Father, Son, and Spirit. Ponder the way the Father is revealed though the pages of Scripture. Remember the embrace of the Son to a multitude of unlikely candidates. Recall the transformation of the disciples at Pentecost. If God will be who God has been, and if God will do what God has done, could it be that we can expect new versions of church to spring into being? Perhaps in the future we will participate in communities of surprise, embrace, and witness. The nature of our triune God leads us to expect nothing less.

Bibliography

Andrews, Dave. *People of Compassion*. Blackburn, Victoria: TEAR Australia, 2008.

Barth, Karl. *Church Dogmatics*. 1/1. Translated by G. W. Bromiley. 2nd ed. Edinburgh: T. & T. Clark, 1975.

Bebbington, David. *Evangelicalism in Modern Britain: A History from the 1730s to the 1980s*. Grand Rapids: Baker, 1989.

Bellah, Robert N., et al. *Habits of the Heart: Individualism and Commitment in American Life*. Berkeley: University of California Press, 1985.

Chesterton, G. K. *What's Wrong with the World*. London: Cassell, 1910.

Forster, E. M. *A Passage to India*. New York: Harcourt, Brace and Company, 1924.

Grenz, Stanley J. "Jesus as the *Imago Dei*: Image-of-God Christology and the Non-Linear Linearity of Theology." *Journal of the Evangelical Theological Society* 47, no. 4 (2004) 617–28.

———. *Revisioning Evangelical Theology: A Fresh Agenda for the Twenty-First Century*. Downers Grove: Inter Varsity, 1993.

Grenz, Stanley J., and John R. Franke. *Beyond Foundationalism: Shaping Theology in a Postmodern Context*. Louisville: Westminster John Knox, 2001.

Griffiths, Michael. *Cinderella with Amnesia: A Restatement in Contemporary Terms of the Biblical Doctrine of the Church*. Downers Grove: InterVarsity, 1975.

Gunton, Colin E. *The One, the Three and the Many: God, Creation and the Culture of Modernity*. The Bampton Lectures 1992. Cambridge: Cambridge University Press, 1993.

Harris, Brian. "Faithful Thinking: The Role of the Seminary in Promoting a Thoughtful Christianity." Baptist World Alliance Annual Gathering, Kuala Lumpur, 2011.

———. "From 'Behave, Believe, Belong' to 'Belong, Believe, Behave': A Missional Journey for the 21st Century." In *Text and Task: Scripture and Mission*, edited by Michael Parsons, 204–17. Carlisle: Paternoster, 2005.

———. *The Theological Method of Stanley J. Grenz: Constructing Evangelical Theology from Scripture, Tradition, and Culture*. Lewiston: Edwin Mellen, 2011.

———. "When Faith Is the Problem." *The Advocate*, April 2007.

Hauerwas, Stanley. *A Community of Character: Toward a Constructive Christian Social Ethic*. Notre Dame, IN: University of Notre Dame Press, 1981.

Hitchens, Christopher. *God Is Not Great: How Religion Poisons Everything*. New York: Twelve, 2007.

Jamieson, Alan. *A Churchless Faith: Faith Journeys beyond Evangelical, Pentecostal and Charismatic Churches*. Wellington: Philip Garside, 2000.

Kinnaman, David, and Gabe Lyons. *Unchristian: What a New Generation Really Thinks About Christianity, and Why It Matters*. Grand Rapids: Baker, 2007.

König, Adrio. *Here I Am! A Believer's Reflection on God*. Pretoria: University of South Africa, 1978.

LaHaye, Tim, and Jerry B. Jenkins. *Left Behind Complete Set, Series 1–12*. Carol Stream: Tyndale, 1990.

Murray, Stuart. *Church after Christendom*. Carlisle: Paternoster, 2004.

———. *Post-Christendom*. Carlisle: Paternoster, 2004.

Rahner, Karl. *The Trinity*. Translated by Joseph Donceel. New York: Crossroad, 1997.

Schmidt, Alvin J. *Under the Influence: How Christianity Transformed Culture*. Grand Rapids: Zondervan, 2001.

Wallis, Jim. *The Call to Conversion*. Herts: Lion, 1981.

10

Romancing the Church

Nineteenth-Century Romanticism in the Twenty-First Century Church

PETER ELLIOTT

ANY FOCUS ON *BEING* the church must surely be interested in the forces that have shaped the church as it is in the early twenty-first century. My intention in this paper is to draw attention to the lasting influence of the Romantic movement on the church, and I will argue that this influence is both profound and, I believe, largely overlooked. We will begin by briefly outlining some key characteristics of Romanticism before considering the ministry of Edward Irving as a case study, and then demonstrating why an understanding of Romanticism is important for those working within today's church.

Isaiah Berlin made a strong statement about the lasting impact of Romanticism:

> The importance of romanticism is that it is the largest recent movement to transform the lives and the thought of the Western world. It seems to me to be the greatest single shift in the consciousness of the West that has occurred, and all the other shifts which have occurred in the course of the nineteenth and

twentieth centuries appear to me in comparison less important, and at any rate deeply influenced by it.[1]

A few pages earlier, Berlin commented that he thought of Romanticism as a revolution that was more profound than the Industrial Revolution in England, the French Revolution, and the Soviet Revolution.[2] These claims are astonishing, and even if they prove exaggerated, indicate that we should reconsider the impact of Romanticism on modern society and thought. However, although Berlin was a profound commentator on Romantic thought, he did not focus on its religious aspects.

Romanticism was a cultural movement that flourished between 1785 and 1825. It was associated with new developments in poetry, politics, music, and more. Beyond that lies a great deal of argument because Romanticism is a diverse and slippery beast, which I have examined in detail elsewhere.[3] Let me summarize: Romanticism followed the rationalism of the Enlightenment era and was largely a response to it. Romanticism was convinced that rationalism had produced a society that was reductionistic, mechanistic, and utilitarian.[4] For many in that era, rationalism reached its zenith with the French Revolution and its excesses and was tarnished as a result.[5] By contrast, Romanticism was not obsessed with finding neat answers to everything, rejected the precision of classicism in the arts, and embraced mystery, the unknown, and the numinous.[6] Valuing emotion as well as intellect, Romantics found a place for the subjective in the search for valid perception and truth; it was therefore a significant development in epistemology and a challenge to the Enlightenment myth of the objective observer. Essentially, this led Romantics to a place where diversity was seen not as a problem to be avoided but as the natural human context.[7] Unanimity became far less important than personal integrity; the struggle to discover meaning was seen as noble in itself.

In this brief list of Romantic characteristics it is easy to recognize the foundations of both existentialism and postmodernism, as scholars have

---

1. Berlin, *Roots of Romanticism*, 1–2. This book is a transcript of lectures originally delivered in the 1960s.

2. Berlin, *Roots of Romanticism*, xiii.

3. For a more detailed examination see my discussion in Elliott, *Edward Irving*, 1–16.

4. Abrams, *Natural Supernaturalism*, 170–71.

5. Reardon, *Religious Thought*, 92.

6. Brown, "Romanticism and Enlightenment," 38.

7. Berlin, *Roots of Romanticism*, 138.

frequently pointed out.[8] This indicates something of the substance beneath Berlin's assertion of the importance and ongoing influence of Romanticism. It is natural therefore, to expect Romanticism to have had an impact on the church. We will now explore this impact by examining the ministry of Edward Irving as a case study.

The London-based ministry of Edward Irving was short, stellar, and controversial. Born in South West Scotland in 1792 and educated at Edinburgh University, Irving served as parish assistant to Church of Scotland minister Thomas Chalmers in Glasgow for three years from 1819 to 1822. In 1821, he received an unexpected call from the Caledonian Chapel in London for him to preach for them with a view to becoming their next minister, an invitation that was probably less of a compliment to Irving than a reflection of the dwindling fortunes of the congregation.[9] Irving preached for them during December 1821 and took up the position as their minister in July 1822.[10] Twelve years later, in December 1834, Irving was dead at the age of forty-two. These twelve years from 1822 to 1834 saw a rapid rise and gradual decline in Irving's ministerial career, if not his hopes, as during this time he became London's most popular preacher, a published author, and a theological innovator. He embraced a heterodox (heretical in the eyes of many) Christology, a premillennial eschatology, and the charismatic gifts.[11]

The reason for focusing on Irving is that he was at the forefront of integrating Romanticism and Christianity in the 1820s and 1830s. This integration is particularly fascinating in the area of Irving's ecclesiology, to which we will now turn.

Irving's Church of Scotland background had immersed him in Presbyterian polity, so he was on the one hand very respectful of church tradition (which leads some to conclude he was basically conservative), yet he was simultaneously frustrated with the progress of the church in general and he spoke and acted out of this frustration (which leads some to conclude he was radical). An early indication of the trajectory of Irving's thought occurred in his 1822 farewell address to St John's Glasgow where he had served under Chalmers. Just before taking up his London pastorate, Irving made clear the type of minister he admired and aspired to be. The ideal preachers were "adventurers, with the Bible as their chart, and the necessities of their age

---

8. For example, Prickett, *Romanticism and Religion*, 134.

9. The congregation had dwindled to about fifty at this time and was barely able to pay a minister's salary. Dallimore, *Edward Irving*, 31.

10. Oliphant, *Edward Irving*, 68, 76.

11. This paragraph summarizing Irving's ministry is drawn from my chapter "Irving's Hybrid," 139.

as the ocean to be explored, and brought under authority of Christ."[12] They would suffer opposition from those who preferred the ways of conformity, but it was precisely ministers like this that society needed: "Such adventurers, under God, this age of the world seems to us especially to want. There are ministers enow [enough] to hold the flock in pasture and in safety."[13]

Irving was setting his own course of nonconformity because the past may have provided safe pastures, but it had not yielded the desired results. It was the declaration of a Romantic quest, one which he already knew would be criticized by the majority, but it was chosen because he saw no alternative: the glory of God must lie elsewhere, down little travelled and more adventurous paths. Yet this was still expressed in quite general terms. Further elaboration came in an address that he gave to the London Missionary Society in 1824. By this stage, Irving was London's most popular preacher, and the Society no doubt thought that by inviting him, they would gain increased financial support. They were sorely mistaken. Irving's three-and-a-half-hour address took aim at several targets, including the institution of missionary societies!

> What are missionaries but the prophets' order enlarged from the confines of the land of Israel, to roam at large over the world? God's messengers to the nations, telling them their several burdens if they repent not, and shewing them salvation if they repent. Each a Jonah to the several quarters of the heathen world: not servants of this or that association of men, but heralds of Heaven, who dare not be under other orders than the orders of Christ. It is a presumption hardly short of Papal, to command them. They are not missionaries when they are commanded. They are creatures of the power that commandeth them.[14]

Although on this occasion the subject was missionary activity, several themes from the St John's address reemerged: adventure, willing embrace of danger, independence, and the availability of direct (and presumably clear) divine instruction. The message was plain: missionaries should not follow the directions of organizations but hear directly from heaven themselves; to do otherwise was to invalidate their calling. Elsewhere in this address, Irving made clear that this also applied to finances: missionaries needed to depend fully on God for all their needs. To Irving, the watchword of "prudence" was a virtual blasphemy, a synonym for lack of faith in God.[15]

12. Irving, "Farewell Address," 350.
13. Irving, "Farewell Address," 351.
14. Irving, "Missionaries," 504.
15. Irving, "Missionaries," 488.

The anti-institutional element is prominent and when the two addresses are placed side-by-side, it highlights the tension between independence and institution: Irving's ideal pastor/missionary/Romantic hero was essentially "single-handed and solitary" in his trailblazing.[16]

This tension played out dramatically in Irving's career, as he wrestled with conflicting images of himself as loyal Presbyterian churchman and risk-taking ecclesiastical explorer. Irving's theological distinctives fed directly into this drama, and elsewhere I have argued at length that his theology was comprehensively Romantic.[17] A premillennialist in a postmillennial age, Irving was convinced that Christ would return soon, a belief that facilitated his eventual acceptance of contemporary expressions of the charismatic gifts.[18] Irving was also convinced that Christ assumed fallen human nature, but remained sinless by the power of the Holy Spirit. Arguing from the Cappadocian axiom that what has not been assumed cannot be redeemed, he asserted that anything other than Christ's full identity with humanity *as we experience it* offers nothing but a *faux* salvation.[19] The effect of this was to make Christ's humiliation more profound and simultaneously to optimize human potential through the Holy Spirit. Irving was eventually found heretical for his views, but remained convinced that this label was more appropriate for his critics.[20] Individually, Irving's theological distinctives were not unique; what was unique was his combination of them, the systematic way he defended them, and the Romantic motivation that both permeated them and communicated them so effectively to his contemporaries.

Irving's conviction that Christ's return was imminent was combined with his lofty pneumatology and his desire to lead his people into an adventure for God's glory: his vision was a church revitalized by God's power that would shed the skin of scholastic Protestantism and timid evangelicalism to embrace fully the supernatural wonders that were the church's inheritance. Irving's beliefs were threatening to the church of his day, but also anticipated many of the characteristics and tensions of the church of

---

16. Irving, "Farewell Address," 350.

17. See especially, Elliott, *Edward Irving*, 148–83.

18. Irving's eschatology gained initial impulse from Hatley Frere, a former lieutenant turned student of biblical prophecy. Oliphant, *Irving*, 104. His initial Presbyterian cessationism first wavered in the face of arguments put by his assistant, Sandy Scott, that the gifts remained accessible through faith, and then when charismata were reported in Scotland in 1830 and later appeared in his own congregation. Irving, "Facts." For evidence that Irving saw the church as in decline, see Grass, "Edward Irving," 101–7.

19. Irving's preface to *Doctrine of the Incarnation*, 4–5.

20. For a detailed, pamphlet-by-pamphlet examination of the view of Irving and his critics, see Dorries, *Edward Irving*. Few today consider Irving a heretic.

the early twenty-first century. Although his congregation remained loyal to Irving through the allegations of heresy, the trustees eventually moved against him after he allowed the charismata into the congregation. The wording of their formal objections showed their concerns revolved around order in the church and the issue of allowing women and unordained men to participate in public worship (the trustees actually used the words "interrupt" and "disturb").[21] It was not Irving's Christology that disturbed them, but his ecclesiology.

At this point in his ministry then, we can see Irving as proclaiming an egalitarianism of the Spirit. This is not to say that he was completely anti-hierarchical—far from it—but that he made a greater place for the movement of the Holy Spirit amongst the laity than was common in his day, and he had been led to this position by a combination of personality, theology, and experience immersed in the Romantic milieu. He argued his position exhaustively from Scripture, patristics and Reformation history. In this, we can see Irving as something of a pioneer of the many possibilities that are open to believers in the contemporary church, a reviver and reinterpreter of Luther's priesthood of all believers (at least one notable contemporary referred to Irving as a new Luther[22]) in the face of a rigid Protestant clergy-laity gulf. From the wider cultural perspective, Irving's stance was completely coherent with Romanticism's tendency to reject the assertion of traditional authorities.

When the trustees forced him out, the majority of parishioners (about 800) followed Irving into a new building.[23] How would Irving reconfigure his leadership in this new group, freed from the constraints of Presbyterianism? He seemed to hark back to the role of bishop and congregational autonomy in the earliest days of the church.[24] A year or so earlier, in the context of disagreement over the charismata, he had written to the trustees.

> Now, my dear brethren, it is well known to you, that, by the word of God, and by the rules of all well-ordered churches, and by the trust-deed of our church in particular, it lies with the angel or minister of the church to order in all things connected with the public worship and service of God. For this duty I am responsible to the great Head of the Church, and have felt the burden of it upon my conscience for many weeks past; but consulting for

21. Oliphant, *Irving*, 355–56.
22. Coleridge, "Aphorisms," 378.
23. Oliphant, *Irving*, 369. In itself, this was a harbinger of the many splits in twentieth-century congregations over the charismatic gifts.
24. In an 1827 ordination address for a friend, Irving exhorted him to "Be thou then a bishop" to his congregation. "Ordination Charge," 533.

the feelings of others, I have held back from doing that which I felt to be my duty, and most profitable for the great edification of the church of Christ, over which the Lord hath set me.[25]

Here is the echo of Irving's earlier statements of independence and a solitary path; his obedience to Christ superseded any earthly responsibilities, including those to his own trustees, and he was trying to depict this independence as fully aligned with Presbyterian polity. But there was an obvious potential tension between the charism of angel and that of the newly authorized prophets within the congregation, for Irving saw both as Spirit-authorized. And like all Romantics, Irving was not going to sacrifice his epiphany on the reductionist altar of reason.

> That because this gift of tongues and prophesying, which is its fruit, are the constant demonstrations of God dwelling in a man, and teaching him all spiritual things by the Holy Ghost, without help of any third thing or third party, to the great undervaluing and entire disannulling of the powers of natural reason and speech as a fountain-head of divine instruction: therefore they must ever be fatal to the pride of intellect, to the prudence and wisdom of the world, to the scheming, counselling, and wise dealing of the natural man; to all mere philosophers, theologians, poets, sages, and wits of every name; yea, makes war upon them, brings them to nought . . .[26]

The potential tension between Irving's view of his own God-given responsibility as angel and that of the charismatically gifted in his congregation may have been defused if Irving himself had manifested the charismata, but he did not. As this drama played out in the final two years of Irving's life, the tension remained essentially unresolved: Irving's own writings proclaimed an exalted view of both the pastor-bishop and the charismatically gifted laity. In the end, it was the latter group that rose to preeminence within the group that, after Irving's death, would become known as the Catholic Apostolic Church.[27]

We can now begin to see how Irving's Romanticism led him to pioneer a number of innovations in church worship and government with which we are familiar today. One of these, obviously, was the exercise of the

---

25. Anon., *Trial*, 4. Irving used the term "angel" as synonymous with "minister," deriving this from Revelation.

26. Irving, "On the Gifts," 558, which first appeared in two parts, in *The Morning Watch*, Vol. II of 1830 and Vol. III of 1831.

27. Complicating the issue was the arrival of the office of apostle. Elliott, *Edward Irving*, 202–5.

charismata. Certainly, Irving's group was not the first in the modern era to make these claims; for example, the Quakers of the mid-seventeenth century were well known for prophesying, but Irving was unique in welcoming the charismata into an established Protestant denomination. This was controversial enough in the charismatic movement of the 1960s, so it was truly revolutionary in 1830s London. Romanticism provided the context for its occurrence. Secondly, Irving was at the forefront of allowing the laity in general and women in particular a role in public ministry. Again, this had long been a feature of dissenting groups, but had certainly not been a characteristic of churches in the Reformed tradition. Under John Wesley, women had briefly been allowed to preach in Methodist circles, but this opportunity was removed after Wesley died, some decades before Irving's ministry.[28] Later in the nineteenth century, the Salvation Army would make its own contribution in this area, and some of the early Pentecostal denominations also offered opportunities, but this was eighty years after Irving. Irving's advocacy of the charismata and thereby the participation of women and the laity in public worship naturally led to a breaking down of the Protestant clergy-laity division, and contributed to the egalitarianism which is a prominent feature of today's church.

Thirdly, for Irving, theology had to "work": it had to make a difference in the lives of individuals, churches, and the accomplishment of God's work on the planet. If it failed to do this, then something was seriously wrong and diagnosing the problem was a priority. Evangelicalism's focus on conversion was well established by Irving's day: lives and societies were supposed to be changed.[29] Theology was nothing if not practical.

Finally, Irving created a new model of the pastor-minister. We have seen Irving's impatience with intermediary bodies, be they mission societies or presbyteries. His belief that God was clearly capable of communicating directly with the minister or missionary meant intermediaries were at best a waste of time and at worst opposed to God's will. Institutions were seen more as obstacles than opportunities. Theologically, this derived from Irving's pneumatology and Christology; culturally, it derived from the anti-authoritarian element within Romanticism that yearned to break through existing barriers to a new level of enlightenment and inspiration. Romantics did not accept authority for its own sake, but they molded their own vision of what could be.[30] Irving advocated a much greater independence for the role of pastor than was normal in his day.

28. Barker-Benfield, "Sensibility," 111.
29. Hindmarsh, *Evangelical Conversion*, 52.
30. Berlin, *Roots of Romanticism*, 116, 119.

It is in the combination of these factors: the charismata; the acceptance of the laity and women in public worship; the breaching of the clergy-laity divide; the insistence on theology making a practical difference; and the recalibration of the role of minister that Irving contributed in a significant way to the church as we know it today. This is not to say that Irving was the first, the only, or even the most significant contributor in any of these factors, but it does indicate ways in which the thought of the Romantic age was a major force in shaping the church and that Irving played a key role in this. Irving's ecclesiology played out on a wide screen: the whole was greater than the sum of the parts.

In the years since Irving's death, it has been fascinating to note how the church has in many ways drifted towards these positions. Obviously, churches that regard themselves as Pentecostal or charismatic would have broadly similar views to Irving's on the issue of spiritual gifts. The cessationism of Irving's day has gradually receded, but certainly not disappeared. Even among churches that are essentially cessationist, it is probably fair to say that there has been a broadening in their view of how the Holy Spirit operates amongst the laity. In churches of all stripes, the wall between clergy and laity has lowered considerably, and there is an increasing awareness of the vitality and centrality of lay ministry. Books on preaching universally emphasize the need to explain clearly the direct link between doctrine and daily life, answering the unspoken "so what?" question. Yet it is the last element on the list that is possibly the most fascinating: the recalibration of the role of minister.

Irving's vision of the minister as bishop is broadly similar to the view that has arisen in recent times of senior pastors as chief executive officers and/or visionary leaders.[31] The minister was directly responsible to Christ (Irving's terminology) for "receiving the vision" (contemporary terminology) and exhorting the congregation to follow it; on the other hand, individual members could also prophetically discern the voice of the Spirit to share with the congregation. In these cases, the minister needed to exercise discernment about the content of the messages, but once accepted they were also binding on the minister himself. As Irving wrote in the last few months of his life, the role of angel was to rule, discern, and then obey the word of the Lord spoken in the congregation.[32] This was obviously a complex dynamic: it was egalitarian in the sense that it potentially gave all congregation members a "voice," but hierarchical in that the minister retained the "veto."

---

31. Irving, *Confessions of Faith*, li–lii.

32. Letter to Henry Drummond dated April 7, 1834, C/9/37 in the Alnwick collection. Accessed and used by permission of His Grace, the Duke of Northumberland.

In Irving's case, as he neither spoke in tongues nor prophesied, it is perhaps not surprising that some of the "gifted ones" came to question the suitability of the "ungifted" Irving assessing their utterances.

At the heart of this tension is the perennial question of authority that the church regularly addresses: put crassly, under Christ "who runs the church"? Is it the minister or the people? Or the synod, or the denomination? The church has continually reframed its answer to this question. Irving's theology and the struggles he faced in the later years of his ministry show him wrestling with this tension in a way that is particularly poignant in the early twenty-first century. In the past few decades, we have seen many moves to encourage the role of pastor as visionary leader and even more moves to encourage and empower the laity. We talk not only about power but also about serving and try to reconcile the two in the context of reciprocal responsibility. Perhaps we sometimes wonder if our attempts to empower both the laity and the senior leadership will lead to some form of congregational meltdown. Essentially, I believe this is what happened at the end of Irving's life, and his failure to achieve a satisfying reconciliation between the two led to a tragic denouement.[33] I suspect that this tension is prevalent in the ongoing drama of congregational life and has led to numerous situations that lie somewhere on the spectrum from awkward to devastating.

I am personally aware of churches in which staff members attempted a "coup" against a senior minister who was not seen as "spiritual enough"; I am also aware of congregations in which the senior minister wields authority with a heavy hand. Irving also sailed these difficult waters and his ministry journey sheds light on how Romanticism has helped to shape some of the issues in contemporary ecclesiology.

In closing, I would like to make some general observations about the impact of Romanticism on other aspects of church life. One key area is biblical hermeneutics. Romanticism legitimized subjectivity, and thereby paved the way for later developments such as redaction criticism at one end of the spectrum and random application of scriptural texts at the other. Careers were forged as scholars tried to "peel back" the layers of cultural and theological subjectivity imposed by the original authors on the text. More prosaically, many Christians treated Scripture like a "promise box," taking texts out of context and boldly proclaiming "this is what the Spirit is telling me through this verse," blissfully unaware (or unconcerned) that their cloistered approach flew in the face of the original setting and two millennia of interpretation. These two phenomena both seem very different,

---

33. For details of this fascinating story, see Grass, *Edward Irving*.

but perhaps the underlying risk is similar—too great a confidence in one's abilities to deal with the subjectivities involved. Romanticism, therefore, has not only played a role in constructing certain hermeneutical approaches which have been important in the development of liberal theology; it has also contributed to modes of thought that have been common in evangelicalism and fundamentalism. It is ironic to think of such apparently different expressions of Christianity all being informed by a common source, but it is expressive of the enduring and pervasive power of Romanticism.

Another key area in which the influence of Romanticism can be seen is that of spiritual experience within evangelicalism. Although religion was not his focus, Isaiah Berlin saw Pietism's emphasis on heartfelt devotion as an influence on Romanticism.[34] It appears that eighteenth-century evangelicalism's emphasis on the conversion experience may have helped pave the way for Romanticism.[35] Be that as it may, when Romanticism arrived as a force in the late eighteenth century, it lent cultural and philosophical credibility to subjectivism. Writers like Samuel Taylor Coleridge demonstrated the difficulty in separating perception and interpretation; in a world where objectivity was not possible, subjectivity should not be demonized.[36] The cherished Enlightenment myth of pure objectivity was in decline.

In this context, it is easy to see Romanticism reinforcing one of the classic Evangelical distinctives (from David Bebbington's quadrilateral definition)—conversionism.[37] Evangelicalism emphasized that true Christian conversion should encompass a subjective and emotional crisis experience that could be readily recounted as a testimony. One scholar of Evangelical conversion narratives concluded that the form flourished in modern societies in which pluralism and therefore greater potential for self-determination flourished.[38] Romanticism provided just such a context. Romanticism took the empiricist emphasis on experiment and observation and twinned it with subjectivity to elevate personal experience as an important criterion in the search for truth. Later philosophical developments would make subjectivity the *only* criterion for truth, thereby relativizing it and launching frontal attacks on any overarching truth claims.

---

34. Berlin, *Roots of Romanticism*, 36.

35. Jonathan Edwards's classic, *A Treatise on the Religious Affections* (1746) is the best-known early evangelical exploration of the role of emotions in the religious life.

36. Prickett, *Romanticism and Religion*, 62.

37. The Bebbington definition derives from his *Evangelicalism in Modern Britain*, 2–3. For evidence that this has become the standard definition in the years since see Larsen, "Reception Given," 25.

38. Hindmarsh, *Conversion Narrative*, 337–39.

What then can we say of Romanticism's legacy in the twenty-first century church? Its pursuit of transcendent goals has influenced the contemporary church's fascination with visionary leaders yet somewhat paradoxically, its egalitarian impulse has facilitated the rise of the laity in church life. This lingers with us in many ways through unresolved issues of authority, discipline, and accountability (all "touchy" words) within the local church which of course relate profoundly to church government. Romanticism's embrace of subjectivity has both heightened sensitivity to the indwelling of the Holy Spirit and simultaneously encouraged idiosyncratic and self-centered spirituality. Romanticism's awareness of the subjectivity of the writers of Scripture has fostered redaction criticism which has fueled much liberal theology; at the other end of the spectrum Romanticism has encouraged the often subjectivist interpretations of fundamentalist groups. Also, the links between Romanticism, existentialism, and postmodernism have been widely noted, as typified by Berlin's quote at the beginning of this chapter. To the degree that the twenty-first-century church is influenced by the latter two, it is inevitably also influenced by Romanticism. This is not an exhaustive list, but I hope it is sufficient to indicate that what Isaiah Berlin claimed for Romanticism in general is also true for the church specifically, namely, that Romanticism has had an enormous—and ongoing—influence. Reflecting on the cultural behemoth of Romanticism will help us better understand the church of today and its tensions. The nineteenth century seems a long time ago, but it is much closer and more influential than we suspect.

Bibliography

Abrams, Meyer H. *Natural Supernaturalism: Tradition and Revolution in Romantic Literature.* New York: W. W. Norton and Co., 1971.

Anon. *The Trial of the Rev. Edward Irving, M.A. before the London Presbytery; Containing the Whole of the Evidence; Exact Copies of the Documents; Verbatim Report of the Speeches and Opinions of the Presbyters, &c.; Being the Only Authentic and Complete Record of the Proceedings: Taken in Short hand by W. Harding.* London: W. Harding, 1832.

Barker-Benfield, Graham J. "Sensibility." In *An Oxford Companion to the Romantic Age: British Culture 1776–1832*, edited by Iain McCalman, 102–13. Oxford: Oxford University Press, 1999.

Bebbington, David. *Evangelicalism in Modern Britain: A History from the 1730s to the 1980s.* London: Unwin Hyman, 1989.

Berlin, Isaiah. *The Roots of Romanticism.* Princeton: Princeton University Press, 1999.

Brown, Marshall. "Romanticism and Enlightenment." In *The Cambridge Companion to British Romanticism*, edited by Stuart Curran, 34–55. Cambridge: Cambridge University Press, 2010.

Coleridge, Samuel T. "Aphorisms on Spiritual Religion B, Aphorism XXIV." In *Aids to Reflection*, edited by J. Beer, 155–381. London and Princeton: Routledge and Princeton University Press, 1993.

Dallimore, Arnold. *The Life of Edward Irving: The Fore-runner of the Charismatic Movement*. Edinburgh: Banner of Truth, 1983.

Dorries, David. *Edward Irving's Incarnational Christology*. Fairfax, VA: Xulon, 2002.

Elliott, Peter. *Edward Irving: Romantic Theology in Crisis*. Studies in Evangelical History and Thought. Milton Keynes: Paternoster, 2013.

———. "Edward Irving's Hybrid: Towards a Nineteenth-Century Apostolic and Presbyterian Pentecostalism." In *Episcopacy, Authority and Gender: Aspects of Religious Leadership in Europe, 1100-2000*, edited by J. W. Buisman, M. Derks, and P. Raedts, 139-48. Leiden: Brill, 2015.

Grass, Tim. "Edward Irving: Eschatology, Ecclesiology and Spiritual Gifts." In *Prisoners of Hope? Aspects of Evangelical Millennialism in Britain and Ireland, 1800-1880*, edited by C. Gribben and T. F. C. Stunt, 101-7. Carlisle: Paternoster, 2004.

———. *Edward Irving: The Lord's Watchman*. Carlisle: Paternoster, 2011.

Hindmarsh, D. Bruce. *The Evangelical Conversion Narrative: Spiritual Autobiography in Early Modern England*. Oxford: Oxford University Press, 2005.

Irving, Edward. *The Confessions of Faith and the Books of Discipline of the Church of Scotland, of Date Anterior to the Westminster Confession. To Which are Prefixed a Historical View of the Church of Scotland from the Earliest Period to the Time of the Reformation, and a Historical Preface, with Remarks*. London: Baldwin and Cradock, 1831.

———. "The Doctrine of the Incarnation Opened." In *The Collected Writings of Edward Irving*, vol. 5, edited by G. Carlyle, 3-446. London: Alexander Strahan and Co, 1865.

———. "Facts Connected with Recent Manifestations of Spiritual Gifts." *Fraser's Magazine*, January 1832, 754-61.

———. "Farewell Address at St John's Glasgow." In *The Collected Writings of Edward Irving*, vol. 3, edited by G. Carlyle, 343-62. London: Alexander Strahan and Co, 1865.

———. "Missionaries after the Apostolical School." In *The Collected Writings of Edward Irving*, vol. 1, edited by G. Carlyle, 427-523. London: Alexander Strahan and Co, 1864.

———. "On the Gifts of the Holy Ghost, Commonly Called Supernatural." In *The Collected Writings of Edward Irving*, vol. 5, edited by G. Carlyle, 509-61. London: Alexander Strahan and Co, 1865.

———. "Ordination Charge to the Minister of the Scots Church, London Wall, March 15, 1827." In *The Collected Writings of Edward Irving*, vol. 1, edited by G. Carlyle, 527-40. London: Alexander Strahan and Co, 1864.

Larsen, Timothy. "The Reception Given *Evangelicalism in Modern Britain* Since Its Publication in 1989." In *The Emergence of Evangelicalism: Exploring Historical Continuities*, edited by M. A. G. Haykin and K. J. Stewart, 21-31. Nottingham: Apollos, 2008.

Oliphant, Margaret. *The Life of Edward Irving*. 5th ed. London: Hurst and Blackett, n.d.

Prickett, Stephen. *Romanticism and Religion: The Tradition of Coleridge and Wordsworth in the Victorian Church*. Cambridge: Cambridge University Press, 1976.

Reardon, Bernard M. G. *Religious Thought in the Victorian Age: A Survey from Coleridge to Gore*. London: Longman, 1980.

11

Cultural Exegesis

*Missiological Pragmatism or
Theological Imperative?*

Stephen Garner

Introduction

For some Christians, culture and the Christian faith are diametrically opposed to each other, and the faithful response to the gospel to be "in the world, but not of it," necessarily rejects culture having anything of significance to say to the church. At the other end of the spectrum there are those who, perhaps uncritically, see God as fully present in human activity, and seek to shape Christianity to resonate with prevailing worldviews. Most of us, though, probably oscillate between those two positions; there are things that we identify as unhelpful or opposed to the Christian faith in culture and other things that we consciously appropriate from culture into our life of faith. Moreover, there are aspects of culture that shape the Christian faith without us being aware of them, and which are present invisibly in our living out of the gospel in private and public spheres.

This ambiguous relationship with culture and the wider world often leads to a pragmatic engagement with culture that tends to be "thin" and, to be honest, motivated by missiological ends. For example, the apostle Paul's engagement with Greek thinkers in Athens (Acts 17) is for some a classic example of how cultural awareness is a means to an end; the effective translation of the gospel into the thought forms of the day. However, this is often interpreted as a one-way conversation rather than a genuine dialogue with culture, where the gospel is somehow distilled from one's own context into some sort of "pure" form that is then translated into a new form seen as compatible with a target context. As practical theologian Angie Pears notes, this raises a number of critical questions: Are the people doing the translation skilled enough at understanding not only the target culture, but also their own culture? Is the complexity of cultural diversity truly understood? Is there some core universal Christian truth that can always be shaped into another context? And what about expressions of Christianity already present in the target culture?[1]

However, if, as Kathryn Tanner asserts, God is in some form of relationship with all aspects of creation, then a deeper exploration of culture, and in particular the shape of everyday life, needs to take place if only to glean some insight into those relationships.[2] This move towards a deeper engagement with culture connects with what Kevin Vanhoozer calls cultural exegesis and hermeneutics, moving beyond the identification of ideas and "texts" within culture, to understanding how they occur in their contexts, how they shape interpretive worldviews within those contexts, and how the church and its members are also shaped by that culture. Identifying these things and developing a "thick" description of culture leads, he argues, to theology that understands how faith is shaped by the everyday world and how faith should be embodied in this world.[3]

This richer development of theological engagement with culture is to be commended, but perhaps it doesn't go far enough. It can still be taken to be a one-way relationship, of the church pragmatically undertaking cultural analysis to achieve the church's ends, and not allowing culture to speak back critically and constructively to the church. If God is connected to all things in the world, then the liturgical imperative "Hear what the Spirit is saying to the Church" might be articulated in unfamiliar and surprising cultural locations and forms.

Theology and the Everyday World

Theology is a communal process by which the church seeks to understand its faith and the world around it through reflection upon Scripture, tradition,

1. Pears, *Doing Contextual Theology*, 15–16.
2. Tanner, "Theological Anthropology," 567–70.
3. Vanhoozer, "Everyday Theology," 15–60.

reason, and experience. One of the more common definitions of Christian theology is that of Anselm of Canterbury (c. 1033–1109), who saw it as "faith seeking understanding" (Latin: *fides quaerens intellectum*). Anselm's description was rooted in his own medieval context, and every generation rearticulates what theology is in relation to the sociocultural situation of their day thus involving some sort of dialogue between theology and culture. For example, "faith seeking understanding" might be tied to a sense of "faith seeking intelligent action" in the world, which by necessity demands an understanding of that world, or maybe as Vanhoozer puts it, an everyday theology that seeks a "grasp of what is going on in ordinary situations (and why), an attempt to make sense of one's surroundings."[4]

This in turn ties in with the observations of theologians Kathryn Tanner and Douglas Hall about both the breadth of theology and its connection to the very real everyday world. For Tanner, theology must be comprehensive as it explores what it means to be human beings in relationship with God, for if God is the Lord of everything then no aspect of the world, no matter how ordinary, is exempt from being understood in relation to faith.[5] Moreover, as Douglas Hall puts it:

> Theology is "thinking about everything all the time." Everything! For there is no subject under the sun that is unimportant to someone who tries to understand a little about God and God's world; and if you have that as your object, you have to be at it—simply at it—*all the time.*[6]

This kind of theological reflection is a kind of contextual theology, which locates itself as a theological endeavor seeking to articulate, critique, and express a practical theology rooted in the experience of the individual or community through an explicit dialogue between the past (represented by Scripture and tradition) and the present (represented particularly by personal and community experience).[7] This dialogue is critical because it forces us to ask the two key questions: How does the world we live in affect our faith? And how should we live out our lives in the "shapes of everyday life"?[8] As Bevans sums it up, "[t]he contextualization of theology—the

---

4. Vanhoozer, "Everyday Theology," 16.
5. Tanner, "Theological Anthropology," 567.
6. Hall, "What is Theology?," 172.
7. Bevans, *Contextual Theology*, 4–7.
8. Vanhoozer, "Everyday Theology," 16.

attempt to understand Christian faith in terms of a particular context—is really a theological imperative."[9]

Connecting Theology and Culture?

So, if faith seeking understanding or faith seeking reflective agency in the world are part and parcel of the Christian life as we seek to join with God's work in the wider world, how then might we go about it? And, moreover, how do we look at the world, not just as something to be sallied forth into for occasional missions excursions, but rather as the place in which we live and breathe mission? Are we, as the late Baptist theologian Stanley Grenz puts it, open to the idea that the Holy Spirit is operative in a variety of locations both inside and outside of the church?[10] And if this is the case, how might the Holy Spirit alert us to elements within human cultures that bear the Spirit's "fingerprints" and serve as a voice to speak back critically to the community of faith? Furthermore, how does our vision of the world to come shape how we live our lives in the worlds and cultures of this age?

In pondering these kinds of questions, Vanhoozer contends that we need to develop "cultural hermeneutics," ways in which the church critically reads, interprets, and understands the cultures it encounters or is embedded within. To do this, the church will need to avoid the twin temptations of being dazzled by culture in a way that results in uncritical acceptance, or simply rejecting it as something that Christians should have nothing to do with.[11]

Interpretation of culture is a tricky business, not the least because there are no culturally unbiased positions, whether we're talking about theology or simply the culture that has colonized our own lives and communities. Missiologist Lesslie Newbigin talked about this when he posited that there is no "culture-free" gospel, and to claim that there is one is a denial of the good news as word made flesh. That said, Newbigin does not reject the power of the gospel to critique culture:

> Every statement of the gospel in words is conditioned by the culture of which those words are a part, and every style of life that claims to embody the truth of the gospel is a culturally conditioned style of life. There can never be a culture-free gospel. Yet, the gospel, which is from the beginning to the end embodied

---

9. Bevans, *Contextual Theology*, 3.
10. Grenz, "Hollywood," 309.
11. Vanhoozer, "Everyday Theology," 32–33.

in culturally conditioned forms, calls into question all cultures, including the one in which it was originally embodied.[12]

For Newbigin, the birth, life and ministry, and death and resurrection of Jesus Christ changed things universally across the world and through history, and therefore must speak to every human culture now caught between this age and the age to come. Similarly, Vanhoozer and Grenz also both see culture as unavoidable, but that the gospel as ministered through the Spirit shapes how the church engages with its own and other cultures.

For Grenz, the Spirit's work in culture always aligns with the truth revealed in Scripture, and how well we discern the work of the Spirit in culture is also determined by how open we are to the Spirit through Scripture.[13] For Vanhoozer, the goal of this process is a deepening of the Christian faith, brought about by reading and interpreting cultural texts—such as a particular cultural artefact like a film or the web of meaning or a worldview provided by culture—in light of the gospel of Christ. The texts are read both on their own terms, to avoid reading into them something that isn't there (destroying their own meaning or aesthetic effect in a quest to find Christian meanings), and also in light of the biblical text.[14]

In order to do this, Vanhoozer proposes a method for reading cultural texts that respects both the text in its own right, as well as in light of the biblical or Christian reading. Both of these approaches provide different dimensions to the "thick" description of cultural discourse being developed. The description is "thick" because it draws upon multiple disciplinary perspectives when examining the text in question such as history, economics, film and media studies, social sciences, and theology.[15] This means that we are not narrowly focused upon a single point of view or way of looking at text. This is reminiscent of the prophets such as Amos in the Old Testament who brought not just a theological perspective to their prophesying about their culture, but also nuanced it with an understanding of the social, political, and economic dimensions at play in their context, thus providing a thick description of the cultural discourse to engage with.

In the initial instance, the cultural text, whether it is a film, song, or idea, is examined in terms of who made the text and why it was made. This is the world behind the text, and narrowly this means identifying and researching the author or authors of a text (e.g. ascribing some sort

---

12. Newbigin, *Foolishness*, 4.
13. Grenz, "Hollywood," 310.
14. Vanhoozer, "Everyday Theology," 44.
15. Vanhoozer, "Everyday Theology," 45–48.

of authorial intent). However, it also means going further and identifying whose interests or power is being served by the text.[16]

The next key question to ask, is "what meaning is being created by the text and how is that meaning communicated to the recipients?" This requires us to become familiar with the text at several levels, from a simple reading of the text in question (e.g. viewing a film or reading a political speech), through to identifying the kind of text it is (i.e. genre) and acknowledging how those texts communicate their message, and then finally analytically distilling what meanings, values, and ethos are being expressed.[17]

And finally, we ask "what effect does this text have upon those who receive, use, or consume it?" Just as we use other disciplines in the other steps, here the social sciences, media and cultural studies, as well as the narratives of those who consume and reuse the cultural material, are helpful. What people consume or receive this text? How do they appropriate it? How does it shape their everyday rhythms of life and their perception of the world? Vanhoozer argues that cultural texts communicate "root metaphors," typically a single hermeneutical key that is then used to interpret the surrounding world.[18] One is asked to step into that world, take on board the narrative being offered, and then live their life accordingly.

And this is where the second aspect of the process comes into play. We have an understanding of the cultural text on its own terms which includes the root metaphor it offers for interpreting the world, but then we need to look at that text through the lens of the gospel. Thus, we ask questions of the metaphor being communicated: Does it draw us towards Christ or away from Christ into some form of idolatry? Through the communal process of faithful and prayerful reflection upon Scripture can we also discern if the Spirit might be saying something to us about our own Christian lives, our community of faith, and how we live that out in our culture?

Exegeting Popular Culture

One particular way in which we might explore this process is to examine popular culture, which intersects with the idea that we are wrapped in media, so much so that it has become the environment in which we "live and breathe and have our being."

Popular culture can be a slippery beast to define, but a useful way of thinking about it is offered by practical theologian Gordon Lynch, who

16. Vanhoozer, "Everyday Theology," 48–50.
17. Vanhoozer, "Everyday Theology," 50–52.
18. Vanhoozer, "Everyday Theology," 52–54.

suggests that it might be better to think of popular culture as "the shared context, practices, and resources of 'everyday life.'"[19] This emphasis on the broad, everyday world means that examining popular culture deals not only with its "texts" or cultural products such as films or music, but also with the study of how these things are produced and "consumed" in society, thus giving insight into the wider structures, patterns, and activities of meaning-making taking place in everyday life. Additionally, it also highlights that popular culture exists alongside a number of different competing and complementary cultures.[20]

These connections with the everyday, with meaning-making, and with the experiential highlight four key dimensions of culture that Kevin Vanhoozer argues we need to be aware of in our theological engagement with culture: (a) culture communicates; (b) culture orients; (c) culture reproduces; and (d) culture cultivates.[21]

First, culture communicates not only information but also interpretations of that information. It does this at many levels, including the content of its messages as well as the form that content may take. Advertising messages are an ideal example of this, where the glossy magazine picture of a group of friends enjoying drinks in a tropical island paradise conveys not only information about the particular alcoholic beverage being sold, but also the idea that purchasing said beverage would, by implication, let you live "the good life."

If culture provides narratives to interpret the world, the implication of that brings us to the second dimension of culture, that is, its power to orient individuals and communities in the world. First, culture communicates both information and interpretation to provide a worldview, and then that worldview can be used to orient us towards the world, shaping how we live our lives. This is not just our thinking about ourselves and our context, but also how we feel about those things, defining understandings of right and wrong, and the character of our environment. This is echoed by Australian media scholar Lelia Green, when she notes that popular culture is "that subsection of mass media which are appropriated by people in their daily lives and remodeled as the raw material through which they communicate their values and enthusiasms, and through which they connect to others."[22]

Furthermore, these worldviews are not static or limited to a single location, for, third, culture reproduces or transmits beliefs, values, and practices

---

19. Lynch, *Understanding Theology*, 13.
20. Lynch, *Understanding Theology*, 15–16.
21. Vanhoozer, "Everyday Theology," 28–32.
22. Green, *Technoculture*, 156.

from one social group to another. This might be through the imposition of these worldviews by an authority such as a school, government, church, or family, or simply through the imitation of others that we come into contact with. Developments in mass media and the Internet, including new media, provide constant avenues for both of these kinds of cultural reproduction.

And last, information, values, narratives, and worldviews that are transmitted and reproduced shape the spirit of who we are and the character of our societies. Culture cultivates, forming the human spirit, and providing the soil and nutrients for flourishing or, in some cases, stunting growth.

In light of this kind of power that popular culture exerts, Lynch identifies some parallel questions that could stand alongside Vanhoozer's two questions of "how does our world affect our faith?" and "how should we live out our lives in the 'shapes of everyday life?'" Examining popular culture allows us not only to map broadly what is happening in our contemporary culture, but also what images, texts, ideas, and values are being used to: (a) build healthy and responsible communities; or (b) stunt the growth of those kinds of communities? Additionally, what are some of the ways we can identify in which people are using popular culture to critique and resist dominant ideologies in their society, and to manifest authentic forms of self-expression?[23] And to that, I'd add, if it is to be a true conversation between faith and popular culture, what is popular culture saying back to the church? In what ways might we prayerfully and faithfully listen to see if we can hear the Spirit speaking not just to the wider world, but also back to those who follow Jesus Christ?

In order to think about these questions I'll use some examples from popular culture including a number related to the theme of belief, religious authority, and lament, to think about not only how we might "decode" what is going on here so we can speak into it, but also how it might be speaking into our own lives.

bro'Town: Family, Friends and Your Heart in the Right Place

For five years the television show *bro'Town* (2004–2009) represented a novel and somewhat controversial approach to telling stories about New Zealand society in mainstream media.[24] The particular characters and setting were connected to immigrant Pacific Island and urban Maori communities, but the stories being told were broader than that and resonated with the

23. Lynch, *Understanding Theology*, 19.
24. The Naked Samoans, and Firehorse Films, *Bro'Town*.

wider New Zealand public. It was more than just a comedy and satirical social commentary, drawing out the themes of liberation, respect, love, and authentic well-being played out in the *bro'Town* narratives, in the lives of Sione, Vale, Valea, Mack, and Jeff. Their slogan "Morningside for life!" was a contemporary metaphor for the need to find friends, love, respect, and home in an often complicated and conflicted world, and to find something to believe in to hold all that together.

Each episode begins and ends with the interaction of a semi-irreverent Pacific contextualization of God the Father and Jesus in heaven discussing a particular issue, which is then played out through the schoolboys who are the main characters in the show. The show explores their own hybrid existence at the meeting of different cultures, whether that is church, gender, ethnicity, sexuality, family, or socioeconomic status.

The show is helpful for raising a number of questions, from the ways in which God might be represented by different cultures or by the church to the wider community, the notion of whether something is offensive or even blasphemous within a pluralistic society, and the "afterimages" of Christendom within postcolonial societies, issues to do with constructing identity in bicultural and multicultural societies.

Exegeting such a text leads us into an act of listening as we develop a "thick" understanding of the show. This starts with the stories of the Samoan comedians who created the show by drawing on their own experiences. We observe the world that the program creates, a world that communicates an understanding of a slice of contemporary New Zealand life, complete with a mixture of sympathetic and critical engagement with Christianity, and a root metaphor of belief in friends, family, and having your heart in the right place as the key to the good life. The final step would be to then look at how that root metaphor was received in real life, shaping the lives of a range of New Zealanders. This act of listening precedes a twofold response: first, to examine the critique of the enculturation of Christianity and to see what truths that might reveal, and then second, how one might tell the story of Jesus and extend that into the new and existing categories and contexts described in the show.

Firefly and *Serenity*: You Need to Believe in Something

Science fiction is another form of popular culture that opens itself up to a meaningful dialogue with questions of faith. By its very nature science fiction is speculative, providing a safe space to ask critical questions about our current world within imaginative environments used to focus upon those questions. As theologian Stephen May comments, "[s]uch invention can either suggest a universe as strange as possible (with equally strange creatures inhabiting it), or one like ours—except for one vital difference."[25]

For example, the reimagined television series *Battlestar Galactica* (2004–09) explored the crisis that arises when the vibrant, militant fundamentalism of the Cylons clashes with listless, nominal faith represented by human beings, as well as responses to terrorism.[26] Similarly, the television series *Terminator: Sarah Connor Chronicles* (2008–09) is interwoven with questions about what it means to be human, the potential of human technological agency for harm and for good, and, as Yvonne Sherwood puts it, the way that biblical "afterlives" exist as part of some cultural legacy or representation in popular culture through the explicit use of biblical themes and characters to tell its stories.[27]

The theme of belief is a dominant thread woven through the texts of Joss Whedon's short-lived science fiction television series *Firefly* (2002) and its cinematic sequel *Serenity* (2005). Examining the "world-behind-the-text" tells us that Whedon has also created television shows like *Buffy the Vampire Slayer* (1997–2003), *Angel* (1999–2004), and *Dollhouse* (2009–10), is a movie director, composer, and a comic book writer. Additionally, he's a self-identified atheist and feminist, and exhibits an interest in the existentialism that influences his work.

Looking at the "world-in-the-text" in *Firefly* and *Serenity*, we identify that it mixes the Western and science fiction genres, develops a narrative about a dominant culture seen from the margins of that society, and continually comes back to the idea that for human beings to construct and maintain meaningful lives they need to have something to believe in. This isn't necessarily God, but anything that gives shape and vitality to life. Without that, people are somewhat less than they could be. This concern for belief filters through into dialogues such as the preacher Book's comment in *Serenity*, "I don't care what you believe. Just believe it," and his conversation in *Firefly* with the girl River, about the Bible and faith ("Jaynestown"):

> Book: River, you don't fix the Bible.
>
> River: It's broken. It doesn't make sense.
>
> Book: It's not about making sense. It's about believing in something, and letting that belief be real enough to change

---

25. May, *Stardust and Ashes*, 15.
26. Marshall and Wheeland, "Cylons," 96–97.
27. See Sherwood, *A Biblical Text and Its Afterlives*.

your life. It's about faith. You don't fix faith, River. It fixes you.

Whedon's work in *Serenity* explores belief from a variety of perspectives including those who lose their faith in something and need to find it again, those whose belief drives them to engage positively in the world, and those whose belief in an absolute means that "normal moral impulses of compassion and empathy must be subsumed to concepts of righteousness."[28]

Approaching the "world-before-the-text" invites us to think about how this text might be received by its audience, how it shapes those who view it, and what worldview the "root metaphor" of needing to believe in something invites us to enter into. At one level the church community might use these themes to expound to those outside of the church the metaphor that every human being has a "God-shaped hole" inside of them or that the need to believe and have purpose are the essence of a relational-social being made in the image of God. But what might it be saying *back* to the church? Might it be saying that we have failed to clearly communicate and live out what it is that we believe, failed to demonstrate how our faith and our gospel narrative provides meaning, purpose, and a vitality of (abundant) life found in Jesus Christ through the power of the Spirit? Certainly, Whedon's work might provide some with an alternative narrative for making sense of the world around us, and how to live in it, demonstrated by responses to his work such as *What Would Buffy Do?* and *The Vampire Slayer as Spiritual Guide*.[29]

Comic Books: Religious Authority and the Problem of Evil

Contemporary comic books and graphic novels are rich in imagery and characters drawn from existing religious and spiritual traditions, often mixing and matching these traditions in interesting and novel ways, as well as providing worldviews and commentaries on faith and religion. While the most obvious way in which Christianity engages with this form of popular culture is typically through adapting the biblical text to a graphical format in an effort to make it more appealing to a younger, more visual culture, or through creating comic book tracts, much more is provided by the medium.[30]

---

28. Greene, "Good Book," 86–89.
29. Riess, *What Would Buffy Do?*
30. See Ross, *Blinded*; Ross, *Marked*; Siku and Akinsiku, *Manga Bible*; and, Anderson et al., *Lion Graphic Bible*.

Mainstream superhero comics, that also engender films and television shows, contain within them remarkably well-developed cosmologies with natural and supernatural dimensions, and worldviews that shape morality. For example, David Hughes asks:

> Why this sudden fascination with comic book heroes? Perhaps because so many directors and studio executives grew up (as I did) on Marvel and DC comics—an entire generation learned about morality, heroism and the difficult choices faced by heroes not from the classics, but from Spider-Man and The Hulk, with mythologies as potent and powerful as those of the gods of ancient times.[31]

Mainstream superhero comics have, perhaps because they predominantly originate in the US and UK, tended to assume cosmologies that are oriented around the combination of Judeo-Christian religious and post-Enlightenment scientific cosmologies, augmented by other spiritual, religious, and metaphysical traditions, thus reflecting the worldviews that closely parallel our own pluralistic world.

Faith, spirituality, and comics also intersect in material produced in order to critique or explore spiritual or theological ideas without being caught up in a preexisting comic book universe. Examples of this can be found in graphic novels such as Craig Thompson's *Blankets*, Joann Sfar's *The Rabbi's Cat*, Will Eisner's *A Contract with God*, and J. Michael Straczynski's *Midnight Nation* series. In particular, *Blankets* is an autobiographical exploration of growing up in American fundamentalist Christianity, while atheist Straczynski's *Midnight Nation* deals with the concepts of theodicy and free will.[32]

One consistent theme running through contemporary comic books across the spectrum is an interest in the way religious authority is manifested and potentially abused. For example, Douglas Rushkoff's *Testament* series interweaves his own reinterpretation of the Hebrew Scriptures with contemporary commentary post–9/11 America.[33] The Superman stories *Angel* and *Redemption* fall into this category, where the writers use the well-known figure of Superman to explore the notion of misplaced faith.[34] In *Angel* the writers explore the idea of recovering faith in oneself rather than an external force in order to change the world for good, while in *Redemption* we see the notion of fundamentalist belief given in "good

---

31. Hughes, *Comic Book Movies*, 1.
32. Sfar, *Rabbi's Cat*; Thompson, *Blankets*; and Eisner, *Contract with God*.
33. Rushkoff and Sharp, *Testament*.
34. Busiek and Nicieza, *Superman*.

faith" empowering someone to do "evil." In the latter we hear Superman commenting, "This is about a good if misguided—young man who needs to *control* his actions . . . even if those actions are guided by his *beliefs* . . . No, I have no problem with religion. I have a problem with abusing one's power in the name of *anything*."[35]

So perhaps here we see the concept of freedom of religion and belief within a Western liberal democracy being expressed in the language of tolerance and pluralism, provided it doesn't seek to impose itself in the public sphere in a way that is perceived as "hurtful" or "abusive."

The nature of religious institutions and the authority they wield is also a dominant theme running through the genre, and especially the issue of how those in power can be corrupted by it, leading to the manipulation of those they oversee. This is a theme in the *Magdalena* comics, where the current "warrior nun" Magdalena, Patience, has lost her faith in the church because of the way she sees herself and all those who have gone before her used by that institution for their own, and not God's, agenda.[36] The ongoing narrative contains the stories of those who represent institutional powers of oppression, along with those of people who are trying to reform the church. This is also intermingled with discussions of how gender roles are shaped within churches and "means-justifies-the-ends" pragmatism in serving God.

Patience believes, barring the occasional crisis of faith, in her vocation and also in the God who calls her to that vocation. This is not necessarily a passive acquiescence to this vocation though, and the narratives show the very real struggles that people of faith might have with the life they feel called to and the way in which they work that out. Indeed, Patience's struggles in *The Magdalena*, represent not a loss of faith in the Christian God, but rather in the institutions that represent that God and also a searching for an assurance (almost a Wesleyan "warming of the heart") that the vocation chosen is being followed authentically. Moreover, the characters often highlight how religious faith must deal at times not with absolutes, but with the moral ambiguities of the contemporary world.

As such, the comic book narratives that permeate and shape popular culture offer a rich source of theological and cultural reflection in how they engage audiences through a visual medium able to address complicated and relevant issues, and how they provide moral frameworks that can shape how people live (e.g. Spider-Man's "With great power comes great responsibility"). Thus they provide dialogue partners for the church in asking questions

---

35. Nicieza and Goldman, *Superman*.
36. Marz and Blake, *Magdalena*.

about how authority is manifested within religious communities, how faith might be misused even for good purposes, how society views the place of religion in the public sphere, as well as a genuine warmth towards people who are wrestling with questions about their faith.

Lament and New Media

In late 2010, the tragedy resulting from the loss of twenty-nine miners' lives in the Pike River mine accident on the West Coast of New Zealand created a deep sense of national mourning. One of the most publicized responses to this widespread grieving was incorporated into the U2 concerts held just after the tragedy. Here, lead singer Bono's short reflection on the tragedy, the performance "One Tree Hill" (a song about loss with New Zealand connections), and the projection of the names of lost miners on video screens, combined to create a space where the audience could share in and express the rawness and grief that affected the nation at that time.

Perhaps U2's (and in particular Bono's) response at the time, of being able to create such a space for lament was because they understood the power of cultural exegesis and hermeneutics, and particularly the power and role that lament possesses. In the past, U2 have used the psalms of lament to good effect in their music (e.g. "40" based on Ps 40), and in his reflection on the book of Psalms, Bono comments: "That's what a lot of psalms feel like to me, the blues. Man shouting at God, 'My God, my God why hast thou forsaken me? Why art thou so far from helping me?'"[37]

In their performance, U2 managed to look at an event in a contemporary setting, understand the event, connect it to the local cultural context through popular culture (e.g. the empathy and meaning contained in the song selected and the visual imagery used), and provide a space for participation and response from the audience. Again, the question can be asked, what can the church learn from this kind of reading the culture, its connection to the hearts, minds, and spirits of everyday people?

Conclusion

Culture is inescapable, and if we're living out the gospel narrative of Jesus Christ, and proclaiming it in the world, then we need to be wise about the role and power that culture possesses in the world, in the church, and in our own lives. If all that is in the heavens and the earth is God's, and if the

---

37. Bono, "Book of Psalms," 136.

triune God is present in the world working in surprising, embracing, and witnessing ways, then we are called to read culture carefully, prayerfully, and faithfully. This is so that we can not only communicate and live out the gospel in our mission, becoming active culture creators and agents in our own right, but also so that we are aware of the Spirit speaking back to us through culture. As such, cultural exegesis becomes a theological imperative that allows us first to listen with the ears of the Spirit and then to act wisely in the world.

Bibliography

Anderson, Jeff, Mike Maddox, and Steve Harrison. *The Lion Graphic Bible*. Oxford: Lion, 1998.
Bevans, Stephen B. *Models of Contextual Theology*. Faith and Cultures Series. Rev. and expanded ed. Maryknoll: Orbis, 2002.
Bono. "The Book of Psalms." In *Revelations: Personal Responses to the Books of the Bible*, edited by Richard Holloway, 135–40. Edinburgh: Canongate, 2005.
Busiek, Fabian, and Kurt Nicieza. *Superman: Redemption*. New York: DC Comics, 2007.
Eisner, Will. *A Contract with God and Other Tenement Stories*. New York: DC Comics, 1996.
Green, Lelia. *Technoculture: From Alphabet to Cybersex*. Crowsnest, NSW: Allen and Unwin, 2002.
Greene, Eric. "The Good Book." In *Serenity Found: More Unauthorized Essays on Joss Whedon's Firefly Universe*, edited by Jane Espenson and Leah Wilson, 79–93. Dallas: BenBella Books, 2007.
Grenz, Stanley J. "What Does Hollywood Have to Do with Wheaton? The Place of (Pop) Culture in Theological Reflection." *Journal of the Evangelical Theological Society* 43, no. 2 (2000) 303–14.
Hall, Douglas John. "What Is Theology?" *Cross Currents* 53, no. 2 (2003) 171–84.
Hughes, David. *Comic Book Movies*. Virgin Film. London: Virgin, 2003.
Lynch, Gordon. *Understanding Theology and Popular Culture*. Malden, MA: Blackwell, 2005.
Marshall, C. W. and Matthew Wheeland. "The Cylons, the Singularity, and God." In *Cylons in America: Critical Studies in Battlestar Galactica*, edited by Tiffany Potter and C. W. Marshall, 91–104. New York: Continuum, 2008.
Marz, Ron, and Nelson Blake, II. *The Magdalena*. Los Angeles: Top Cow, 2010–12.
May, Stephen. *Stardust and Ashes: Science Fiction in Christian Perspective*. London: SPCK, 1998.
Newbigin, Lesslie. *Foolishness to the Greeks: The Gospel and Western Culture*. Grand Rapids: Eerdmans, 1986.
Nicieza, Fabian, and Allan Goldman. *Superman: Redemption*. New York: DC Comics, 2007.
Pears, Angela. *Doing Contextual Theology*. London: Routledge, 2010.
Riess, Jana. *What Would Buffy Do? The Vampire Slayer as Spiritual Guide*. San Francisco: Jossey-Bass, 2004.
Ross, Steve. *Blinded: The Story of Paul the Apostle*. New York: Seabury, 2008.

———. *Marked*. New York: Seabury, 2005.
Rushkoff, Douglas, and Liam Sharp. *Testament: Akedah*. New York: DC Comics, 2006.
Sfar, Joann. *The Rabbi's Cat*. New York: Pantheon, 2005.
Sherwood, Yvonne. *A Biblical Text and Its Afterlives: The Survival of Jonah in Western Culture*. Cambridge: Cambridge University Press, 2001.
Siku. *The Manga Bible: NT-Extreme*. London: Hodder and Stoughton, 2007.
Tanner, Kathryn. "The Difference Theological Anthropology Makes." *Theology Today* 50, no. 4 (1994) 567–79.
The Naked Samoans, and Firehorse Films. *Bro'Town*. Auckland: Firehorse Films, 2004–09.
Thompson, Craig. *Blankets: An Illustrated Novel*. Marietta, GA: Top Shelf, 2003.
Vanhoozer, Kevin J. "What Is Everyday Theology? How and Why Christians Should Read Culture." In *Everyday Theology: How to Read Cultural Texts and Interpret Trends*, edited by Kevin J. Vanhoozer et al., 15–60. Grand Rapids: Baker Academic, 2007.

12

The Goldilocks Planet—When It's Just Not Right

Psalm 24, The Environment, and Human Responsibility

DAVID J. COHEN

Introduction

THE MAJESTY OF PSALM 24 is self-evident to any who read, pray, or sing it. Striking in its all-encompassing vista, the psalm offers some probing theological insights at both cosmic and personal levels. Though deeply doxological in its view of God, the psalm moves beyond the vision of a praised cosmic warrior,[1] who brings order out of chaos, inviting a thoughtful human response to this divine reality. The psalm culminates rather paradoxically with an eschatological vision of Yahweh on the move, the one who possesses creation, being welcomed into creation by those who have been created. But could it be, that in the interim, humankind has been invited to undertake a significant role in the development of creation leading up to the eschatological culmination described at the end of Psalm 24?

As humankind has embarked on another millennium of being on earth it has become increasingly clear that all is just *not* right on our "Goldilocks

---

1. Bergant, "Earth," 72.

planet."[2] A careful reading of Psalm 24 brings to light some significant insights for Christians both individually and collectively as we live in times of climate change and the resultant environmental issues never before confronted. As people of faith it challenges us to step outside, beyond the four walls of our church buildings, in cooperation with one another and with the God of creation. First, the psalm invites us to explore how we understand God as the agent of creation. Second, it offers a vision of humankind as coagent (with God) in creation and, finally, the psalm reaches a climax where God is envisaged as the agent of the eschaton. Each of these insights implicitly, and at times explicitly, raises questions about our fundamental understanding of the relationship between God, creation, and humankind and, from this, a clearer vision emerges of dynamic divine engagement with our world. But we also discover our responsibility as human beings to ensure dynamic human engagement with creation as an expressed response to divine activity. I will argue that in being aware of this dynamic process we are invited, and enabled, to become fully human as we live, love, and work in relationship with God, ourselves, others, and the environment. Clearly this work extends beyond the four walls of the church.

Before exploring the issues identified above in detail it is important to sketch briefly the possible historical contexts of Psalm 24 and highlight some literary considerations relevant to this exploration. Both aspects deepen our appreciation of the psalm as a profound liturgical statement, a carefully crafted piece of literature, and also alert us to the psalm's clarion call for human response to both God and the environment.

The genre of Psalm 24 is often identified as an "entrance liturgy"[3] creating an inclusio with Psalm 15, as a psalm of the same genre.[4] Gerstenberger prefers the more general classification of "entrance liturgy" over some earlier suggestions arguing for specific cultic contexts.[5] In considering the idea of "entrance liturgy," which now seems generally agreed upon by more recent scholarship, there are those who then want to expand the idea of "entrance liturgy" to include a remembrance of the ark of the covenant's entry into Jerusalem.[6] Despite these suggestions, a simple reading of the

2. NASA Science, "Goldilocks Zone."
3. McCann, "Book of Psalms," 732, 772.
4. Miller, "Kingship," 279–97. Miller provides a starting point for this kind of study.
5. Gerstenberger, *Psalms: Part 1*, 119. By "entrance liturgy" Gerstenberger has in mind an entrance procession to the temple. He also discusses the views of Gunkel, Mowinckel, and Kraus in particular but surmises that there is scant evidence for concrete conclusions to be drawn.
6. Westermann, *Living Psalms*, 277. Westermann makes the connection between this psalm and 2 Samuel 6.

psalm itself suggests very little concerning its initial, or ongoing, cultic setting. One could suggest a historical allusion with the title *l^e dāwîd* although, again, this is not liturgical instruction and its historical value is arguable. Speculations about specific cultic contexts aside, one issue is clear. The inclusion of Psalm 24 in the Psalter implies *some kind* of cultic usage and significance. While the original setting of the psalm may be indeterminate, the ongoing employment of this psalm as a part of Israel's cultic practice remains a given. This leads Eaton to conclude that, "Such psalms were thus not merely songs incidental to ceremonies, but texts which carried worship forward and unfolded the meaning of the rites."[7] They formed a part of Israel's hermeneutic of life as they attempted to make sense of themselves and their world. The Christian tradition has continued the practice in the case of Psalm 24 by incorporating it into the church's liturgy for Ascension Day.

In addition to questions about cultic setting, the literary form of Psalm 24 has generated much discussion. A superficial reading of it suggests a rather disjointed amalgam of three disparate sets of ideas. The way in which this psalm evolved into its final form is unclear. However, we now have a literary whole and are left to make sense of the content *as a whole*. Mays discusses the issue at length and reaches the conclusion that "there is, however, a theological unity."[8] In doing this he reminds us that the psalm is presented as a whole in the text we possess and should be read as such. So, in summary, it is fair to say that Psalm 24 formed a part of the liturgical life of ancient Israel and possesses a theological unity from which a number of practical implications can be drawn.[9]

Yahweh as Agent and Owner of Creation (vv. 1–2)

There can be no doubt that God, in this case identified by use of the divine name Yahweh, is designated as both the agent behind and the owner

---

7. Eaton, *Psalms*, 126.

8. Mays, *Preaching and Teaching*, 153. He then describes how he sees this theological unity in the content saying, "Each of the parts of the psalm expresses a basic assumption that is integral to the entire Bible, and, so, to Christianity. First is that God has created the world and, therefore, is its Lord. The second is that we have to appear before God to be questioned, how it stands with our righteousness. The third is that God comes to his own and seeks entrance." I am not fully convinced of Mays's second point on the basis of this psalm despite the fact that it appears in other sections of Scripture.

9. I place liturgical function and practical implications together as a reflection of the Hebraic concept of worship which reflects life both inside and outside the temple/synagogue.

of creation.[10] The use of the divine name here is notable. It is not the more generic term ʾēl but, rather the Tetragrammaton indicating that the psalm is specifically designating Israel's God as creator and owner.[11] However, the idea here of Yahweh as agent and owner of creation is not predicated so much on the identity of this God.[12] Rather, it is predicated on what this God did in the act of creation. Vos observes the careful use of language in verses 1 and 2 saying that, "The use of poetic strategies serves to emphasize that the earth and the world are Yahweh's *carefully ordered creation.*"[13] This, of course, presents a contrasting view to commonly held beliefs in the ancient Near East about the dangerous unpredictability of creation and its perceived threat to human beings.[14] Bergant is even more forthright in her understanding of the divine imagery of a god who orders creation here in Psalm 24 calling God the "omnipotent . . . cosmic warrior."[15] While the vision of Yahweh presented here could be viewed as a contrast, or even a polemic directed towards existing ancient world beliefs, it also clearly emphasizes the psalmist's desire to affirm that Yahweh, Israel's God, is both the agent behind, and owner of, creation.[16] Mays concludes that "the [statement that the] Lord is owner is an intentional denial that anyone else is."[17] Ownership is not only exclusive to YHWH but is also all-encompassing. Wolf and Gjerris describe this all-encompassing divine ownership as one which reflects the "integrity" of creation or "an interpretation of the world which sees the world as a whole."[18] The link they make between an "integrated creation" and ownership by one god is a unique theological statement for the ancient world. It would have been profoundly significant for the way in which Israel

---

10. Goulder, "David and Yahweh," 470, draws an interesting comparison between the opening to this psalm and the opening of Psalm 23 noting that Psalm 23 emphasizes "Yahweh's providential guidance" while Psalm 24 emphasizes Yahweh as "creator and owner."

11. Contrast this to Psalm 19 which addresses similar issues but prefers the use of ĕlōhîm when speaking of God in relation to creation. It is only when the psalmist begins to raise the concept of tôrâ that the language shifts to YHWH.

12. Again, this is in contrast to Psalm 19 where no reason is given for God's glory being declared by creation.

13. Vos, *Theopoetry*, 144, emphasis added.

14. Vos, *Theopoetry*, 144. Vos goes on to discuss this perception at some length.

15. Bergant, "Earth," 72.

16. Mays, *Psalms*, 120. He discusses in some detail the idea of this psalm presenting a polemic against existing perceptions of creation, gods, power, and control in the ancient world.

17. Mays, *Psalms*, 120.

18. Wolf and Gjerris, "Religious Perspective," 130–31.

viewed and made sense of its world and is pregnant with significance for people of faith in today's world.

Contained within the psalm's affirmation declaring Yahweh as creator and owner is the presence of an interesting linguistic nuance. Gerstenberger makes the observation that the psalm begins with the preposition $λ^e$ which expresses the idea that "The earth . . . and all that is in it, the world, and all who live in it" are viewed as being "to Yahweh" or "for Yahweh."[19] Translated either way the implication is that while Yahweh is the *agent of* creation, creation is also relationally *connected to* Yahweh and/or creation is *for* Yahweh. Gerstenberger goes on to make the point that the placement of the preposition *before* the subject is unusual syntax.[20] With this nuance the psalmist has expressed two underpinning concepts for the Israelite worldview. First, that creation should be viewed primarily as being "for Yahweh" and not Yahweh being viewed primarily as "for creation." Second, accepting the principle that creation exists "for Yahweh," as the owner, implies some kind of ongoing divine interest and engagement with creation.[21] A worldview underpinned by these two principles challenges an anthropocentric view of creation, challenging any claims to outright ownership of, and therefore, unmitigated anthropogenic destruction of, creation by humankind.

In light of the relational connection between Yahweh and creation expressed in Psalm 24, one might well ask the question, "How does this relationship function?" Clifford suggests that,

> Nature is more than just the object of human duty . . . and it is not solely a vehicle for God's glory to be displayed [but] God working through and with nature to communicate with human beings.[22]

If creation is to be viewed as "for Yahweh," as suggested by the opening statement of Psalm 24, and Yahweh is relationally connected with creation, communicating through it as Clifford suggests, then humankind is left with an important question to answer. Are we listening to what creation is saying about God, humankind, and our relationship with God and the integrated

---

19. Gerstenberger, *Psalms*, 117. It should be noted here that we are speaking of verse 1 in English versions of the Bible rather than the Masoretic Text which considers the title to be verse 1.

20. Gerstenberger, *Psalms*, 117.

21. This is based on the concept that by owning something the owner is, self-evidently, concerned with and interested in that which is owned. This principle, in relation to God, is clear throughout both the Hebrew Bible and the New Testament.

22. Clifford, "All Creation," 7. Cf. Psalm 19:1–6.

creation of which Wolf and Gjerris speak?²³ A further question might be, "What are God and creation together saying to us as humankind?"²⁴

So here the paradox of divine being beyond creation and yet divine presence in creation comes into sharp focus. Psalm 24 concurrently expresses a transcendent view of God *over creation* and an immanent view of God in ongoing relationship *with creation*. In a general way Mays responds to the questions posed above by saying, "the one who is beyond our world is the final truth and meaning to all that is in it."²⁵ From here then, we journey into the territory of human response to God and the environment on the basis of understanding Yahweh as the agent and owner of creation.

Humankind as Coagents of Creation (vv. 3–6)

For people of Judeo-Christian heritage, the view of God espoused by the opening verses of Psalm 24 together with many other sections in both the Hebrew Bible and the New Testament ought to evoke a positive response. The psalmist anticipates this response by moving dramatically from the cosmic vista of verses one and two to the hands, heart, and soul of the person of faith. The action of "going up" and "standing" in verse three echoes the practice of the community going up to the temple in Jerusalem, which symbolized the presence of Yahweh amid the faith community. The temple was a place of worship and sacrifice, possible within the context of covenant relationship. It was a place where sins could be forgiven, and thanks could be expressed. Brueggemann views the poetic images of clean hands and pure heart together with the idea of going up to the temple in terms of *tôrâ* obedience saying that, "they [Psalms 15 and 24] suggest that only the obedient persons may enter into God's presence. But it is important to recall that this spirituality reflects only a *well-oriented community*."²⁶

It is arguable whether a "well-oriented community" is *all* that Psalm 24:3–6 reflects but Brueggemann's concept is nonetheless helpful. If the community of faith becomes well-oriented towards Yahweh in the context of cultic practice within the temple then this can serve as a motivator to live differently outside the temple. Mays makes the observation that, "What has been made holy is marked off from everything else by its identification

---

23. Wolf and Gjerris, "Religious Perspective," 130–31.
24. Cohen, "Journey to Center," 15–35. In this chapter I discuss the issue of God's communication through creation in some depth.
25. Mays, *Preaching and Teaching*, 153.
26. Brueggemann, *Message*, 42. Emphasis added.

with God."²⁷ His observation highlights the relational connection between Yahweh and creation (in this case, specifically with humankind) and also the prerequisites for those who not only exist within covenant relationship with God (a given in the broader context of Psalm 24) but have also been set apart *for* Yahweh to accomplish Yahweh's purposes in the world. McCann makes the astute observation that "praise involves 'activity' as well as 'identity.' Indeed, it is impossible and undesirable to separate these concepts too sharply."²⁸ Another way of conceptualizing McCann's idea is that the people envisaged in Psalm 24 will act according to their identity as opposed to their actions creating an identity for them.²⁹

Out of the affirmation of identity found in Yahweh's presence and the reorientation experienced by the community through cultic practice, the motivation to live differently emerges, acknowledging that while the temple is at the center of the community of faith it is not the place where the people live. The temple was a place to go up to and also a place to return from into everyday life. But are affirmation of identity and reorientation the only things carried down from the temple? The answer to this is both yes and no! Verse five is rather ambiguous in its language and yet deeply profound. It could be translated "He will receive blessing from the Lord and vindication from the God who saves him," which reflects the majority of English versions. Alternatively, it could be translated as "He will carry³⁰ blessing from the Lord and rightness³¹ from the God who saves him." The second is a more literal translation which I argue captures both the Hebrew and the broader context of the verse in Psalm 24.

The ambiguity in the Hebrew means that each English attempt above presents quite a different stance for the person of faith. The first reflects one who *receives in* Yahweh's presence while the second reflects one who *carries*

---

27. Mays, *Psalms*, 121.

28. McCann, *Theological Introduction*, 71.

29. This is a fundamental understanding of the nature of covenant in the Hebrew Bible.

30. The verb *nāśā* is more naturally translated "carry" or "bear" given the imagery of hands and the actions of lifting up (same verb two times) in v. 4. The LXX uses *lambanō* which emphasizes the action of "receiving" *and*, beyond that, also the action of "taking." An extensive discussion of the meaning/s of *lambanō* can be found in Delling, "λαμβάνω."

31. Goldingay, *Psalms*, 360, argues convincingly against the translation of *ṣᵉdāqā* as "vindication" and prefers "mercy" (as expressed in the LXX). Although this is helpful, my usage of "rightness" incorporates the idea of Brueggemann's "well-oriented community," and, notwithstanding its shortcomings as a plain English translation, I would argue that the word "rightness" is helpful in this context.

from[32] Yahweh's presence. Perhaps the ambiguity is appropriate in that both apply. However, given a covenantal understanding which is founded on identity *and* activity, as expressed above, I suggest that the second reading is more appropriate. Goldingay reinforces this view by concluding that, "Blessing characteristically refers to God's involvement in the everyday recurrences of life, making it fruitful."[33]

What might this "blessing" and "rightness," which Israel carries from the Lord, look like? I suggest that it might have been a life which reflected the character of the God Israel worshipped. This raises a further question: "What does a God characterized by blessing and rightness look like?" This question, in part, takes us back to the imagery of Yahweh's dominance over the seas and rivers found in verse 2. Given the fear, in the ancient world, of the seas, this divine dominance could be viewed as an ordering of chaos. In fact the imagery echoes the first creation account in which "the earth was a formless void and darkness covered the face of the deep, while a wind from God swept over the face of the waters" (Gen 1:2).[34] Again the idea of a god ordering the chaos is unique to Israel and their belief in Yahweh. Le Mon states that "Israel's testimony that *Yahweh* created order from chaos stood in direct opposition to myths of other ancient Near Eastern peoples."[35] The kind of language and imagery here is indicative of divine power and control *over* creation. While it may not be difficult for some to envisage God with this kind of influence over creation, any description of human beings as coagents with Yahweh acting with power and control over creation evokes some strong responses.[36] Habel, for example, classifies Genesis 1 where it speaks of "subdue" and "have dominion" as "grey texts" which remain difficult to understand and even more difficult to enact.[37] As a counterview Le Mon argues that "God's creation is also an act of ordering, and it is *incumbent upon God's people* to promote the order God establishes."[38] It is a fair observation by Habel that historically this "incumbency" has often been misunderstood and abused by people of faith and others.[39] But should we,

32. Cf. also *JPS Hebrew-English Tanakh* which translates it as "he will carry away."

33. Goldingay, *Psalms*, 360.

34. As a further example, Job 38:8–11 also expresses the idea of order from chaos in the context of creation.

35. LeMon, "Psalm 24," 106.

36. Micah Challenge, "Theology," 7. Here the writers seem to view the concepts of "subdue" and "have dominion" (Gen 1:28) as pejorative and redefine the role as "gardeners."

37. Habel, *Inconvenient Text*, 7.

38. LeMon, "Psalm 24," 106, emphasis added.

39. Habel, *Inconvenient Text*, 7.

on this basis, dismiss the whole idea of humankind taking a coagent role with Yahweh in creation?

One response to this question is captured well by Hauerwas and Willimon when they observe that, "We can only act within that world which we can see. So the primary ethical question is not, What ought I now to do? but rather, How does the world really look?"[40] Following on from this the next question might be, "What *could* the world look like?" For people of faith this question takes us back to God and *God's view* of how the world should look.[41] Reifsnyder says, "It is the psalmist's conviction that ethics flows from and depends on our perspective on reality. Clear-sighted understanding of who God is and confidence in God's reign shape the psalmist's ethical choices."[42]

The logic proceeds as follows: Through relationship with God human beings progressively discover what God is like and how God originally intended creation to function. From this the "blessing" and "rightness" is discovered for the self and for the whole of creation. This is then carried by the individual and the community of faith into the world as a mandate to bless and reorient creation (rightness). Through such a process people of faith act as coagents with Yahweh in creating what God intended for both humankind and the rest of creation. Admittedly this kind of human power and control (reflected in the terms, "subdue" and "have dominion" found in Gen 1:28) is open to abuse and has been abused historically. Nonetheless the examples of abuse do not invalidate the ideal.

The psalmist clearly states in verse six that "This is the generation who seeks him [God]." The universality of the descriptor cannot be ignored here.[43] While the vision of God and God's people may begin with Israel it certainly does not end there. In keeping with the opening to Psalm 24 the coagency of God with humankind is not limited to ethnic groupings, with God's ultimate goal being for the whole of humankind to carry "blessing" and "rightness" into creation.[44]

In sum then, the middle section of Psalm 24 presents a vision of humankind working as coagents with God in creating what God intended. This coagency, however, is not something which begins with, nor is it entirely dependent on, humankind; it begins with, and is ultimately dependent on, God. As human beings grasp the character, nature, and vision of God

---

40. Hauerwas and Willimon, *Resident Aliens*, 88.
41. See, for example, Gen 1 and 2; Isa 61; Matt 5; Rev 21.
42. Reifsnyder, "Psalm 24," 286.
43. Vos, *Theopoetry*, 146.
44. Vos, *Theopoetry*, 146.

they carry the blessing and the "rightness" of God into a world desperate for restoration. In Craigie's words, "the motifs of order and chaos are transformed into moral concepts, *good* and *evil*."[45] It challenges people of faith to know the difference between good and evil and to live ethically and morally in relation to the environment. However, it is fascinating to observe that Psalm 24 moves beyond the vision of humankind as coagents with Yahweh in creation to present Yahweh as the agent of the eschaton.

Yahweh as Agent of the Eschaton (vv. 7–10)

The final section of Psalm 24 combines a sense of occasion, proclamation, and imminence primarily by employing an antiphony between imperatives and interrogatives, and emphatically reinforcing the opening verses of the psalm creating a theological inclusio. However, even a cursory examination of verses 7–10 reveals intrinsic qualities of incongruity and oddity in its antiphony.

The incongruity is found most distinctly in the predicate to the imperative found in both verses 7 and 9. "Lift up your heads, O gates! and be lifted up, O ancient doors! *that the King of glory may come in*."[46] Why would it be stated *"that the King of glory may come in"*? Has the psalm not already affirmed that the earth and all that is in it is "the Lord's"? But the incongruity harbors a mystery. While the psalm does clearly affirm Yahweh's *ownership of* all creation and does affirm Yahweh's *power over* all creation, a role for humankind is evident in opening the gate to divine presence *in* creation. Vos states that, "In this psalm, God stands outside the gate, not as a threat but as a welcome arrival. He is seeking access to the center of his own world—the sanctuary from which, blessings are disseminated to all parts of the world."[47]

Vos's observation captures the essence of Psalm 24 as an expression of worship within the cultic construct of ancient Israel. The imperatives can be viewed as recognizing the reality of divine presence in the form of a liturgical "welcome" by the community of faith.[48] Does this suggest that

45. Craigie, *Psalms 1–50*, 212.

46. NRSV with emphasis added. The NRSV assumes the jussive form of *bôʾ* along with TNIV, ESV, NJB, TNK, et al. Interestingly the NET translation renders *bôʾ* as an imperfect which is also allowable. The NET translation concurs with the LXX on this point.

47. Vos, *Theopoetry*, 152.

48. This can be experienced in many Christian communities of faith where the Holy Spirit is "welcomed" through song, prayer, or other means even though the New Testament clearly affirms the presence of the Spirit with the church gathered.

divine presence and activity in creation is contingent upon humankind opening the gate and welcoming the King of glory? That question cannot be answered categorically. It is part of the mystery. However, the question does underscore the concept of human coagency discussed earlier. Divine entry into creation, at least as perceived from a human perspective, comes first and foremost through the acknowledgement of Yahweh by the faith community.

An oddity is also present at the close of this psalm in the form of a repeated question. "Who is this?" Surely the psalm has already clearly indicated that *this* is "the Lord." But the response to the question presents us with fascinating images of the *nature* of this Lord. Mays, in his commentary on the Psalter, notes the uniqueness of the title "King of Glory," linking it to the use of "God of Glory" found in Psalm 29:3. In both cases the psalms clarify this concept with images of a divine warrior in battle.[49] Goldingay concludes that these kinds of questions are "often . . . a question about the world's security."[50] So, where is security found in an insecure world for people of faith? Vos states categorically that the "emphasis fall[s] on the identity, the glory, and the might of Yahweh."[51] These are significant observations. The psalmist emphasizes clearly that creation is primarily "to" or "for" Yahweh. The primary relationship for God is between creation and Godself. God is willing to work with humankind in creating but there is a divine prerogative beyond this partnership which will culminate in a new creation.[52]

While we are presented with an incongruity and an oddity in verses 7–10 which initially may be confusing, they can be viewed as expanding the purview of the community of faith beyond the present to see this "King of glory" as the initiator of the eschaton. In employing the imagery of divine warrior in these final verses together with the imagery of verses 1 and 2 we encounter a God who both initiated and will ultimately culminate creation.[53]

49. Mays, *Psalms*, 121. The phrase "King of glory" is only found in this exact form in this psalm.

50. Goldingay, *Psalms*, 357.

51. Vos, *Theopoetry*, 142.

52. The imagery of divine warrior used here should not be interpreted as suggesting a form of violence but, rather, one which emphasizes the power of this divine warrior to bring creation to its intended culmination as a strong human warrior might ultimately impose his/her will on an enemy.

53. Wright, *Don't Understand*, 166, contrasts an ancient understanding of eschatology and some contemporary Christian views suggesting that the expected coming of Christ, for Christians, should be viewed as "believers welcoming their Lord on his return to his rightful place as Lord and King of the whole earth." This New Testament

Holding such a perspective on creation placed Israel in a unique situation. It is a tension and a tenuous tension at that. The tension found in Psalm 24 lies in a recognition of divine activity in coagency with humankind while at the same time wanting to acknowledge the way in which divine power transcends that of humankind. It is a tenuous tension because Israel could have been tempted to view this divine warrior as one who would impose the divine will on creation irrespective of human response. In this case Israel could consider their responsibility to creation abrogated in the light of irresistible divine will. However, this does not appear to be the case, at least in terms of covenant, where human responsibility encompasses care and concern for all of creation.[54] A second temptation may have been for Israel to take up their responsibility of caring for creation as a way of trying to manipulate Yahweh to provide for them. Although perhaps attractive to Israel, given their ancient Near Eastern cultural context, there is little, if any, evidence to suggest that care for creation was ever used as leverage for divine favor.

In spite of, or perhaps because of, the temptations and the tension inherent between divine and human wills, the ideas were ensconced in the cultic practice of ancient Israel utilizing psalms such as Psalm 24. The repeated use of psalms like this in the liturgy reinforced both divine prerogative and the importance of human responsibilities before Yahweh. Craigie summarizes this well when he concludes:

> The kingship of the Lord is not merely a religious affirmation—it is the basis for worship and praise. Those who worship are those who recognize the kingship, who accept the rule of the sovereign God. But the genius of the psalm lies in the linking together of cosmological belief and historical experience . . . From the perspective of cosmology, the world is created and thus represents order; that order was established by God the king. But historical experience, characterized by war and conflict, suggests a different reality, namely that the world is marked by chaos. The psalm offers a resolution of the dilemma.[55]

For Craigie then, the resolution of chaos is firmly and ultimately within the domain of divine action. Hence, Yahweh is the God of the eschaton.

---

image reinforces this concept of Yahweh, as agent of the eschaton, as creation is culminated in a decisive and definitive manner.

54. E.g. Lev 25:4–7. It must be acknowledged here that there may well have been a divergence between covenant requirements and the actual practices of the people in this regard.

55. Craigie, *Psalms 1–50*, 214.

However, this does not, by definition, preclude the coagency of humankind with God in moving towards a new creation which will ultimately be an eschatological reality as we are "invite[d] to enter the extraordinary new world of God's reign."[56]

Conclusion

I conclude now with some reflections on the responsibilities we have to the whole of creation as people of faith based on the exploration of Psalm 24. While I am reflecting on the issues primarily from a Christian perspective, I also acknowledge the importance of this text to the other two great monotheistic religions of Judaism and Islam, humbly suggesting that some of the implications from the text may well relate to people of those traditions as well, as they live out their faith in response to God.

In a faith context it is clear from Psalm 24 that any discussion of the environment begins and ends with the clear understanding that God is the one who brought creation about and the one who has ultimate ownership of the whole. On this basis it must be acknowledged that responses to the environment by people of faith cannot exclude God from considerations. The psalm also precludes a view which might allow people of faith to abrogate their responsibility to the environment. If God owns all creation, and we are God's people, then caring for and conserving the environment is a natural corollary. While people of all faiths and people of no faith might share a concern for the environment, Psalm 24 provides a clear articulation of why people of faith *should care*. Morrison puts it well when he suggests that:

> The world must take responsibility for the well-being of the environment. But my problem is precisely this: we are focused on an object rather than a subject. The work of caring for the environment depends first on the love of one's neighbor and in more hidden ways, on the love for God.[57]

The subject is always God. Genesis 1:1 affirms this with the resounding announcement, "In the beginning God . . ." Everything else flows from this reality. A focus on God as the subject has the additional effect of challenging an anthropocentric view of creation. It reminds humankind what we are and what we are not. As David Suzuki said in a radio interview in 2010, "We are trying to be gods but we don't know how to be gods."[58]

56. McCann, "Book of Psalms," 774.
57. Morrison, "Thinking Otherwise," 5.
58. ABC, "The Legacy."

If Psalm 24 ended at this point it could be tempting to leave the fate of the environment and everything else in the hands of the creator. After all, if God is the agent and owner, why would any form of human responsibility or response be necessary? Here lies the mystery with which this psalm attempts to grapple. A divine-human partnership is imagined where we, as divine image bearers,[59] carry blessing and a mandate to put the world right, *together with God*. As people of faith we care for the environment *because* God cares. The way in which we care for the environment should reflect God's creative activity woven through the fabric of Scripture. From a Christian perspective Spencer argues that: "Christians should care for creation because it has an eternal destiny in Christ: it will be transformed along with our own bodies in the new creation, and the work we do now to shape and to care for the world is of eternal significance."[60]

This is a profound statement of substance for the present and hope for the future. While some might argue that we need to care for creation for the sake of generations to come (and this is most certainly a meaningful response), people of faith have an added horizon of "eternal significance." The role of humankind as coagents in restoring creation is clear from Psalm 24 and is found throughout the pages of both the Hebrew Bible and the New Testament.

This leads us to reflect finally on the conclusion to Psalm 24 and the idea of Yahweh as the agent of the eschaton. In considering this idea the words of David Suzuki quoted earlier echo strongly: "We are trying to be gods but we don't know how to be gods." While there is most definitely a role for humankind to play as coagents with God, Psalm 24 clearly affirms that ultimately creation's emergence and creation's destiny lie with God. While we work with God, we are not God, and there are some tasks which only God can complete. This is the tension which was present for ancient Israel and persists today for people of faith. The question is, "Do we fall to the temptation of abrogating our responsibility and wait for divine intervention or do we take seriously the mandate embedded in the creation stories to work with God in bringing order out of chaos?" We are called to respond to this question both individually and collectively. Spencer captures the tension Christians live with when he concludes by saying: "Christians are called to live in a way that announces the future kingdom of God, and to model the reality that, at least in part, the kingdom of God is here already, while

---

59. Spencer, *Christianity*, 81. Taking up the idea of being image bearers Spencer categorically states, "Why care? Because it is part of what it means to be human."

60. Spencer, *Christianity*, 75.

realizing that it will be brought about completely by the decisive intervention of Christ's return."[61]

In an emphatic manner Psalm 24 presents a fresh vision for the faith community beyond its four walls demonstrating that divine concern for, and engagement with the whole world, is fundamentally God's prerogative but not God's alone. The outworking of this divine prerogative is provocatively invitational. It sounds a clarion call for the church to reflect on what a truly divine-human partnership looks like in carrying blessing and rightness into a Goldilocks world that is just *not* right, *yet*. Psalm 24 reflects both liturgical and missional actions as the church confronts the spiritual, sociological, and environmental challenges facing us in the twenty-first century. All that remains is the challenge to embrace this narrative as both gathered and scattered communities living out our faith in recognition of our role *with* God in creation.

Bibliography

Alter, Robert. *The Book of Psalms: A Translation with Commentary*. New York: W. W. Norton, 2007.

ABC. "The Legacy: An Elder's Vision for Our Sustainable Future." *Mornings with Margaret Throsby*. ABC Classic FM, December 15, 2010.

Bergant, Dianne. "'The Earth is the Lord's': A Biblical Reflection on Psalm 24:1." *Mission Studies* 15, no. 2 (1998) 66–74.

Brueggemann, Walter. *The Message of the Psalms: A Theological Commentary*. Augsburg Old Testament Studies. Minneapolis: Augsburg, 1984.

Clifford, Paula. "'All Creation Groaning': A Theological Approach to Climate Change." *Christian Aid*. https://www.christianaid.org.uk/sites/default/files/2017-08/all-creation-groaning-theological-approach-climate-change-development-june-2007.pdf.

Cohen, David. "Journey to the Center of the Heart: Psalm 19 as Transformation." In *In Praise of Worship: An Exploration of Text and Practice*, edited by David J. Cohen and Michael Parsons, 15–35. Eugene, OR: Pickwick Publications, 2010.

Cooper, Alan. "Psalm 24:7–10: Mythology and Exegesis." *Journal of Biblical Literature* 102, no. 1 (1983) 37–60.

Craigie, Peter C. *Psalms 1–50*. Word Biblical Commentary. Waco: Word, 1983.

Delling, Gerhard. "λαμβάνω." *Theological Dictionary of the New Testament*. Grand Rapids: Eerdmans, 1967.

Eaton, J. H. *The Psalms: A Historical and Spiritual Commentary*. London: T. & T. Clark, 2005.

Evangelical Alliance. "Christians and Climate Change." *EA*, n.d. http://www.ea.org.au/site/DefaultSite/filesystem/documents/public%20policy/Climate%20Change.pdf.

Feuer, Avrohom Chaim. *Tehillim/Psalms 2 Volume Set: A New Translation with a Commentary Anthologized from Talmudic, Midrashic, and Rabbinic Sources*. New York: ArtScroll, Mesorah, 1986.

---

61. Spencer, *Christianity*, 94.

Fretheim, Terence E. "The Color of God: Israel's God-talk and Life Experience." *Word and World* 6, no. 3 (1986) 256–65.

Gerstenberger, Erhard. *Psalms: Part 1, With an Introduction to Cultic Poetry*. The Forms of the Old Testament Literature. Grand Rapids: Eerdmans, 1988.

Goldingay, John. *Psalms*. Grand Rapids: Baker Academic, 2006.

Goulder, Michael. "David and Yahweh in Psalms 23 and 24." *Journal for the Study of the Old Testament* 30, no. 4 (2006) 463–73.

Grogan, Geoffrey. *Psalms*. The Two Horizons Old Testament Commentary. Grand Rapids: Eerdmans, 2008.

Habel, Norman. *An Inconvenient Text: Is a Green Reading of the Bible Possible?* Adelaide: ATF Press, 2009.

Hauerwas, Stanley, and William H. Willimon. *Resident Aliens: Life in the Christian Colony*. Nashville: Abingdon, 1989.

Howell, James C. "The Psalms in Worship and Preaching: A Report." In *Psalms and Practice: Worship, Virtue, and Authority*, edited by Stephen Breck Reid, 123–42. Collegeville, Minn: Liturgical Press, 2001.

Hunter, Alastair G. "'The Righteous Generation': The Use of DÔR in Psalms 14 and 24." In *Reflection and Refraction*, edited by Robert Retzenko et al., 187–205. Leiden: Brill, 2006.

LeMon, Joel M. "Psalm 24." In *Psalms for Preaching and Worship: A Lectionary Commentary*, edited by Roger Van Harn and Brent A. Strawn, 105–8. Grand Rapids: Eerdmans, 2009.

Mays, James Luther. *Preaching and Teaching the Psalms*. Louisville: Westminster John Knox, 2006.

———. *Psalms*. Louisville: Westminster John Knox, 1994.

Mazor, Yair. "Psalm 24: Sense and Sensibility in Biblical Composition." *Scandinavian Journal of The Old Testament* 7, no. 2 (1993), 303–16.

McCann, J. Clinton. "The Book of Psalms." In *New Interpreter's Bible: 1 and 2 Maccabees, Job, Psalms*, edited by Robert Doran et al. Nashville: Abingdon, 1996.

———. *A Theological Introduction to the Book of Psalms: The Psalms as Torah*. Nashville: Abingdon, 1993.

Micah Challenge. "Theology of Climate Change." May 2009. http://www.micahchallenge.org.au/assets/pdf/Theology-of-climate-change.pdf.

Miller, Patrick D. "Kingship, Torah Obedience, and Prayer: The Theology of Psalms 15–24." In *Neue Wege der Psalmenforschung*, edited by Klaus Seybold and Erich Zenger, 127–42. Herders Biblische Studien. Freiburg: Herder, 1994.

Morrison, Glenn. "Thinking Otherwise: Theology, Inculturation and Climate Change." *Australian eJournal of Theology*, no. 16 (2010). http://researchonline.nd.edu.au/theo_article/69.

NASA Science. "The Goldilocks Zone." *Science News*. http://science.nasa.gov/science-news/science-at-nasa/2003/02oct_goldilocks/.

Newbigin, Lesslie. *The Gospel in a Pluralist Society*. Grand Rapids: Eerdmans, 1989.

Poorthuis, Marcel. "King Solomon and Psalms 72 and 24 in the Debate between Jews and Christians." In *Jewish and Christian Liturgy and Worship*, edited by Albert Gerhards and Clemens Leonhard, 257–78. Boston: Brill, 2007.

Pope, Mick, and Brian Edgar. "EA Climate Change—Problem or Opportunity?" *EA*, n.d. http://www.ea.org.au/site/DefaultSite/filesystem/documents/public%20policy/Climate%20Change%20-%20Problem%20or%20Opportunity.pdf.

Reifsnyder, Richard W. "Psalm 24." *Interpretation* 51, no. 3 (1997) 284–88.
Spencer, Nick. *Christianity, Climate Change and Sustainable Living*. Illustrated ed. London: Society for Promoting Christian Knowledge, 2007.
Steussy, Marti J. "Psalms." In *Chalice Introduction to the Old Testament*, edited by Marti J. Steussy, 183–208. St. Louis: Chalice, 2003.
Vallianatos, Angelos. "Creation, Koinonia, Sustainability and Climate Change." *Ecumenical Review* 49, no. 2 (1997) 194–202.
Vos, C. J. A. *Theopoetry of the Psalms*. Pretoria: Protea, 2005.
Westermann, Claus. *The Living Psalms*. Edinburgh: T. &T. Clark, 1989.
Wolf, Jakob, and Mickey Gjerris. "A Religious Perspective on Climate Change." *Studia Theologica* 63, no. 2 (2009) 119–39.
World Wildlife Fund. *Does the World Believe that Climate Change Exists?* July 20, 2006. http://wwf.org.au/articles/interview-with-tim-flannery/.
Wright, Christopher J. H. *The God I Don't Understand: Reflections on Tough Questions of Faith*. Grand Rapids: Zondervan, 2008.

13

Atonement and Church

Scot McKnight

Missionaries

THREE FACTS, ONCE CLEAR in our minds, revolutionized a segment of Judaism to become what we now call Christianity. Long ago, in the generation before this one, Judaism was considered a missionary religion. In fact, the first century was considered the missionary age of Judaism *par excellence*. Such a viewpoint was routinely claimed by no less than the German scholar Joachim Jeremias, but he was either standing on the shoulders of others, like Bernard J. Bamberger, W. G. Braude, Karl Georg Kuhn, and G. F. Moore, or his line of thinking was being developed by the next generation of German scholars, like Dieter Georgi.

But this conclusion has been all but disproven to the point that now the consensus is that Judaism at the time of Jesus, Peter, and Paul *was not a missionary religion* in the way Christianity became a missionary religion. This conclusion has been established by a number of scholars, including Martin Goodman of Oxford, Michael Bird in Australia (though he wrote the book while in Scotland), and if I may stake a claim in this, by a study I published in 1991 called *A Light Among the Gentiles*. In the last two decades the former consensus has been overturned, and while some are stronger in the denial than others, and while there are nuances to be grown on each textual flower, the fact is that Judaism was not a missionary religion and

Christianity became such, and Peter in Acts 10–11 and Paul in his Aegean mission are the originators of evangelizing the Roman empire.

Judaism, to be sure, had pockets of presence all over the Roman Empire but the practice of evangelizing in order to convert into a universal faith was so rare that one can only say they were exceptions to the general absence of missionary concerns among the Jews. But where then did the Christians, like Peter and Paul, get not only the idea but the *chutzpah* to evangelize through synagogues and then form *ecclesia* that increasingly became gentile? All sorts of explanations have been offered, none of which need to be taken as the singlemost factor, but they include Jesus's own table fellowship practice in Galilee, the Great Commission (though never once quoted outside its single occurrences in Matthew and Luke), the power of Pentecost, the decisive impact of persecution, and just the sheer rethinking of Israel's Scriptures by the apostles.

But what concerns us are not the specific historical conclusions we may wish to draw. What concerns us is *missionary activity itself*, and that begins with Jesus. There are two notable "missions" by Jesus: he sent out the Twelve, now recorded in Mark 6, Matthew 10, and Luke 9, and then later sent out the seventy (or seventy-two) in Luke 10. The Great Commission involves a sending, and John's famous line "As the Father has sent me, so I am sending you" (John 20:21) also confirms this. The early Christians had a conviction to go out, and a set of beliefs that compelled them to go out, and to tell others the gospel.

The Very Presence of Jesus

Now for a second fact, and this one and the next one will be briefer for fear that this, like a German monograph, will be mostly methodology, prolegomena, and bibliography. There's a word of Jesus in the Gospel of Matthew that staggers me every time I read it. In preparing the Twelve for their mission to fellow Jews, Jesus said this:

> Anyone who welcomes you welcomes me, and anyone who welcomes me welcomes the one who sent me. Whoever welcomes someone known to be a prophet will receive a prophet's reward, and whoever welcomes someone known to be righteous will receive a righteous person's reward. And if anyone gives even a cup of cold water to one of these little ones who is known to be my disciple, truly I tell you, that person will certainly be rewarded. (Matt 10:40–42)

In addition to this, is "Mother Teresa's gospel" in Matthew 25:40: "The King will reply, 'Truly I tell you, whatever you did for one of the least of these brothers and sisters of mine, you did for me.'"

While I'm not convinced this has to do with visiting orphans in Zimbabwe who have never heard the gospel but is instead about Jesus's missionaries, the general point can now be drawn: *Jesus believed his own presence was extended in his followers, wherever they were, and whenever they were doing his kingdom ministries.*

There's nothing quite like this in Judaism, though there is the famous rabbinic line that "the one sent is as the one who sent him," a comment about ambassadors in *Mishnah Berakot* 5:5. Which now leads me to the third fact.

Temple

Judaism at the time of Jesus was marked by a common theological idea of the ancient Near East. God was located in a shrine. For Judaism (while there are clear exceptions to the belief that God can be contained in a dwelling) believed that YHWH dwelt in the temple above the old city of David. That *shekinah* was gloriously obvious during the kingdom of Solomon and was ingloriously dethroned in the Babylonian captivity in 587 BC, and that glory never fully returned. Hence, Tom Wright made famous the notion that Israel was still in captivity and the exile was not yet over, so long as that glory had not returned to Israel, until the king returned to Zion. Whether you buy into his very suggestive idea that Jesus's triumphal entry was in fact that Zecharian return of the king to the temple, or not, there can be very little disagreement that *Jesus and the earliest followers of Jesus had some very unusual ideas about both the temple and the presence of God.*

St. Stephen, with his feet to the fire and emboldened beyond measure to recapture Israel's history in a gospel-ish reading of the Bible, slips in near the end of his sermon and in the climactic conclusion to his sketch of history these words: "However, the Most High does not live in houses made by human hands" (Acts 7:48). He pulls in a passage from the messianists' favorite prophet, Isaiah, that announces, "Heaven is my throne, and the earth my footstool. What kind of house will you build for me?" (7:49). Thereafter Stephen accuses his hearers and they put him death. Many of us then see the presence of Saul, or Paul, and we forget the powerful counter-theology of Stephen: he sketched history to make one point: God does not dwell in a house made by humans.

Of course, there were other critics of the temple, not the least of whom is the community that took up residence at that hot and dusty Qumran awaiting the apocalyptic act of God to destroy the wicked priest in Jerusalem and reinstate a proper priest which meant that they—the Essenes—would be vindicated as the truly faithful in Israel. Of course they weren't, and the ruins of Qumran are a witness to a sectarian madness more than faithful embodiment of the covenant God had made with Israel. Qumran stands not far north of Masada, another site that witnesses to courage, some might say madness, as a way of faithfulness to God.

What the Essenes failed at their next-door neighbor achieved. His name was John and instead of offering purification in a *mikvah* or in the temple, he said they had to begin all over again in the Jordan River, enter into the land one more time and his special messianic follower, Jesus, would divide the apostles into twelve, for twelve new tribes for Israel. And Jesus said something like this in the second chapter of John: "Destroy this temple and I will raise it again in three days" (2:19). Jesus was notoriously critical of the temple and the temple establishment, predicted its destruction within a generation, and then in a breathtaking evening had the *chutzpah* to reveal that his body and his blood, found now in the Passover's bread and wine, would be the means of atonement. This has to be taken as rebellion against the temple and revolution in the inner courts of the temple.

Stephen was extending a Jewish and especially Johannine and Jesus tradition here, and so we are not surprised that four other apostolic writings remind us of the very same revolution. Paul, too, taught a revolutionary understanding of the temple, and it is only because we aren't first-century Jews that we fail to hear just how wild and crazy his ideas were. I quote now three texts:

> Don't you know that you yourselves are God's temple and that God's Spirit dwells in your midst? If anyone destroys God's temple, God will destroy that person; for God's temple is sacred, and you together are that temple. (1 Cor 3:16–17)

> What agreement is there between the temple of God and idols? For we are the temple of the living God. As God has said:
>
> > "I will live with them
> > and walk among them,
> > and I will be their God,
> > and they will be my people." (2 Cor 6:16, citing perhaps Lev 26:12; Jer 32:38; Ezek 37:27)

> In him the whole building is joined together and rises to become a holy temple in the Lord. (Eph 2:21)

We can't pause to exegete these texts except to observe that Paul thought the followers of Jesus, not unlike what Jesus said about his missionaries, *were the presence of God, the temple itself, on earth wherever they were and whenever they carried on the kingdom work.* My, my, these are massive claims.

Peter, briefly. Somehow Peter can't avoid such an idea even if it is not developed, but here are his words: "As you come to him, the living Stone—rejected by human beings but chosen by God and precious to him—you also, like living stones, are being built into a spiritual house to be a holy priesthood, offering spiritual sacrifices acceptable to God through Jesus Christ" (1 Pet 2:4–5). The church has in some senses become both the temple and its personnel, not to fail to mention they are also the royalty of Jerusalem too! (See 2:9–10.)

Where does one even begin to speak of the temple in Hebrews? Again, notice these words from 3:6: "But Christ is faithful as the Son over God's house. And we are his house, if indeed we hold firmly to our confidence and the hope in which we glory." Jesus is not only over the house as Son, he's the high priest and the followers of Jesus are priests (cf. 2:17; 4:15—5:10; 6:19—10:18; 2:1-12). But the temple appears now to be the all-encompassing presence of God in the heavens (8:1-2). My, my, what must have the Essenes thought when they heard these claims!

One more, and I thank you for your patience in trotting out this evidence. I promise we are going somewhere with all of this. The author of the Revelation brings that heavenly temple in Hebrews down to earth, and it is all part of the final restoration of all creation: the new heavens and the new earth and a new Jerusalem. But there is an unheard of, revolution beyond revolutions claim made in the Apocalypse and it is found in Revelation 21:22, and by the way it is the most gospel-ish of statements in the entire New Testament. Here's what the seer says: "I did not see a temple in the [new Jerusalem] city, *because the Lord God almighty and the Lamb are its temple.*"

Atonement and Church: General Observations

Our goal is to talk about atonement and the church, but I wanted these three facts—the sudden development of missionary activity, the presence of God among God's people, and the temple revolution from John to John—in order to say something fresh beyond what I said in *A Community Called Atonement*.[1] In that book I argued that "atonement" needs to be used for

1. McKnight, *Community*.

the comprehensive theory of God's action on our behalf in this world and that it is multidimensional because of the history of atonement theory. I also argued that the various atonement theories—ransom, satisfaction, penal substitution, exemplary, governmental, and even the Girardian scapegoat theory—are each one club in a golf bag full of clubs and that the wise "golfer-theologian" knows which club to play at the right time but that no one can camp on one club as either the most important club or the "right" club.

A friend of mine, David Neff, a former chief at *Christianity Today*, however, suggested that penal substitution was the putter and that we use a putter on every hole, making it the central metaphor. I countered that I sometimes, especially when I was younger, hit the ball into the hole from off the green, and he said, "I suppose there are exceptions but exceptions prove the rule." I thought this was playing my metaphor too hard, so I called all such critics to show me that New Testament texts either *always or almost always* draw our attention to God's wrath and our punishment whenever atonement language appears. However, this simply isn't the fact. And because it isn't, I think it is unwise to think there is such a thing as a biblical *central metaphor*. What we see instead with chat about the "central metaphor" is the skill of theologians to make each text say what they believe. I don't say this because I have any beef with penal substitution, though it is not as prominent as some think, and I say this as one who learned atonement theory at the hand of an Aussie, Leon Lamb Morris.[2] I say this because I want to be biblical, even if I have taken the meaning of "atonement" from the history of discussion and not just from a single biblical term, like the *hilasterion* word group.

So let me now draw these three facts together into a double thesis I want to expound: first, the missionary activity, the presence of Christ among his followers, and the temple revolution *democratized the mediation of God's redemption in the world*. We are all involved; we are all involved at all times. Second, again taking the larger sense of "atonement," atonement is now mediated by ordinary people in the form of a community through gospelling, baptism, and eucharist, and Spirit-shaped fellowship. This, too, is a significant discussion among theologians. That is, they are asking "where is the church?" and "when is the church?"[3] This issue of mediation asks, "when is the church truly being the church?" This has to do with the nature of the church: is it a fellowship or a communion, or is it an institution? Some are troubled today by limiting the means of grace to the age-old sacraments Eucharist and baptism, and so it is worth our while to reconsider this issue

---

2. Morris, *Apostolic Preaching*.
3. Jenson and Wilhite, *Church*.

of ecclesial mediation in light of atonement theory and how it is that God mediates through the church in our world today.

Theme Verses

Second Corinthians 5:17–20 are the theme verses in what follows, and we need to read them to see that missionary calling, the presence of Christ, and the dispersion of the temple are all at work in the one central calling we each have: *reconciliation*, and that term is at the heart of atonement theory.

> Therefore, if anyone is in Christ, the new creation has come: The old has gone, the new is here! All this is from God, who reconciled us to himself through Christ and gave us the ministry of reconciliation: that God was reconciling the world to himself in Christ, not counting people's sins against them. And he has committed to us the message of reconciliation. We are therefore Christ's ambassadors, as though God were making his appeal through us. We implore you on Christ's behalf: Be reconciled to God.

Briefly, then. The *intent* of atonement or God's redemptive design is "new creation." The *work* of atonement is accomplished by God the Father who "reconciled us to himself through Christ." The emergent critics of the so-called divine child abuse need to read texts like this more carefully. The Father is not angry at us and it is not Christ who steps in to take the hit from the Father, but it is entirely the work of the Father, Son, and Spirit. A simple reading of John Stott's *The Cross of Christ* ought to have settled this long ago. The *goal* of God's atoning, reconciling work is to reconcile "the world to himself in Christ." I have no desire here to get into the problems of universalism and particularism and hope we can leave that for another time or another discussion.[4] The *manner* of God's atoning work is "not to count our sins against us," which shows a commercial and perhaps legal metaphor is at work inside the relational context and metaphor of "reconciliation." But the *modus operandi* of God is to assign this task to "us." It is to us that the "message of reconciliation," this *logon tes katallages* has been given (5:19). Paul is as committed as Jesus to how significant we are: we are not only ambassadors, but it is "as though God were making his appeal *through us*: we implore you on Christ's behalf, be reconciled to God!" The more we stare

---

4. Parry and Partridge, *Universal Salvation?*

at this perhaps the more we need to use the term of two Aussie brothers, Michael Frost and Alan Hirsch, "the faith of leap."[5]

My thesis, then, is that instead of everyone coming to Zion to see God and experience God's presence on the temple mount, God changed in midstream by dispensing his presence into his people and sent out Jesus's followers to a global mission of reconciliation. This atoning work, then, is assigned to us as we call people to Jesus Christ. Boiled into a stock broth, then, *we are a community called atonement, or a community called reconciliation.* How do we do this? I suggest in these ways: atonement is now mediated by ordinary people in the form of a community through gospelling, baptism, and Eucharist, and Spirit-shaped fellowship.

Through Gospelling

Whether we go back to Jesus's sending out of the Twelve and the Seventy, to the Great Commission, or to the presence of Christ in his followers, or to the temple's completion in the very presence of God and the Lamb, where no temple will even be needed, the *fixation of these texts is on Jesus Christ.* This christological driver shapes the story of Israel and it completes the story of Israel, so that the gospel itself is the declaration of Jesus Christ as the center of God's mission in this world.

Gospelling is how the church mediates the atoning work of God in this world. Once more this means that we tell people about Jesus by preaching the Gospels as the gospel, we teach God's people the core elements of the gospel through the lens of the apostolic gospel in 1 Corinthians 15, and we learn how to gospel by watching the apostles gospel in the book of Acts.

When will we ever learn as churches and as pastor-teachers that *all we have to offer, all we have to tell people about, and all we have to show people is Jesus?* We like our music and our acting groups; we are now more and more driven to act justly in social ways by engagement with the poor and despised; we do everything we can to make the gospel relevant by toning down offenses and oddities about our first-century Jewish message and Messiah; we have shaped and reshaped our churches according to business and entertainment models so we are attractional; and we work hard at being normal, honest, and authentic. We even study business strategies and use consumer satisfaction surveys to become more managerial and sensitive, all the while thinking these are the tricks of the trade. What made the movie *Chocolat,* starring Juliette Binoche, so incredibly evocative was that the chocolate itself was more healing than the church. And that might be

---

5. Frost and Hirsch, *Faith of Leap.*

because the church has too often lost track of what it is designed to do: *mediate Jesus by telling people about Jesus.*

Let me tell you something about myself. For a dozen years I taught in a seminary and then I took a post at a college/university where I taught undergraduates. But it came with a hitch and a warning: the hitch was that 50 percent of my students would not be Christians and hardly any of them would become ministers someday. The warning was this: I had a year to convince the administration that hiring some bald seminary professor wasn't a mistake and that I could in fact communicate with eighteen-to-twenty-two-year-old college students and not just with thirty-year-old seminarians. Well, I somehow convinced my superiors that I could do it, I got to keep the job, and I have learned something. In my first decade of teaching at North Park University between ten and twenty students gave their life to Jesus each year, and it dawned on me that I was not giving them the "gospel" as I had learned it. Instead, I was giving them the gospel as Jesus and the apostles preached it: *I was giving them Jesus.*

My friend Dan Kimball wrote a book that tells the whole story, and you can't forget this as pastors and teachers and leaders: *They like Jesus but not the church.*[6] We tend to dress the church up as the chocolate, but the real chocolate is Jesus. When they bite into church chocolate it can be bitter beyond belief, and sometimes it's rotten on the inside, but if you give them Jesus chocolate there's always a sweet cherry in the middle. Don't forget it, the way we mediate atonement today always begins in the same place: *we tell people about Jesus, we show them Jesus, we live out Jesus, and we do our best to let Jesus be the sole focus of all we do.*

Through Baptism and Eucharist

I grew up Baptist, and the irony of my Baptist heritage is that we believed baptism didn't do us any (redemptive) good but we were stuck with the name because our ancestors chose to believe that baptism upon profession of faith was the only real biblical baptism. The good thing about the irony is that we didn't live down to our theology but well above it. By which I mean, we may have claimed baptism didn't save and that it was purely symbolic, but it was *the distinguishing mark of the true believer*, and that meant—whether we saw this or not—that baptism was genuinely important.

As a seminary student I read through Beasley-Murray's brilliant book on baptism[7] and at that time I concluded there was no such thing as an un-

6. Kimball, *They Like Jesus.*
7. Beasley-Murray, *Baptism.*

baptized believer in the first-century church and that first-century followers of Jesus were driven by social, cultural, and religious instincts to get washed as a way of entering into the Christian faith. As the Qumran folks washed themselves in a purifying manner every day, and as first-century Jews dipped into a *mikveh* (or, as at Capernaum) into a lake or running stream, so the earliest followers of Jesus simply had to get baptized.

Paul nails the theology of baptism on the head in Romans 6, and I quote only verses three and four:

> Or don't you know that all of us who were baptized into Christ Jesus were baptized into his death? We were therefore buried with him through baptism into death in order that, just as Christ was raised from the dead through the glory of the Father, we too may live a new life.

What Paul tells us here is that baptism embodies the story of Jesus and that our baptism is an entrance into the story of Jesus.

Baptism, I am suggesting, is a quintessential gospelling event. When we get baptized, when we baptize, or when we watch a baptism, we are seeing the gospel unadorned and complete. We see a person enter into the story of Jesus as the fitting completion to the story of Israel and we enter into the story of Jesus as the saving story for us. Too many preachers spend too much time explaining baptism and not enough time doing baptism. Explaining it only goes so far; when it is done, we see baptism embodied in reality. The person enters into the water, gets washed, and rises to the surface again—and that is the gospel: we enter into the death of Jesus that forgives our sin and we enter into the resurrection of Jesus as that which justifies us and raises us to life to be the new creation.

Eucharist, too. Many things deserve to be said, and I have space for almost none of them. I begin with this because it crystallizes it all for me: Why did Jesus choose to die on Passover and not Yom Kippur? What are the differences between Passover and Yom Kippur? To begin with, the former is about Israel's historic story of deliverance from slavery, about being protected by the blood of the lamb smeared on the door, and about liberation from Egypt so Israel could return to the land and be God's people where God wanted God's people. Yom Kippur, on the other hand, is primarily about fasting and forgiveness. Jesus's last supper and the place where Jesus officially replaced the temple with himself, is a Passover event because Jesus wants us to ingest the blood as Israel smeared the blood; he wants us to eat the bread as Israel ate the bread and lamb and bitter herbs; he wants us to know that his blood protects us from God's judgment; and he wants us to know that his body is our new life. He wants us to know most completely that his blood and his body bring the true liberation, establishing a new covenant, so that we can be both forgiven and set free.

Whenever we eat this bread and drink this blood, Paul told us, we *gospel* the Lord's death until he comes. *Very slowly now: Eucharist is one of the church's primary instruments for gospelling.* Why? Because like baptism, the gospel is shown and embodied in a way that words can only interpret. We see the death and we see the resurrection; and we ingest as a way of partaking and participating.

I don't know your custom, but you can't do the Lord's Supper too often, and I don't care what others have told you. Kris and I would like to attend an Anglican church if we could find one where the sermons don't undo the liturgy and the lectionary. Why? Because the service aims at leading us to the body and blood of Christ, because the gospel is put on display every time this happens. In my Baptist church as a kid we did communion four times a year, and always tacked it onto a sermon. Often it was rushed and we rushed because the sermon was too long, and the time was getting late, or it was getting hot, or lunch was going to burn (or in our case a roast was going to dry out, which it often did anyway). We once were at a church where you could take the Lord's Supper at a little stand on your way out of the service—oh, my . . .

There is no reason to rush the Lord's Supper because *the Lord's Supper is gospelling at profound levels.* There is no reason to tack it onto a sermon but to let the Eucharist be the sermon. I'm not Orthodox or Catholic with a big "O" or a big "C," but their ornate dramatic liturgies as sacred dramas are organic developments of both the temple itself and of the Lord's Supper itself. The Lord's Supper is a drama, and watching it as a staged drama in which we get to participate is one of the best ways to gospel in our world today.

In the Eucharist *we become the atoning presence of God's work in this world.* Missionary sending, the presence of Christ in us, and the temple revolution all set Baptism and the Lord's Supper on a new level. They combine to show us that these dramatic enactments are atoning works, they are the work of God at work in our midst, and we are the ones called to do them and to show them and to offer reconciliation with God through them. We are God's ambassadors when we offer baptism and when we offer Eucharist. We are calling people to be reconciled to God whenever a baptism takes place or whenever we celebrate communion. We do these things as gospel, reconciling, atoning acts alongside the verbal declaration of the gospel.

Through Spirit-Shaped Fellowship

Back again to being sent on a mission, to the presence of Christ among us, and of the democratizing of God's temple presence in Christ and his people. We would not be the first to observe that the physical temple that sat so high on the temple mount in Jerusalem, which always meant the presence of God, is taken up in new shape and form in apostolic theology. In fact, the temple in some ways becomes the Holy Spirit's presence in us. This is both individual and corporate.

First, our bodies are the housing of the Spirit. Notice 1 Corinthians 6:19–20:

> Do you not know that your bodies are temples of the Holy Spirit, who is in you, whom you have received from God? You are not your own; you were bought at a price. Therefore honor God with your bodies.

Each of us is a dwelling place for the Spirit because the Spirit dwells in us. And this is also corporate, as Paul would fully expound six chapters later in 1 Corinthians, in chapter twelve. There is much to say here.

To begin with, the one Spirit indwells each of us separately "for the common good." We are given the Spirit not for ourselves but for the good of others (1 Cor 12:7). In other words, the Spirit is how God sends us today. The gift we are given determines how we are sent and to whom, but it is the Spirit. The Spirit is given to make a vast collection of all sorts of people to work together as a body. Then the Spirit's work is shaped entirely by love, as Paul says in 1 Corinthians 13. And again, as he says in 1 Corinthians 14:26, all gifts are given for the "strengthening of the church." Another word for this is *koinonia*.

Now I want to probe a bit. In my country—the United States—the younger generation has become obsessed with social justice, and this is leading one student after another into local and state and federal government opportunities. It is leading them to think of politics and of voting in the right candidates. To cut this description short, what it's doing is leading young Christians out of the church and into the public sector to do "kingdom" work. I want to raise a big red flag here. There is no such thing as kingdom work outside the church, for the kingdom is about King Jesus and King Jesus's people and King Jesus's ethics for King Jesus's people. Social justice outside the church is not biblical justice or kingdom work. It is social work. Of course, that's a good thing, but let us not confuse this with the kingdom.

Genuine kingdom work is *koinonia* work. In other words, I plead with my students and readers to reconsider kingdom work, and to work hard at making the church a beachhead of justice, peace, and love in your community, to supply the poor in your church with what they need, to work at alleviating the needs of those who are in your church, and to let that kind of church/kingdom justice work spill over the walls into your community so that people will see the church as the place where the kingdom vision is embodied.

This is countercultural in the church today, and I'm aware of it. I'm aware of it because I see the confusion on the faces of my students when I say working for a government agency is not kingdom work; working through your local church into your community as the way to extend the presence of Jesus, is kingdom work. So, let me say it all over again: kingdom work is not simply justice, which usually means Western democratic principles. True justice is biblical justice; it is being declared right and growing in being made right, as we embody the reconciling *koinonia* that Jesus came to embody. True justice is found in the *Magnificat* and in Acts 2 and Acts 4. It is found in 1 Corinthians 12 and in Ephesians 4. True justice is found in Revelation 20–22, not in the Democrats or the Republicans, not in Labor or the Liberals (or the Greens) here in Australia. True justice is living under the true King.

Now back to missionary sending, the presence of Christ among us, and the dispersion of the temple. If our local church sees itself as sent by Christ, as the presence of Christ and as the new temple, it will seek to sanctify the place, and it will seek justice and peace and love. If we live like this, we will be a kingdom called atonement, right here, wherever we live. And wouldn't *that* be something?

Bibliography

Beasley-Murray, G. R. *Baptism in the New Testament*. Grand Rapids: Eerdmans, 1973.
Frost, Michael, and Alan Hirsch. *The Faith of Leap: Embracing a Theology of Risk, Adventure and Courage*. Grand Rapids: Baker, 2011.
Jenson, Matt, and David E. Wilhite. *The Church: A Guide for the Perplexed*. New York: T. & T. Clark/Continuum, 2010.
Kimball, Dan. *They Like Jesus But Not the Church: Insights from Emerging Generations*. Grand Rapids, MI: Zondervan, 2007.
McKnight, Scot. *A Community Called Atonement*. Living Theology. Nashville: Abingdon, 2007.
Morris, Leon L. *The Apostolic Preaching of the Cross*. Grand Rapids: Eerdmans, 1960.
Parry, Robin A., and Christopher H. Partridge. *Universal Salvation? The Current Debate*. Grand Rapids: Eerdmans, 2004.

14

The Spirit—Beyond Christ?
Christian Witness in a Plural World

CAROLYN ENG LOOI TAN

Introduction

THE TWENTY-FIRST CENTURY IS characterized by globalization and the increasing awareness of the multiplicity of cultural and religious paradigms. How can the church of today share the gospel of Jesus in this marketplace of competing worldviews and religions? This question is not unique to our generation. We sometimes forget that the church of the first century faced the same challenge. However, Veli-Matti Kärkkäinen correctly points out that this challenge confronts us now with greater urgency, not because of plurality but because of the pervading mindset of pluralism. This is a mindset that acknowledges a rough parity among all religions, giving no final authority to any particular truth claim.[1] The pluralistic principle currently plays out in educational and workplace policies in several democracies including Australia, and for many people, it seems a fair and straightforward approach to cultural and religious diversity, encouraging tolerance and mutual respect. Christian thinkers seeking to engage in meaningful interfaith dialogue have increasingly turned to pneumatology. Kärkkäinen writes: "The acknowledgement of the gifts of God in other religions by virtue of the

---

1. Kärkkäinen, *Religious Pluralism*, 2.

presence of the Spirit—as well as the critical discernment of these gifts by the power of the same Spirit—means a real trinitarian basis to Christianity's openness toward other religions."[2]

Kärkkäinen suggests that the presence of the Holy Spirit can be discerned in non-Christian religions which are therefore, to some extent at least, divinely sanctioned and gifted. This idea is anchored in his understanding of God's Spirit as "the principle of all life" and offers the attractive possibility of pneumatological interfaith interaction based on the Spirit as the touchstone of human commonality.[3] Arguing in favor of this view, Amos Yong proposes a "foundational pneumatology" as a methodological principle and common platform for interfaith conversations.[4] This foundational pneumatology is defined by the basic notion and experience of divine presence and agency in individuals and human communities. It is framed by three axioms: first, that God is universally active and present in the Spirit; second, that the Spirit is God's life-breath of the *imago Dei* in every human and the presupposition of all human relationships; and third, that everything that exists, including all religions, are "providentially sustained by the Spirit of God for divine purposes."[5]

For Christians the first and second axioms are uncontroversial from the biblical standpoint (Gen 1:27; Ps 139:1-7). However, Yong's third axiom, one which is critical for his foundational pneumatology, is problematical. He attributes to the Spirit not only humanity's religious impulse but also the variety of expressions of that impulse.[6] The existence of such an impulse is widely recognized. John Calvin describes the *sensus divinitatis*,[7] Friedrich Schleiermacher a "God-consciousness" and "sense of absolute dependence,"[8] Rudolph Otto the "experience of the numinous."[9] Paul himself alludes to humanity's intimation of a Creator but only to point out

---

2. Kärkkäinen, *Religious Pluralism*, 179. See also Yong, "Spirit Gives Utterance," 299–314. Note the reorientation of Catholic theology towards greater openness and recognition of other faiths in the Second Vatican Council's 1965 "Declaration," in *Nostra Aetate*, 738–42.

3. Kärkkäinen, *Religious Pluralism*, 175. See also Kärkkäinen, "How to Speak," 47–70.

4. Yong, *Beyond the Impasse*, 67–72.

5. Yong, *Beyond the Impasse*, 44–46.

6. Yong, *Beyond the Impasse*, 46.

7. Calvin believed that within every human was "an unshakeable sense that there is a God who ought to be honored and worshipped." See Steinmetz, "Theology," 121.

8. Schleiermacher, *Christian Faith*, 17 (§4.4). Schleiermacher does not attribute "God-consciousness" to the work of the Spirit.

9. Otto, *Idea of the Holy*, 9–30.

how this has been subverted (Rom 1:18–19). However, the idea that all human activities are expressions of the Spirit[10] seems to dissolve pneumatology into anthropology. This pneumatological trajectory leads inevitably to the ascription of evil to God. Perhaps in anticipation of this criticism, both Yong and Kärkkäinen caution that discernment is necessary in order to detect the true voice of the Spirit.[11] However, the criteria for such discernment cannot exist in a vacuum, but are formulated through epistemic, cultural, religious, social, and philosophical presuppositions. Yong himself looks to the Bible for support for his concept of a foundational pneumatology. He cites Acts 2:17 which he interprets as "the Holy Spirit is being poured out universally," and Acts 10:34 from which he deduces that God welcomes all people "regardless of race or ethnicity, gender, social standing, religious affiliation, or geographical location."[12]

The first disciples were Jews who were convinced that Jesus was their divinely promised Messiah on the basis of his anointing with God's Spirit and resurrection from the dead. Who was the Holy Spirit to these early Jewish Christians? Clearly, they recognized him as the Spirit of God who empowered and inspired their prophets and leaders, and the eagerly awaited eschatological Spirit. After Jesus's death and resurrection, these Christians testified to a widespread experience of God's Spirit and divine empowerment of ordinary people from every strata of life. They believed that the *eschaton* had begun in Jesus. The terms Spirit of Jesus, Spirit of Christ, and Spirit of the Son emerged in their writings (Acts 16:7; Rom 8:9; Phil 1:19; Gal 4:6; and 1 Pet 1:11). What did the New Testament writers mean by these terms, and how were these terms related to the Holy Spirit?[13] Perhaps their elucidation with close attention to their theological contexts will help assess if these New Testament writers understood the Holy Spirit in ways that are congruent with Yong's foundational pneumatology.

---

10. Yong's appeal to Acts 17:28 ("In him [God] we live and move and have our being") as scriptural support for his view that the Spirit "sustains intersubjective communications, interpersonal relationships, and intentional, rational, moral and spiritual life" is reading far too much into this Greek quotation that the Lukan Paul used in his address at the Aeropagus; see Yong, *Beyond the Impasse*, 45.

11. Kärkkäinen, *Religious Pluralism*, 175; Yong, *Beyond the Impasse*, 73.

12. Yong, *Beyond the Impasse*, 131.

13. Unfortunately, genitives are notorious for their ambiguity. Hence the importance of the theological context in which these terms appear.

"Spirit of Jesus/Christ/Son"

Acts 16:6–7

> They went through the region of Phrygia and Galatia, having been forbidden by the Holy Spirit to speak the word in Asia. When they had come opposite Mysia, they attempted to go into Bithynia, but the Spirit of Jesus (*to pneuma Iēsou*)[14] did not allow them.

In Acts, the Holy Spirit is portrayed as the agent of divine power promised by God and poured out by the exalted Jesus on his disciples, and as the director of the church's evangelistic mission.[15] The term "Spirit of Jesus" appears just once here in Luke-Acts[16] and it appears at a critical point in Paul's evangelistic outreach. He is prohibited from evangelizing in Asia and Bithynia, and is instead redirected westward to Macedonia (Acts 16:4–10).

The juxtaposition of the "Holy Spirit" in verse 6 with the "Spirit of Jesus" in verse 7 has been understood to indicate that both titles refer to the same Spirit, on the basis that the *divine* prohibition to Paul's initial plans was given not once but twice.[17] It is unlikely that Jesus's human spirit or character is indicated here, although Bruce speculates that a prophetic utterance in Jesus's name may have occurred. Against that idea Marshall and Bock correctly point out that the actual manner of guidance is not detailed. Instead, they suggest that Luke wishes to emphasize that Jesus himself was guiding the progress of the gospel through the Spirit.[18] In Luke's narrative Jesus appears at key points of the mission: at the beginning of the entire mission (Luke 24:47–48; Acts 1:8), at Paul's commissioning as the apostle to the gentiles (Acts 9:1–19), and here as the "Spirit of Jesus" at the start of the Aegean mission. "Luke's change of expression here is not simply for stylistic variation but to recall an important theological perspective about the Spirit's relation to the ascended and enthroned Messiah."[19] Thus the use of the term "Spirit of Jesus" here asserts the Christocentricity of the Holy Spirit.

---

14. The word *kyriou* is substituted for *Iēsou* in C and a few Coptic versions, but the far greater weight of textual evidence is for *Iēsou*; see Nestle-Aland, *Novum Testamentum Graece*, 369.

15. Acts 1:8; 2:33; 8:29; 10:19–20; 13:2, 4; 16:6; 20:28.

16. Ju Hur observes that the phrase "Spirit of Jesus" finds no comparable expression in the Jewish Bible or in intertestamental literature; *Dynamic Reading*, 141–42.

17. See Bruce, *Book of Acts*, 306–7; Marshall, *Acts*, 262–63; Fitzmyer, *Acts of the Apostles*, 577–78; Bock, *Acts*, 527–28; Peterson, *Acts of the Apostles*, 454–55.

18. Bruce, *Book of Acts*, 307; Marshall, *Acts*, 263; Bock, *Acts*, 527.

19. Peterson, *Acts of the Apostles*, 455.

Romans 8:9

> But you are not in the flesh (*en sarki*); you are in the Spirit (*en pneumati*), since the Spirit of God (*pneuma theou*) dwells in you. Anyone who does not have the Spirit of Christ (*pneuma Christou*) does not belong to him.

In Romans 8, Paul contrasts life controlled by the flesh (*en sarki*) to life controlled by God's Spirit (*en pneumati*). He asserts that the indwelling of God's Spirit (*pneuma theou*) is *the* criterion for life in the Spirit's domain (Rom 8:9), and that the Spirit-controlled life is in Christ (Rom 8:2). Not only are believers "in Spirit" (*en pneumati*),[20] but "God's Spirit dwells in you" (*pneuma theou oikei en hymin*), hence a mutual indwelling. Paul uses similar phrases to describe the union between Christ and his followers: they are "in Christ" (*en Christō*, Rom 8:1-2) and "Christ in you" (*Christos en hymin*, Rom 8:10).[21] Thus being in Christ and having Christ in us means also being in God's Spirit and having his Spirit dwell in us. He insists that those without the "Spirit of Christ" (*pneuma Christou*) simply do not belong to Christ (Rom 8:9). Significantly, by the intentional juxtaposition of "Spirit of God" and "Spirit of Christ" not only does Paul see "the Spirit as integrally related to Christ as well as to the Father,"[22] but he identifies God's Spirit with Christ's Spirit. What, then, does Paul mean by the phrase "Spirit of Christ," and why mention it if he has already spoken of God's Spirit?

Gordon Fee observes a chiasmic pattern in Romans 8:8-11 and posits that the main point of Paul's argument is found in verses 10 and 11, "which express the result of the reality of the indwelling Spirit."[23] According to Fee, since God's Spirit is none other than the Spirit of Christ, the believer gains life as a result of Christ's work,[24] and since God raised Christ from the dead through the Spirit, believers are assured of bodily resurrection because the

---

20. An anthropological understanding of *en pneumati* in verse 9 is considered less likely in view of the thrust of Paul's context; so Fitzmyer, *Romans*, 290.

21. *En Christō* is, of course, an important theological phrase for Paul, and appears more frequently than *Christos en hymin*.

22. Morris, *Romans*, 308.

23. Fee, *God's Empowering Presence*, 545.

24. In verse 10, Paul's switch from "Spirit of Christ" to "Christ" has been variously interpreted. Morris insists that there has been no change of subject, merely that the Spirit's indwelling is impossible without union with Christ (*Romans*, 309). Fee even suggests that "Christ in you" is Pauline shorthand for "Spirit of Christ in you" or "Christ in you by his Spirit" (*God's Empowering Presence*, 548). Osborne sees a shift in focus from the Spirit onto Christ's atoning work as the basis for the indwelling of the Spirit (Osborne, *Romans*, 200-1). Importantly, all three agree that in Romans 8:9-11, the work of Christ and the work of the Spirit are tightly integrated.

Spirit lives in them. Byrne concurs, adding that the ways that Paul refers to the Spirit, as "Spirit of God," "Spirit of Christ," and "Spirit of the One who raised Jesus from the dead" (Rom 8:9, 11), ties the eschatological Spirit to the person and "career" of Jesus, so that anyone who does not have the Spirit of Christ is not destined to share in Christ's resurrection.[25] Dunn sums up simply and succinctly that "for Paul the Spirit is the Spirit of Christ."[26] However Moo rightly cautions that although Christ and the Spirit are "so closely related in communicating to believers the benefits of salvation that Paul can move from one to the other almost unconsciously," this does not mean "that Christ and the Spirit are equated or interchangeable."[27]

Philippians 1:19

> For I know that through your prayers and the help of the Spirit of Jesus Christ (*tou pneumatos Iēsou Christou*) this will turn out for my deliverance.

Paul writes from prison.[28] He had received a gift from the believers in Philippi by way of Epaphroditus and the latter was returning to Philippi after a serious illness. Paul took the opportunity to send the Philippians a letter of thanks and to update them on Epaphroditus's illness and his own situation. While he himself is facing an impending trial and possible martyrdom, Paul exhorts his beloved Philippians to reject false teaching, to keep united and to remain true and loyal to Christ, sharing steadfastly with him the fellowship of Christ's sufferings.[29] Christ is the focus of this letter, particularly since Paul's imprisonment is the consequence of his evangelism for Christ, and because his life has become wholly defined by Christ (Phil 1:21). Even imprisonment is viewed not from the perspective of his own personal safety but from the standpoint of the spread of Christ's gospel, and from that latter perspective, imprisonment has had a positive rather than a negative outcome (Phil 1:12–18). Hence, in the midst of his suffering, Paul rejoiced!

In verse 19, Paul describes his confidence that he will be delivered[30] through the prayers of the Philippians, and through the "help" of the "Spirit

25. Byrne, *Romans*, 240.
26. Dunn, *Romans 1–8*, 429.
27. Moo, *Romans*, 491.
28. The traditional location of this imprisonment is Rome (corresponding to Acts 28:30), although Caesarea and Ephesus have been proposed; see the discussion in Martin, *Philippians*, 20–39.
29. Martin, *Philippians*, 46.
30. The word translated "deliverance" is *sōtērian*, interpreted variously as release

of Jesus Christ." Fee highlights that the noun *epichorēgias* which is widely translated as "help," denotes "supply or provision" and was used in its non-compounded form as "a term for supplying choristers and dancers for festive occasions" or the generous provision of a husband for his wife.[31] This provision may indicate the help that the Spirit gives, or the provision of the Spirit himself.[32] Since Paul uses the participle form in Galatians 3:5 to mean that God supplies *the Spirit*, the second interpretation seems more likely here.[33] Furthermore, Fee notes that Paul links "prayer" and "supply of the Spirit" together in one prepositional phrase, indicating that Paul requests prayer for a fresh anointing of the Spirit so that he will be empowered to speak boldly, and that whatever the outcome of his imprisonment Christ will be exalted in him (Phil 1:20). "The Spirit" is itself qualified by the genitive "Jesus Christ" for which an anthropological or ethical interpretation (that is, Jesus's human spirit or fortitude) would make little sense because the context is prayer for God's provision of spiritual assistance. The scholarly consensus is that *tou pneumatos Iēsou Christou* refers to the Holy Spirit.[34]

However, could not the phrase "Spirit of God" or "Holy Spirit" have sufficed for Paul's prayer request?[35] Why specifically "the Spirit *of Jesus Christ*"? In this letter, Paul sees the humiliation-exaltation of Christ as

---

from imprisonment or escape from death (Hawthorne), vindication (Fee, Martin) or eternal salvation (Hansen, Schreiner). The exact phrase *touto moi apobēsetai eis sōtērian* ("this will turn out for my deliverance") is used by Job in his appeal before God (Job 13:16). If Paul is citing this passage, then "deliverance" probably means vindication rather than release from imprisonment or spiritual salvation. See Hawthorne, *Philippians*, 40; Fee, *God's Empowering Presence*, 737–38; Martin, *Philippians*, 82; Schreiner, *New Testament Theology*, 485; Hansen, *Philippians*, 77–79.

31. Fee, *God's Empowering Presence*, 740–41. Its verbal root *epichorēgeō* is used in the background of Greco-Roman public service and marriage contracts with the sense of "providing generous support"; BDAG, 386–87. See also 2 Pet 1:11 and Col 2:19.

32. *Epichorēgias* is seen here as a verbal noun, so that *tou pneumatos* may be interpreted as a subjective or objective genitive (so Hawthorne, *Philippians*, 40, and Hansen, *Philippians*, 79, n. 156).

33. Thus Fee, *God's Empowering Presence*, 740–41, and Hansen, *Philippians*, 79. Hawthorne's argument for the subjective genitive seems weak. It is based on the "idea of the Spirit bringing assistance to Christians, especially as they bear witness to their faith when they are brought before judges," an idea which he draws from non-Pauline New Testament writings (Hawthorne, *Philippians*, 40–41).

34. For example, see Lightfoot, *Saint Paul's Epistle*, 90–91; Schweizer, *Spirit of God*, 60; Dunn, *Jesus and the Spirit*, 318; Motyer, *Message*, 85; Hawthorne, *Philippians*, 41; Ladd, *Theology*, 503; Fee, *God's Empowering Presence*, 735; Schreiner, *New Testament Theology*, 485; Hansen, *Philippians*, 80.

35. Elsewhere in his letter Paul refers to the sharing (*koinōnia*) in the Spirit by the believers (Phil 2:1), and when he describes "those who worship in the Spirit of God" (Phil 3:3).

central not only to the content of his gospel, but also as the paradigm for the new life in Christ. By belonging to Christ, Paul shares in the spirit of the one who was imprisoned, tried, tortured and killed, and who rose from the dead. The Spirit who enabled and empowered Jesus through his own suffering, is the very Spirit who now dwells in Paul. This "Spirit of Jesus Christ" will see Paul through his imprisonment, impending trial and possible martyrdom, help him speak with all boldness and to imitate Jesus (just as Paul exhorts the Philippians to imitate him; Phil 3:17), guaranteeing Paul's eschatological resurrection and eternal destiny with Christ (Phil 3:14; 21). Hence Fee is right in stating that the phrase "Spirit of Jesus Christ" "is the key to Christ's being glorified in every way: by Paul's being 'supplied' the Spirit of Jesus Christ, who will live powerfully through Paul as he stands trial."[36]

Galatians 4:6

> And because you are children (*huioi*, "sons"), God has sent the Spirit of his Son (*to pneuma tou huiou autou*)[37] into our hearts, crying, "Abba! Father!"

Paul makes this statement in the context of his polemic against agitators who insisted that Torah observance was necessary for Christians to remain in right relationship with God, and for gentile Christians, that meant circumcision and adherence to Sabbath and food laws. At the heart of the argument is the fundamental question about how people become Abraham's true sons (Gal 3:6; "descendants" in the NRSV).[38] Paul argues that the Abrahamic covenant predates the giving of the Torah by centuries (Gal 3:17–18), that it is the *Spirit* that God promises (Gal 3:14), and that the true heir of Abraham's promise is Christ, God's Son (Gal 3:16; 4:4). The Torah was given as a pedagogue to the people prior to the coming of Christ (Gal 3:19–23), and has now outlived its purpose (Gal 3:24–25). Hence it is only by belonging to Christ, Abraham's heir, through faith, that both Gentile and Jewish believers inherit God's promise, the Spirit (Gal 3:29). In Christ Jesus, they have been adopted as God's sons (Gal 3:26; 4:5; "children" in the NRSV) with all the legal privileges that sonship brings, regardless of race, social status, and gender (Gal 3:28). *Because*[39] they are sons (*hoti de*

---

36. Fee, *God's Empowering Presence*, 743.

37. *Tou huiou* is omitted only in P46 but is present in all other ancient manuscripts; Nestle-Aland, *Novum Testamentum Graece*, 498.

38. Fee, *Galatians*, 7.

39. According to Bruce, this is the most natural reading of *hoti*; Bruce, *Commentary on Galatians*, 198. In agreement are Longenecker, *Galatians*, 173; Hansen, *Galatians*,

este huioi) and no longer slaves, God sent forth (*exapesteilen*) the Spirit of his Son into their hearts, and like Jesus, they can address God by the family endearment "Abba" (Gal 4:6).[40] Since the Galatians have undoubtedly received the Holy Spirit (Gal 3:2–5), they are already validated as sons of Abraham, as God's sons. Therefore, subsequent submission to the Torah is a renegade step, relinquishing the freedom of life in the Spirit through Christ to return to "a yoke of slavery" under the Torah (Gal 5:2).[41]

The word "son" is the key to Galatians 4:4–7. Inclusion into divine sonship, evidenced by receiving God's promised Spirit (the Spirit of the Son), is based on faith in Christ, the Son of God. Hence the "Spirit of the Son" is identified with God's Spirit. Fee notes the parallelism between "God sent his Son (*exapesteilen ho theos ton huion autou*)" with "God has sent the Spirit of his Son (*exapesteilen ho theos pneuma tou huiou autou*)," and observes that "Paul deliberately conjoins the work of the Son and the Spirit."[42] According to Longenecker, Paul's intentional choice of terminology "highlight[s] the integral nature of sonship and the reception of the Spirit."[43]

1 Peter 1:10–11

> Concerning this salvation, the prophets who prophesied of the grace that was to be yours made careful search and inquiry, inquiring about the person or time that the Spirit of Christ within them (*to en autois pneuma Christou*)[44] indicated when it testified in advance to the sufferings destined for Christ and the subsequent glory.

In addressing Christians who were living in a hostile society and facing persecution, Peter[45] encourages and exhorts them by drawing their attention to Jesus Christ who suffered, died and was raised in glory. He persuades them that their salvation is not based upon trumped up unsubstantiated

---

120; Martyn, *Galatians*, 391.

40. For the discussion concerning the differences between the order of sonship and reception of the Spirit in Rom 8:14–15 and Gal 4:6, see Bruce, *Commentary on Galatians*, 198; Longenecker, *Galatians*, 173, Fee, *Galatians*, 152–53.

41. This brief summary of Paul's argument follows Fee, *Galatians*, 147–51.

42. Fee, *God's Empowering Presence*, 405.

43. Longenecker, *Galatians*, 174.

44. The word *Christou* is omitted only in Codex Vaticanus but is present in all other ancient manuscripts; Nestle-Aland, *Novum Testamentum Graece*, 599.

45. While Petrine authorship of 1 Peter has been challenged (see Jobes, *1 Peter*, 5–19), Petrine authorship will be assumed in this paper as the question of authorship does not impact the issues discussed here.

ideas but is grounded in the foreknowledge of God the Father, in the Holy Spirit's sanctifying work and in the shedding of Jesus's blood for their sins (1 Pet 1:2, 10; 2:5, 24). Like the ancient Hebrews, the recipients of Peter's letter are foreigners and sojourners in this hostile world, looking forward to their heavenly home (1 Pet 2:11). Their heavenly citizenship requires them nonetheless to behave as God's holy priesthood and spiritual household, God's own people (1 Pet 2:5, 9). Their example and role model is none other than Jesus himself. Peter stresses that Jesus's suffering and sacrificial death were divinely planned, revealed to God's prophets beforehand and manifested at the right moment in history.

Peter explicitly identifies the Spirit who inspired Israel's prophets as the "Spirit of Christ." The interaction between those prophets and the "Spirit of Christ" precludes an anthropological interpretation of that term because it is presented in the context of divine revelation. Commentators concur that by "Spirit of Christ" Peter means God's Spirit.[46] This is the same Holy Spirit "sent from heaven,"[47] the Spirit of empowerment (1 Pet 1:12) and sanctification (1 Pet 1:2), who builds Christ's followers into *oikos pneumatikos* (a spiritual house) of which the cornerstone is Jesus Christ (1 Pet 2:5–6), and who is the s/Spirit[48] of glory (and of the glorified Christ) and of God that now rests upon Peter's persecuted hearers (1 Pet 4:14).[49] Thus "Peter says, in effect, that the Spirit who inspired the prophets also inspired the evangelists and gave them insight into the true meaning of the prophets."[50] In the context of Peter's message, the phrase "Spirit of Christ" becomes the lynchpin that holds Israel's prophetic traditions and the gospel together in one divine strategy of redemption for humanity.[51]

---

46. See Marshall, *1 Peter*, 47; Michaels, *1 Peter*, 44; McKnight, *1 Peter*, 70, 73; Jobes, *1 Peter*, 101, 103; Achtemeier, *1 Peter*, 105; Skaggs, *1 Peter*, 21.

47. Possibly a reference to the Spirit's coming at Pentecost; see Marshall, *1 Peter*, 46; Hillyer, *1 and 2 Peter*, 40.

48. The parallelism between *to doxēs* and *to tou theou* as adjectival genitives of *pneuma* strongly suggests that the capitalized "Spirit" applies to both "Spirit of glory" and "Spirit of God"; thus NIV, TNIV, NAU, NJB, NKJV and ESV, contra NRSV and KJV.

49. 1 Peter 1:2, 12; 2:5–6; 4:13, 14.

50. Marshall, *1 Peter*, 47. "In 1 Peter 1:11 the point seems to be that the Spirit who was the agent of revelation to the prophets of old is the same Spirit of Christ known to the first century church." See Jobes, *1 Peter*, 101. The discussion as to whether this passage supports the preexistence of Christ will not be entered into here.

51. "This phrase points therefore to the continuity between prophets and gospel: both have the same inspirer and ultimately the same content." Achtemeier, *1 Peter*, 110. "Peter contends that this salvation, which the Asian Christians have enjoyed and for which they earnestly hope, is the very salvation that the ancient prophets (cf. Matt 13:17) were seeking in all its details but never found" (McKnight, *1 Peter*, 73).

Discussion

In Jesus's birth narratives, baptism, and ministry, the evangelists had the divine spirit of Yahweh in view when the Holy Spirit was mentioned. For example, Luke understood that Jesus was the prophesized Spirit-anointed servant (Isa 61:1–2; Luke 4:1–19), and the Spirit that was poured out at Pentecost was God's prophetically promised Spirit (Joel 2:28–29; Acts 2:17–18). However, a new understanding of God's Spirit seems to emerge with the appearance of the names we have identified above, names which would have represented a startling concept to devout first-century Jews, particularly if these names are intended to denote God's Spirit.[52] As discussed in the previous section, these terms are not arbitrary but carefully chosen for specific reasons: in Acts 16:7, to emphasize Jesus's leadership, through the Spirit, of the Western gentile mission; in Romans 8:9, to anchor life in the Spirit's domain to the work of Christ; in Philippians 1:19, to show that Paul views his imprisonment, earthly life, and eternal destiny completely through a christological lens, and that he participates in Christ's suffering and glory through his Spirit; in Galatians 4:6, to assure the gentile believers that they are truly sons of Abraham and sons of God because they have already received their inheritance, viz. the Spirit of God's Son; and in 1 Peter 1:11, to highlight that Christ is the centerpiece of the whole of God's redemption plan in which the Holy Spirit's work is integral.[53] In all these passages, God's Spirit is in view rather than Jesus's human spirit, or an attitude that Jesus displayed. Yet these writers also distinguish the Holy Spirit from Jesus Christ.[54] How then should we interpret these terms?

The contexts in which all these terms appear are pneumatological. In Acts 16:6–10, Luke affirms that the Holy Spirit, as the director of the apostolic mission, is the Spirit of Jesus. In Romans 8:1–17, Paul's discourse concerns the contrast between flesh-life (under the law) and Spirit-life (through Christ), the Spirit being both the Spirit of God and of Christ. In

---

52. Dunn, *Christ and the Spirit*, vol. 2, 329–30.

53. Remarkably, the Johannine writings are absent from this line-up despite John's close association of Jesus with the Holy Spirit (John 14:16; 20:22), his high Christology, explicit pneumatology, and clear depiction of Jesus as the divine Son.

54. Paul, however, seems to come close to identifying the Spirit with Christ in 2 Cor 3:17. Dunn is unconvinced that Paul viewed the Holy Spirit and Christ as one ontological entity, proposing instead a functional identity; Dunn, *Christ and the Spirit*, vol. 1, 115–25; also *Christ and the Spirit*, vol. 2, 78 and n. 31. Fee asserts, as does Dunn, that "the Lord" is a citation from Exodus 34:34 that Paul is quoting, so that Fee's translation reads, "Now 'the Lord' is the Spirit." He continues, "by the words 'the Lord' Paul does not intend either God or Christ; he intends the Spirit." (Fee, *God's Empowering Presence*, 309, 311–12, see also n. 91).

Philippians 1:12–26, the imprisoned Paul is facing possible martyrdom for Christ and asks for prayer to be freshly anointed by the Spirit of Jesus Christ. In Galatians 3:1—4:7, Paul identifies the indwelling of the Spirit of the Son as the criterion for being Abraham's descendants and God's sons. In 1 Peter 1:10–12, Peter affirms that Jesus Christ is indeed the one whom the Israel's prophets foretold, and that it was none other than the Spirit of Christ who made these revelations to them.

Dunn makes an important observation that while an eschatological outpouring of God's Spirit was anticipated by Israel's prophets, "there was no expectation of a messianic figure *bestowing* the Spirit in pre-Christian Judaism."[55] On the other hand, the early Christians claimed that as Messiah, Jesus not only ushered in the eschatological age, but also received and poured out the promised Spirit after his exaltation (Acts 2:33; John 20:22).[56] Thus Dunn posits that the early Christians used the term "Spirit of Jesus/Christ/Son" to closely associate the outpoured Spirit of God to the risen crucified Jesus, and to emphasize that Jesus was *both* the bearer and dispenser of God's Spirit.[57] He also suggests that the cross, and indeed the entire Christ event, changed human perception of the Spirit from the elusive, impersonal *rûah* of the Old Testament to *pneuma* bearing the identity and personality of Jesus. Thus the disciples of Jesus came to perceive *rûah YHWH* in a new way, not only as *pneuma theou*, but also as *pneuma Christou*.

Amos Yong's foundational pneumatology significantly downplays the Christocentricity of the Holy Spirit.[58] In his citation of Acts 2:17 and 10:34, he ignores the fact that the Holy Spirit is poured out in the context of a proclamation about the *risen crucified Jesus*.[59] Peter declared, "Repent, and be baptized every one of you in the name of Jesus Christ so that your sins may

---

55. Dunn, "Towards the Spirit," 7. It is God who bestows the Spirit, not the Messiah.

56. This idea of a Spirit-bestowing messianic intermediary was attributed to John the Baptist in all four gospels (Mark 1:8; Matt 3:11; Luke 3:16; John 1:33). Dunn insightfully argues that if John had God in mind, he would not have spoken about untying the coming one's sandals; "Towards the Spirit," 9.

57. Dunn, *Christ and the Spirit*, vol. 1, 25. "The cosmic power of God, the mysterious and miracle-working action of God in his world, could now be known simply as the Spirit which inspired Jesus and which came from Jesus"; Dunn, *Christ and the Spirit*, vol. 2, 339.

58. This is also noted by Habets; *Anointed Son*, 237–38.

59. Yong is right to point out that the Joel prophecy speaks of YHWH pouring out his Spirit upon all "flesh" (Heb. *bāśār*, Gk. *sarka*). Note however that this phrase is used in the context of Joel's prophecy regarding the restoration of Israel, and "all flesh" is qualified by "your" (Heb. *-cem*, Gk. *hēmōn*) sons and daughters, "your" young and old men. When Joel mentions other nations, he envisions them undergoing judgment in the valley of Jehoshaphat (Joel 3:2).

be forgiven, and you will receive the gift of the Holy Spirit" (Acts 2:38), implying that without repentance and baptism in Christ's name, they will not receive the Holy Spirit. In the event involving Cornelius, Peter recognized that these gentiles had genuinely received the Holy Spirit and responded by saying, "Can anyone withhold the water for baptizing these people who have received the Holy Spirit just as we have?" (Acts 10:47). Hence, reception of the Spirit is once again tied to faith in Christ. Perhaps Yong blurs the christological focus for both of these significant pneumatological events in order to emphasize the universality of the Holy Spirit. It appears that for Yong, a pneumatology that is effective in interfaith dialogue has to be stripped of Christology.[60] But as Yves Congar maintains, there is "no christology without pneumatology and no pneumatology without christology."[61]

Underpinning Yong's pneumatological formulation is Irenaeus's concept of God working in the world through his two hands, the Son and the Spirit, by which Yong envisions the "related yet distinct economies of the Spirit and the Son."[62] However capturing a broader quotation from Irenaeus's *Against Heresies* is illuminating:

> Now God will be glorified in His handiwork, fitting it so as to be conformable to, and modelled after, His own Son. For by the hands of the Father, that is, by the Son and the Holy Spirit, man, and not [merely] a part of man, was made in the likeness of God.[63]

Irenaeus's analogy of "the hands of the Father" is preceded by his affirmation that humanity has been made to conform to *the Son*, and is presented in the context of his insistence that humans are flesh-soul-spirit, aspects that cannot be separated. Yong seems to have read his own presuppositions into Irenaeus's reflections.

While the last few decades have witnessed a pneumatological renaissance, and arguably a very necessary one, the pendulum seems to have swung from neglect in the past to its possible over-ascription as *the* solution to many current theological issues. Within the sphere of interreligious dialogue in particular, a universal pneumatology leaving behind the particular claims of the crucified Christ seems just the right milieu for amiable interaction and commonality. Indeed, a God of love, light, and mercy without

---

60. Yong lauds ecumenical theologians who turn towards pneumatology, expressing regret over those who subsequently "return to Christology"; *Beyond the Impasse*, 97–98, 101.

61. Congar, *Word and the Spirit*, 1.

62. Yong, *Beyond the Impasse*, 103, 169.

63. Irenaeus, *Against Heresies*, 6.1, 531.

the stark shadow of the cross appears much more benevolent and human-friendly. But pneumatology cannot ignore the Christ event. In fact, without the Christ event, pneumatology experienced in the form of the Holy Spirit would not have occurred, even as Jesus would not have been Christ without the Spirit. Paul's concept of the Holy Spirit as the eschatological *arrabōn* ("guarantee"; 2 Cor 1:22; 5:5; Eph 1:14), *aparchē* ("firstfruits"; Rom 8:23) and *sphragis* ("seal"; 2 Cor 1:22; Eph 1:13; 4:30) strongly suggests that the early Christians discerned a distinct difference between the Holy Spirit and the surrounding spirituality in their societies. Nevertheless, Yong is helpful in raising the question of how the Holy Spirit (or the Spirit of Christ) relates to spirituality in general, and while he may be missing the mark by equating the two, he has highlighted the urgency of clarifying this issue.

How does this whole discussion affect our Christian witness in a plural world? Kärkkäinen and Yong correctly point out that there is no room for an imperialistic or triumphalist attitude towards people of other faiths and worldviews, and they stress that Christians should listen closely to what others say. Simply to be alive, people need the presence of God's *rûah* ("breath"), so that the universal presence and operation of the Spirit in humanity (and creation) is clear. However, the New Testament refers to an ongoing alienation between the Spirit and humanity: "This is the Spirit of truth whom the world cannot receive because it neither sees him nor knows him" (John 14:17). Through the work of Christ, this alienation has come to an end. The divine-human reconciliation is located in Jesus Christ, and as this study of the terms "Spirit of Jesus/Christ/Son" indicates, Christian pneumatology cannot be separated from Christology. The Holy Spirit glorifies Jesus Christ (John 16:14). So while the universal presence of the Spirit suggests that many people do have genuine experiences of God, the goal of their encounters is ultimately Christ. We must recognize that as long as the alienation between God's Spirit and humanity is in operation, human understanding of what the Spirit says is tinged with distortion and untruth. The essence of Christian belief is that only in Christ, through his death and resurrection, is there true rebirth into life controlled and transformed by the Holy Spirit. Therefore, as Christ's disciples we are compelled to, indeed we have been *commanded* to, share the good news of God's reconciliation that he has brought about through his Spirit-anointed Son, Jesus. This we must do, humbly recognizing that God's Spirit is also present within every person, and that Spirit-filled Christians living "in between times" continue to experience human fallibility and imperfection. So while we present Christ in a public and global forum, let us pray as Paul did, that we will be generously provided with the Spirit of Jesus Christ, so that we may speak boldly and lovingly, and that Christ may be glorified in us.

Conclusion

Even as plurality is being increasingly recognized as a phenomenon in society today, we are becoming more aware of our common humanity and dignity. Leaving behind imperialistic forms of evangelism, Christians are encouraged to engage people of other faiths in reciprocal exchanges that give serious consideration to different worldviews. To assist in this endeavor, Amos Yong has put forward a foundational pneumatology as a methodological principle. He bases his foundational pneumatology on God's promise to pour out his Spirit on all flesh, proclaimed by Joel and cited by the apostle Peter at Pentecost to explain the unprecedented pneumatological experiences of the first Christians. Within the writings of these early Christians we find the terms "Spirit of Jesus," "Spirit of Christ," and "Spirit of the Son" (Acts 16:17; Rom 8:9; Phil 1:19; Gal 4:6; 1 Pet 1:11). Contextual examination of the usage of these terms by the New Testament writers indicates that they identified the Holy Spirit with the Spirit of Jesus Christ, and that they recognized the Holy Spirit's presence as evidence of belonging to Christ (and therefore to God as his true "sons"), regardless of race, gender, and social status. However, Yong's framework, while being derived from the pneumatological event at Pentecost, ignores its Christocentric and christological basis. It seems untenable to apply the benefits of the Spirit of Christ in a universal fashion without Christ himself. Nevertheless, Yong provides a timely reminder that all humans are spiritual as well as physical beings, and that experiences of God are not limited to Christians. Yet while we share the gospel of Jesus in humility, we must present him to the world with courage and clarity. Yong's scholarship has laid bare the pressing need to elucidate the relationship between the Holy Spirit and spirituality in general, and suggests opportunities for further reflection and research.

Bibliography

Achtemeier, Paul J. *1 Peter*. Hermenia. Minneapolis: Fortress, 1996.
Bock, Darrell L. *Acts*. Baker Exegetical Commentary. Grand Rapids: Baker Academic, 2007.
Bruce, F. F. *The Book of Acts*. Rev. ed. The New International Commentary on the New Testament. Grand Rapids: Eerdmans, 1988.
———. *Commentary on Galatians*. New International Greek Testament Commentary. Exeter: Paternoster, 1982.
Byrne, Brendan. *Romans*. Sacra Pagina. Collegeville: Liturgical, 1996.
Congar, Yves. *The Word and the Spirit*. London: Geoffrey Chapman, 1986.
Dunn, James D. G. *The Christ and the Spirit, vol. 1: Christology*. Grand Rapids: Eerdmans, 1998.

———. *The Christ and the Spirit*, vol. 2: *Pneumatology*. Grand Rapids: Eerdmans, 1998.
———. *Jesus and the Spirit*. New Testament Library. London: SCM, 1975.
———. *Romans 1–8*. Word Biblical Commentary. Dallas: Word, 1988.
———. "Towards the Spirit of Christ: The Emergence of the Distinctive Features of Christian Spirituality." In *The Work of the Spirit: Pneumatology and Pentecostalism*, edited by Michael Welker, 3–26. Grand Rapids: Eerdmans, 2006.
Fee, Gordon D. *God's Empowering Presence: The Holy Spirit in the Letters of Paul*. Peabody: Hendrickson, 1994.
Fitzmyer, Joseph A. *The Acts of the Apostles*. The Anchor Bible. New York: Doubleday, 1998.
———. *Romans*. The Anchor Bible. New York: Doubleday, 1993.
Habets, Myk. *The Anointed Son: A Trinitarian Spirit Christology*. Princeton Monograph Series. Eugene: Pickwick, 2010.
Hansen, G. Walter. *Galatians*. The IVP New Testament Commentary. Downers Grove: InterVarsity, 1994.
———. *The Letter to the Philippians*. The Pillar New Testament Commentary. Nottingham: Apollos, 2009.
Hawthorne, Gerald F. *Philippians*. Word Biblical Commentary. Waco: Word, 1983.
Hillyer, Norman. *1 and 2 Peter, Jude*. Understanding the Bible Commentary. Grand Rapids: Baker, 1991.
Hur, Ju. *A Dynamic Reading of the Holy Spirit in Luke-Acts*. London: T. & T Clark, 2004.
Irenaeus. "Against Heresies." In *Ante-Nicene Fathers*, vol. 1, edited by Alexander Roberts and James Donaldson. Grand Rapids: Eerdmans, 1885.
Jobes, Karen H. *1 Peter*. Baker Exegetical Commentary on the New Testament. Grand Rapids: Baker, 2005.
Kärkkäinen, Veli-Matti. "How to Speak of the Spirit among Religions: Trinitarian Prolegomena for a Pneumatological Theology of Religions." In *The Work of the Spirit: Pneumatology and Pentecostalism*, edited by Michael Welker, 47–70. Grand Rapids: Eerdmans, 2006.
———. *An Introduction to the Theology of Religions: Biblical, Historical and Contemporary Perspectives*. Downers Grove: IVP Academic, 2003.
———. *Trinity and Religious Pluralism: The Doctrine of the Trinity in Christian Theology of Religions*. Aldershot: Ashgate, 2004.
Ladd, George Eldon. *A Theology of the New Testament*. Rev. ed. Grand Rapids: Eerdmans, 1993.
Lightfoot, J. B. *Saint Paul's Epistle to the Philippians*. Classic Commentary Library. Grand Rapids: Michigan, 1953.
Longenecker, Richard N. *Galatians*. Word Biblical Commentary. Dallas: Word, 1990.
Marshall, I. Howard. *Acts*. Tyndale New Testament Commentaries. Leicester: InterVarsity, 1980.
———. *1 Peter*. The IVP New Testament Commentary. Downers Grove: InterVarsity, 1991.
Martin, Ralph. *Philippians*. Tyndale New Testament Commentaries. Downers Grove: InterVarsity, 1987.
Martyn, J. Louis. *Galatians*. The Anchor Bible. New York: Doubleday, 1997.
McKnight, Scot. *1 Peter*. The NIV Application Commentary. Grand Rapids: Zondervan, 1996.
Michaels, J. Ramsey. *1 Peter*. Word Biblical Commentary. Waco: Word, 1988.

Moo, Douglas. *The Epistle to the Romans*. The New International Commentary on the New Testament. Grand Rapids: Eerdmans, 1996.

Morris, Leon. *The Epistle to the Romans*. Pillar New Testament Commentary. Leicester: Apollos, 1988.

Motyer, Alex. *The Message of Philippians*. The Bible Speaks Today. Downers Grove: InterVarsity, 1984.

Nestle-Aland. *Novum Testamentum Graece*. 27th ed. Stuttgart: Deutsche Bibelgesellschaft, 2001.

Nostra Aetate ("Declaration on the Relation of the Church to Non-Christian Religions"). *Vatican Council II: Conciliar and Post-Conciliar Documents*. Vatican Collection, vol. 1. Rev. ed. Edited by Austin Flannery. New York: Costello, 1988.

Osborne, Grant R. *Romans*. The IVP New Testament Commentary. Downers Grove: InterVarsity, 2004.

Otto, Rudolph. *The Idea of the Holy: An Inquiry into the Non-Rational Factor in the Idea of the Divine and its Relation to the Rational*. Translated by John W. Harvey. London: Oxford University Press, 1936.

Peterson, David G. *The Acts of the Apostles*. The Pillar New Testament Commentary. Grand Rapids: Eerdmans, 2009.

Schleiermacher, Friedrich. *The Christian Faith*. Edited by H. R. Mackintosh and J. S. Stewart. Edinburgh, T. & T. Clark, 1928.

Schreiner, Thomas R. *New Testament Theology: Magnifying God in Christ*. Grand Rapids: Baker Academic, 2008.

Schweizer, Eduard. *Spirit of God*. Bible Key Words. London: Adam and Charles Black, 1960.

Skaggs, Rebecca. *1 Peter, 2 Peter, Jude*. The Pentecostal Commentary. London: T. & T. Clark International, 2004.

Steinmetz, David C. "The Theology of John Calvin." In *The Cambridge Companion to Reformation Theology*, edited by David Bagchi and David C. Steinmetz, 113–29. Cambridge: Cambridge University Press, 2004.

Yong, Amos. "As the Spirit Gives Utterance: Pentecostal, Intra-Christian Ecumenism and the Wider Oikoumene." *International Review of Mission* 92 (2003) 299–314.

———. *Beyond the Impasse: Toward a Pneumatological Theology of Religions*. Grand Rapids: Baker Academic, 2003.

15

Transcending Morality

The Church and Christian Living in a Post-Christian World

Andre van Oudtshoorn

On the Problem of Christian Ethics

THE CHURCH OFTEN SEES herself as the final bastion of traditional morals, valiantly defending "Christian culture" against the postmodernist onslaught on all that is right, decent, and true.[1] She thus feels compelled to make weighty pronouncements on diverse ethical issues such as abortion, euthanasia, homosexuality, pacifism, ecology, and so on. Unfortunately, the church does not seem able to speak with one unified voice on most of these ethical concerns. While most Christian ethicists claim to submit to the authority of the Bible, there does not seem to be any agreement on (1) how exactly the Bible is to be used in formulating a response to current ethical issues; (2) how far the Bible's authority stretches when taking the temporal and cultural chasm between its immediate context and ours into account; (3) which principles may be deduced from Scripture as absolute and univer-

---

1. Melden, *Ethical Theories*, 1. The term "ethics" is derived from the Greek word *ethos* which originally covered the semantic domains of custom, habitual conduct, usages, and later, character. Morals or morality is used as an alternative term and is from the Latin term *mores* which encompasses the semantic fields of custom, approval, good, obligatory, right, and worthy.

sally valid and thus applicable to the ethical issue at hand; and, (4) within which ethical system the witness of Scripture should be incorporated and utilized.

Instead of responding to these questions I want to pose a more fundamental question: *Should* the church engage in Christian ethics? Or to put it more radically: *Is Christian ethics possible at all?* To answer this question, I will first of all look at the various ways in which ethics defines itself and then see how the biblical construct of the Christian life differs from ethics. The thesis outlined in this chapter is that the Bible forces the church to take a more dynamic and humble route, in the light of the brokenness of this world, when dealing with questions about right and wrong actions.[2]

One of the first theologians seriously to question the possibility of Christian ethics is the Danish philosopher Søren Kierkegaard. According to Kierkegaard, the Bible shatters the possibility of ethics for people of faith in the story of Abraham who was commanded by Yahweh to sacrifice his son Isaac, and who then set out obediently in faith to do so. Abraham's act of faith, Kierkegaard argues, can only be held to be praiseworthy by those who acknowledge that faith and love always take us beyond the realms of reasonable ethical judgments which are universally valid for all time:

> The ethical is as such the universal, and as the universal it applies to everyone, which from another angle means that it applies at all times. It rests imminent in itself, has nothing outside of itself which is its telos, but is itself the telos for everything outside of itself. The single individual has his telos in the universal, and it is his ethical task continually to express himself in this, to annul his singularity in order to become the universal . . . (But) faith is precisely the paradox that the single individual as the single individual is higher than the universal, is justified before it, not as inferior to it, but as superior . . . that the single individual as the single individual stands in absolute relation to the absolute. This position cannot be mediated.[3]

Banner points out that for Kierkegaard, "The story of Abraham contains a teleological suspension of the ethical."[4] Abraham cannot be considered a tragic hero because in a tragedy the hero may well be forced to make some sort of supreme sacrifice, but such a sacrifice is then usually made in the service of something "greater" or "higher." But how does one determine

---

2. Some aspects of this chapter have been published previously in Oudtshoorn, "Non-Foundational."

3. Kierkegaard, *Fear and Trembling*, 55.

4. Banner, *Christian Ethics*, 83.

what constitutes this higher "something" that has the right to demand such supreme sacrifices from its heroes? It cannot be simply based on opinion for it has to be something that other people will also acknowledge as a valid reason for making the sacrifice. Such universal acknowledgement presupposes an underlying ethic of what is to be considered *good* and right; of what would make such a supreme sacrifice acceptable and just. It is only by making an *ethically* justified sacrifice that the hero gains the right to be acknowledged as a hero. Abraham, however, had no middle term that saves the tragic hero. Far from being any use in explaining what he did, the ethical is entirely beside the point. Ward agrees:

> Whereas the tragic hero relinquishes himself to express the universal, Abraham gives up the universal to express something that is higher that is not universal. This higher particular that Abraham attempts to grasp is his God, who, as love, according to Kierkegaard, is the one who demands absolute love. Real love is always exclusive and tends towards the particular—Abraham could not share his love between his family and God.[5]

In this paper I do not argue for the radical individuation and existential "inwardness" that mark Kierkegaard's perspective on the person of faith, to use as grounds for challenging the construction of "Christian ethics."[6] I do, however, pose the same question that Kierkegaard directed to the philosophical and ethical rationalism propounded by Immanuel Kant, namely: How does faith in God affect the philosophical and religious presuppositions that we bring to ethics?[7] Or, to follow Kierkegaard even further: In what way does faith challenge the very foundations of ethics for Christian believers? I will argue that there is no final foundation on which to ground ethics, and that ethics is virtually impossible to define. Moreover, I will show that the Christian faith contradicts a number of key presuppositions of ethics: the gospel's notion of freedom through the Spirit in the church undermines individual freedom as a necessary precondition for morality; grace places the Christian on the side of the judged, rather than the judge, thereby ceding the neutral position required of ethical decision making; the biblical insistence on unconditional forgiveness undermines the notions of justice, guilt, and moral responsibility which underlie all ethical endeavor; and, finally,

---

5. Ward, in Velásquez, *Love and Friendship*, 312.

6. "Abraham acquires a new interiority of a higher privacy and individuation above the rational and moral order embedded in the community. Abraham therefore, unlike the tragic hero, learns that the soul can feel as well as think, or is heart as well as mind." Ward in Velásquez, *Love and Friendship*, 313.

7. Banner, *Christian Ethics*, 82.

faith and hope, operating within the context of the eschatological kingdom, obstruct the development and engagement of timeless universal principles. Instead of making ethical judgments, it will be argued, Christians are called to express their *faith* through their *actions*.[8]

Moral Foundations?

Let us start by considering the different ways in which ethics may be approached. David Hume, starts his *Inquiry Concerning the Principles of Morals* by considering a number of possible foundations for ethics:

> There has been a controversy started of late, much better worth examination, concerning the general foundation of Morals; whether they be derived from reason, or from Sentiment; whether we attain the knowledge of them by a chain of argument and induction, or by an immediate feeling and finer internal sense; whether like all sound judgment of truth and falsehood, they should be the same to every rational intelligent being; or whether, like the perception of beauty and deformity, they be founded entirely on the particular fabric and constitution of the human species.[9]

If ethics is founded on the constitution of the human species, and if it is the result of that which humans value, its inherent subjectivity, it can be argued, relieves it of any claim to objective truth. This is because the very act of valuing by definition deconstructs the objectivity of that which is valued:

> It is important finally to realize that precisely through the characterization of something as "a value" what is so valued is so robbed of its worth. That is to say, by the assessment of something as a value what is valued is admitted only as an object of man's estimation . . . Every valuing, even when it values positively, is a subjectivizing.[10]

Ethics founded on human values can therefore never be an objective standard for our attitudes, values, and beliefs but rather remains a reflection

---

8. This does not imply that the Christian way of life cannot be described using ethical categories or that the Christian faith cannot, at times, utilize ethical categories for the purpose of indicating how Christians should express their faith in the world. Such uses, however, must be made subservient to the biblical categories within which they are employed.

9. Hume, *Enquiry*, 2.

10. Heidegger, quoted in Hatab, *Ethics and Finitude*, 90.

of them.[11] Bertrand Russell, commenting on the subjective dimension of ethics stated: "I cannot see how to refute the arguments for the subjectivity of ethical values, but I find myself incapable of believing that all that is wrong with wanton cruelty is that I don't like it."[12] Many secular ethicists argue that the absolute character of morality demands something more stable than humanity as a foundation. Some have sought such certainty in religion and God.

Grounding ethics on God and religion rather than humanity, however, raises its own set of problems. Is the God who acts as the final guarantor for ethics (Kant) not simply another rational human construction? Are those who deny God of necessity less moral than those who hold to some form of religion? Atheists and agnostics rightly take exception to such claims. Against this, Hoose argues: "Morality has a certain autonomy. By that I mean that religious faith is not necessary in order to experience and recognize the moral point of view: that is something that is demanded of our humanness or rationality."[13] But even if one should accept that religion is able to provide a true foundation for ethics, it still begs the question: Which religion provides the right foundation? At the heart of each religion is its own unique concept of God. The morality that stems from the worship of a tyrannical God, will of necessity look different from a religion that is centered on a God of mercy and grace. Again Hoose makes the point: "So it has been rightly said that the question of who God is, is the most basic question of moral theology."[14] Religion, furthermore, like culture, speaks with multiple voices, each religion having its own set of presuppositions that ultimately want to silence alternative interpretations. Even within the context of one religion such as Christianity, people make ethical decisions on the basis of what their specific Christian communities have taught them.[15] Religion's ethical pronouncements often uncritically reflect the cultural context from which, and into which, it speaks. Each religion ends up justifying certain ethical positions and abhorring others, often the same positions that are justified as acceptable behavior by another religion. The philosopher Frankena cynically observes: "If morality is dependent on religion then we cannot hope to solve our problems or resolve our differences

---

11. Illies, *Ethical Judgement*, 11.
12. Liu, *Foundations of Ethics*, 1.
13. Hoose, *Christian Ethics*, 152–53.
14. Hoose, *Christian Ethics*, 152.
15. Williams, "Making Moral Decisions," 12.

of opinion about them, unless and in so far as we can achieve agreement and certainty in religion (not a lively hope)."[16]

Another option is to follow Kierkegaard and see morality as existing in and of itself, not being founded on anything else outside of, or apart from, itself. In his *Euthrypo*, Socrates poses the question of whether things are right and good because God wills them, or does God will them because they are right and good? If "right" and "good" exist independently of God, then it presupposes an objective moral order to which even God is subject. Moral realism argues that there are moral facts according to which "judgements on matters of norms and values are literally true."[17] Against this view, however, Nietzsche has convincingly argued that all moral judgments are activities aimed at gaining power for the one making the judgments and are thus biased and fall short of morality's own standards. "Morality" in such cases is, then, nothing more than an instrument of our will to rule over others. A further problem with the idea of "one objective universal ethics" is that in the real world there are many different ethical systems. Montaigne famously questioned how it is possible for something to be considered "truth" in one place, but a lie in another, with only a mountain separating the two places.[18]

It is also possible to ground ethics on reason. According to Kant "our individual duties or obligations arise from universally binding rules of conduct which command that an act be good in itself and therefore necessary for a will which is to conform to reason."[19] "Rationality," Max Weber argues, however, "is an historical concept which covers a whole range of different things."[20] Reason falls short as a foundation for ethics because life has been shown to be value-oriented rather than purely instrumental. Many ethicists accept that ethics must embrace supernatural indefinable properties with the unique power of intuitive recognition. According to Weber, only a specific group of problems which do not involve conflict over ends and values are "solvable" by purely rational means. "The most pressing problems

---

16. Outka and Reeder, *Religion and Morality*, 295.

17. Illies, *Ethical Judgement*, 1.

18. Banner, *Christian Ethics*, 73. In *Leviathan*, Hobbes also reacted strongly against any such objective grounds for morality: "For these words of good, evil, and contemptible are ever used with relation to the person that useth them: there being nothing simply and absolutely so; nor any common rule of good and evil to be taken from the nature of the objects themselves; but from the person of the man, where there is no Commonwealth; or in a Commonwealth, from the person that representeth it; or from an arbitrator or judge, whom men disagreeing shall by consent set up and make his sentence the rule thereof" (Hobbes, *Leviathan*, 32).

19. Banner, *Christian Ethics*, 82.

20. Weber and Parsons, *Protestant Ethic*, 78.

of social life do involve the clash of ends and values and thus . . . cannot be solved in an objectively rational manner."[21]

Some ethicists deny that there is any foundation for ethics. They argue that ethics is linked purely to the biological, instinctive dimension of being human. According to this view, ethics never looks beyond itself to benefit the "other," but always, only, seeks to benefit the one making the ethical decision. A radical materialistic paradigm embeds ethics completely within an evolutionary framework that strives for the survival of the fittest:

> The position of the modern evolutionist . . . is that humans have an awareness of morality . . . because such an awareness is of biological worth. Morality is a biological adaptation no less than are hands and feet and teeth . . . Considered as a rationally justifiable set of claims about an objective something, ethics is illusory. I appreciate that when somebody says "Love thy neighbor as thyself," they think they are referring above and beyond themselves . . . Nevertheless . . . such reference is truly without foundation. Morality is just an aid to survival and reproduction . . . and any deeper meaning is illusory.[22]

There thus seems to be no universal agreement of what ethics "is," on how it is to be accessed, or on what grounds it is to be appropriated. Ethics claims to be absolute and universal, but it is relativized by the particular; it presents its truth objectively, but its truth cannot be separated from human subjectivity and belief systems; it purports to be reasonable but cannot bypass supernatural intuition; it reflects the values of individuals and society but these values become norms by which to criticize other ethical value systems;[23] it may claim to reflect God's will, but it is also used to critically evaluate God and hold him accountable to its norms; it focuses on the other but in the process may serve the self; it claims to be knowable, but nobody knows how it is known or whether, what is known, is "real" in any sense of the word.[24]

---

21. Brubaker, *Limits of Rationality*, 2.
22. Ruse, *Darwinian Paradigm*, 262, 268–69.
23. Those who argue for moral relativism spurn fundamentalists as wrong.
24. Joseph, in Kafka's *The Trial*, knows that he has transgressed an absolute moral law but does not and cannot know its contents. Raskolnikov in Dostoevsky's *Crime and Punishment* comes to see an absolute moral law that is hidden from all minds. "Ethical intuitionism is not popular in contemporary philosophy. There are alternative theories but none of them are popular either. In fact, in contemporary ethics there is little work even being attempted in moral epistemology." Pollock and Cruz, *Contemporary Theories*, 13.

Ethics, by its very nature, presupposes the act of judging between right and wrong, or, good and evil. This motif is also found in the biblical account in Genesis 3 in which the serpent promises that humans will have their eyes opened to be like God, "knowing good and evil" (v. 5). It is clear that the ability, or need, to judge between good and evil, presupposed in ethics, does not belong to God's original good creation but is, instead, at the *center* of the temptation for humankind to sin against God. Exegetically it may be said that this thread of the story is not concerned with a purely intellectual knowledge of good and evil, but with "deciding for oneself what good and evil are."[25] Von Rad indicates that by breaking God's prohibition in the garden humans declared their autonomy from God and ceased to understand themselves as his creatures.[26] Thielicke states: "Thus morality is of the order of the fall."[27] Humanity has, by its disobedience, usurped God's exclusive privilege of determining right and wrong. This did not, however, result in pure ethical discernment by humans. "What actually happened is that by transgressing God's commandment the eyes of man were closed."[28] If ethics is so closely linked to the coming of sin into the world, it goes without saying that Christians should be very careful not to turn ethics into a legitimate, or necessary, Christian enterprise. In Scripture, worship and religious concerns often override ethical considerations.

Transcending Morality—The Distinctiveness of Christian Moral Life

The idea that ethics deals with judgments over right and wrong and that Christian ethics does the same, the only difference being that Christian ethics has the Bible as an extra authoritative resource to help it make more truthful judgments, must be seriously questioned. Nevertheless, as Sell has correctly observed, Christian ethics is and remains a growth area. "It also," he continues drily, "displays certain characteristics of a bomb site."[29] Already in the early seventies Kliever pointed to:

> The mixed bag of technical labels found in [the literature of Christian ethics]—situation ethics, contextual ethics, circumstance ethics, relational ethics, non-principled ethics, pure

---

25. Berkouwer, *Sin*, 271.
26. Berkouwer, *Man*, 78.
27. Berkouwer, *Man*, 148.
28. Berkouwer, *Sin*, 154.
29. Sell, *Testimony and Tradition*, 231.

act-agapism, mixed act-agapism, faith doing ethics, response ethics, Christomorphic ethics, theonomic ethics, and the jaw-breaking cathekontological ethics.[30]

Before embarking on the development of particular Christian ethical approaches and positions, however, it behooves the Christian ethicist to first consider the limitations that the Bible places on some of the other ground rules according to which ethics operate. The first such limitation concerns the difference between the freedom to which Christians are called, and moral freedom.

Moral action requires the free agency of those who endeavor to act morally. If we substitute obedience to orders for morality, then we no longer have morality. "There is no room in morality for commands, whether they are the father's, the schoolmaster's, or the priest's. There is still no room for them when they are God's commands."[31] How does this notion of freedom relate to the freedom to which believers are called in the gospel? Gareth Jones stresses that a shift of identity, by which Christians see themselves as belonging to God and being part of his story, must lie at the heart of Christian action. Christians are called to act, first and foremost, in response to their new identity as children of God.[32]

Christian freedom differs from the freedom demanded by ethics in that it is not a given, something belonging intrinsically to their "being" as believers. Christian freedom is, instead, a by-product of the Spirit's presence; it is a gift from God. Moreover, this freedom is given to believers within the context of the church, and not individually. The Spirit binds believers to "the other." Jones states: "Whereas the democratic theorist will speak of the rights of the individual, Christianity always speaks of God's gifts to the church as a whole."[33]

The presence of the Spirit within believers, and the subsequent "fruit of the Spirit" that shows itself through the actions and dispositions of believers, thus challenge the neutral and objective freedom that ethics requires. Positive or *good* behavior is never the result of the believer's individual free decision alone, but it is the effect of the Spirit's work and presence in the church. "Moral life is transfigured by Christian faith. It is theological."[34] It is, however, exactly within the framework of being bound to God and

30. Kliever, "Moral Argument," 53.
31. De Graff, in Ramsey, *Christian Ethics*, 344.
32. Jones, "Authority," 25.
33. Jones, "Authority," 25–26.
34. Hoose, *Christian Ethics*, 152.

others through the Holy Spirit that believers are given the freedom to make responsible decisions without reference to an objective ethical system:

> And in this sense, it is completely vain to elaborate a Christian morality; there is no Christian morality since, living according to the Spirit, each one is called to make her own decisions as her own responsibility. Each one has the initiative in the conduct of his life provided that it be in Christ.[35]

A second limitation that the Bible places on utilizing the concept of ethics lies in the Gospel's message of grace. Those who are under grace know that they belong on the side of those who are shown to be in the wrong. Grace does not allow those affected by it to take up the position of judging other people or even themselves. Christian ethicists are often concerned about the possibilities that grace offers for libertarianism and immorality, arguing that it needs to be balanced by responsible moral actions.[36] Thus Wogaman states:

> The recurring dilemma is that moral rules and even moral activism, apart from grace, derive from self-centredness; but grace apart from moral actions is empty—indeed, it is not even grace. Somehow Christian ethics must link grace and moral action, even while it affirms the priority of grace.[37]

Grace, however, does not need to be complemented by moral actions. This would only lead the church in the way of the Galatian believers who started with grace but ended with "works." Instead of allowing Christians to flee to their own righteousness, grace binds believers to a deep awareness of being in the wrong; to the conviction that they are in need of forgiveness. Grace always brings believers to the confession that they do not possess "righteousness" in and of themselves, but only indirectly, in Christ. Without faith in Christ, the resurrected human has no possibility of being in the right relationship with God or with other people. Grace thus does not allow the Christian to flee away from his or her own sinfulness into moral righteousness. It is the man who delights in not being like the robbers, evildoers, and adulterers who is sent home unjustified (Luke 18:9–14). There is no objective distance between Christians and those who do wrong. Christians cannot set themselves apart from, or over against the sins of others, for the grace of God convicts them that they, too, are in the wrong; they have to confess their own wrongdoing before God even while becoming aware of

---

35. Ellul and Dawn, *Sources and Trajectories*, 121.
36. Wogaman, *Christian Ethics*, 273.
37. Wogaman, *Christian Ethics*, 274.

the sins of others. Grace convicts Christians that they too are, and will continue to be, in need of God's undeserved kindness and forgiveness.

Forgiveness presents the third difference between Christian faith and morality. Morality cannot forgive. It can praise and blame, but never forgive. The act of forgiveness always needs the personal dimensions of grace and love. Morality may call for sacrificial actions to enable the guilty to redeem him or herself for past transgressions, but morality can never deliver a free pardon to the guilty. This is, however, exactly what God does. The scandal that the unjust is forgiven without having to do anything to deserve it, stands at the very heart of the gospel (Rom 4:4–5). To forgive the guilty, however, is to shatter the moral concept of justice. Forgiveness is always subversive, an act of sabotage against the very edifice of morality. The church, as the gathering of the forgiven, is by definition called to be a forgiving community. Christians are to forgive as they have been forgiven (Matt 6:12, Luke 11:4).

The church continues to live out of the forgiveness of God. "The Christian is certainly in some sense a new creature, but that clearly means not another species altogether, but a creature, a man transformed or renewed, whose transformation and renewal cannot be articulated apart from some understanding of his existence as a creature independent of that renewal."[38] This means that the individual Christian as well as the church as a whole have no supernatural access to God enabling them to always do only what is right; the individual Christian and the church remain fallible, open to making the wrong decisions, leaving them at the mercy of God's forgiveness alone. Sometimes, in a broken world, there are no "right" decisions to make. Morality insists that one should be able to make judgments that, though difficult, ultimately do not condemn you. By following the right process, or acting from the right motives, or having the right goal in mind, people's decisions can be excused, exculpated; and they themselves are exonerated, even turned into heroes. Christians have no such luxury. Christians have to acknowledge that, within this broken reality, they sometimes only have the option of making wrong decisions, that none of the choices that are open to them is compatible with the will of God, that any decision they make will ultimately lead to hurting and damaging some innocent party. Christians are called to be agents of the love of God in the world, but their acts of love in and of themselves are not enough to transform the world. Ramsey points to the gospel's expectation of the return of Jesus in power to finally judge evil and transform the world:

> Jesus himself did not think that his gospel of love would be sufficient by itself to resolve the totality of evil in many life

---

38. Robinson, *Christian Ethics*, 16.

situations, or to defeat the demonic power of evil encompassing even those purely personal relationships which in themselves are often amenable to love's persuasion.[39]

In making their decisions Christians are not able to shift the blame away from themselves. They have to take responsibility for their decisions; they have to own their guilt, confessing their personal sin and the liability for the consequences that flow from their decisions.

> Against orthodox Christianity, the prophetic tradition of Christianity must insist on the relevance of the ideal of love to the moral experience of mankind on every conceivable level . . . But every conceivable order in the historical world contains an element of anarchy. Its world rests on contingency and caprice. The obligation to support and enhance it can therefore only arise and maintain itself upon the basis of a faith that it is the partial fruit of a deeper unity and the promise of a more perfect harmony than is revealed in any immediate situation.[40]

Christians can only make their choices on the basis that God forgives sins. Instead of trying to find reasons to show that they are "in the right," Christians expect to be declared righteous by their faith in Christ alone, the one who embodies God's love for those who are in the wrong and in need of forgiveness.

Christians can only overcome the "anarchy" of the world that Niebuhr describes, through faith and hope. Faith and hope anchor the believers to the narrative of the coming of the kingdom through the salvation-historical eschatological events of the cross and resurrection of Christ. Faith interprets the past and the present in the light of the judgment of the old reality on the cross and the coming of the new creation through Christ's resurrection. Christians are called to respond in obedience to God because they believe the message about their new identity in Christ. They believe that they are God's beloved children who, as members of his body, the church, are bearers of his Spirit.[41] Joachim Jeremias has commented that to read the Sermon on the Mount as an isolated document on ethical behavior is to ignore the broad theological perspective within which it functions. Every word, he suggests, is preceded by something else, by the preaching of the kingdom of God, that says, "you are forgiven; you are a child of God; you belong to the

---

39. Ramsey, *Christian Ethics*, 36.
40. Niebuhr, "Relevance," 243.
41. Hoose, *Christian Ethics*, 151.

Kingdom."[42] The Bible gives us "impressions of the original community's experience of the inbreak of the Kingdom in Jesus and how that issued in a way of life—the logic of faith."[43]

This "logic of faith" implies that Christians can only judge others in the light of the gospel's promise to the other of a new history in Christ; a new past, present, and future by which they will be judged. Faith and hope mean that there is a necessary dynamic to any judgment of someone's character or actions; in Christ they have a past that has been forgiven, a present that is being reshaped in line with God's will, and a future where they will ultimately be "like Christ." The final judgment is ultimately about faith; does the person believe in the new reality in which he/she participates in Christ? In referring to the parable of the seed, Chilton and McDonald say:

> At one end is the divine performance of the kingdom, an inceptive reality which attracts hope. At the other end is human performance, an enacted response which itself elicits action. Hopeful action and enacted hope characterize the parable as a whole, at each point in what is depicted . . . The parable never concerns merely promise alone or action alone. Indeed, the creative interface between the two is of the essence of the Kingdom which is presented.[44]

To live in Christian faith and hope also means to submit to God and not to a set of general principles. "In Christian ethics . . . we have no unambiguous universal principles or rules upon which to rely. It is more a question of performance and improvisation."[45] Ramsey concurs with this view:

> In the face of the inbreaking kingdom, moral decision was stripped of all prudential considerations, all calculation of what is right in terms of consequences which in the present age normally follow certain lines of action. Not only all prudential calculation of consequences likely to fall on the agent himself, but likewise all sober regard for the future performance of his responsibility for family or friends, duties to oneself and *fixed* duties to others, both alike were jettisoned from view . . . All that mattered was complete obedience to God."[46]

---

42. Jeremias, *Sermon*, 35.
43. Hoose, *Christian Ethics*, 154.
44. Chilton and McDonald, *Jesus*, 55, 73.
45. Cunningham, *Christian Ethics*, 135.
46. Ramsey, *Christian Ethics*, 39.

There is no safety net, no broad general system of ethical principles and judgments that can be worked out in the safety of academia, removed from the crisis of the tension between the kingdom of God and the broken world in which the church finds itself. The church lives within the overlap between two radically opposing interpretations of reality. The kingdom of God no longer exists in heaven, apart from and outside of this sinful and broken reality. In Jesus, the kingdom has already come to the earth. As Barth has stated, "The coming of Christ resulted not in a new religion but a new world."[47] The church cannot act and think as if the new creation, the kingdom of God, remains only a future reality. It is, of course, such a future reality, but in Christ and through his Spirit it is a future reality that demands to be made present within the brokenness of the here and now. The church is called to face up to the radical demands of the kingdom of God for the transformation of the world.

> Prophetic Christianity faces the difficulty that its penetration into the total and ultimate human situation complicates the problem of dealing with the immediate moral and social situations which all men must face. The common currency of the moral life is constituted of the "nicely calculated less and more" of the relatively good and the relatively evil. Human happiness in ordinary intercourse is determined by the difference between a little more and a little less justice, a little more and less freedom, between varying degrees of imaginative insight with which the self enters the life and understands the interests of the neighbor.[48]

The rule of God, however, affords no such small compromises. "The Kingdom of God is performative: it is God's performance in which we actively participate."[49] It demands a radical reorientation; a constant seeking in faith after the impossible; a radical commitment to see that which ultimately belongs to the future realized in the present. The reign of God is the "end point which beckons Christian life forward and stands in judgement on every present form of life."[50] Ramsey takes this notion even further by stressing that for Jesus the coming kingdom was already a present reality:

> We frequently hear it said that Jesus' call to the strenuous way of limitless love lays down a method for making all the world a kingdom of God and is to be responded to with this end in view.

47. Barth, in Willis, *Ethics of Karl Barth*, 9.
48. Niebuhr, "Relevance," 241.
49. Stassen and Gushee, *Kingdom Ethics*, 21.
50. Hoose, *Christian Ethics*, 151.

> For Jesus, however, the reverse was the case: the kingdom of God was already effective in this present age and for this reason he believed the strenuous teachings could be lived out.[51]

Replacing "ethics" with radical obedience to the will of God still begs the question: How does the church, finally, determine the will of God in its praxis? The answer to this lies beyond the scope of this paper. From the insights advocated so far, however, we can say that it has to happen in the dynamic tension between the immediate context of broken people within a broken reality; the canon that reflects the new reality in Christ and the obedience that should follow this; and, the Spirit who dynamically actualizes the future reality in the present through the free loving actions of the church. This implies that the will of God can only be discerned in the context of faith, hope, and love and ought to be realized within the context of forgiveness, mercy, and grace, and a free range of practical actions that embody these elements as part of God's new metanarrative for the world.

Conclusion

This essay has shown that the Christian faith cannot allow itself to be directly co-opted by ethics or embrace ethics as part of its own program. Ethics is an elusive concept whose definition suffers many of the same foundational problems as religion. The Bible, however, contradicts some of the basic presuppositions of ethics through its insistence on linking freedom to the Spirit and "the other," as well as by its focus on grace and forgiveness which deny believers a neutral position from which to make ethical judgments. Faith and hope, it has been shown, anchor the actions of believers to the inbreaking of the eschatological kingdom of God in Christ as proclaimed in the message of the gospel. This, in turn, places Christian obedience with the dynamic domain of the Spirit that seeks to bear fruit in the lives of the believers and overcome the broken reality of this world through the faithful, hopeful, and loving actions of the church. It is only as the church turns from a preoccupation with "rights and wrongs" to a preoccupation on how to love others in the context of faith and hope that she will provide a radical and practical alternative to the threat of chaos and despair that is engulfing the Western world today. In so doing, the church will again find herself outside the wall of self-righteousness and judgment, and more clearly reflect the one who died amongst thieves and robbers, radically associating himself with

---

51. Ramsay, *Basic Christian Ethics*, 37.

their condition of despair and sin to bring them the possibility of a new life, a new future, as part of God's new creation.

Bibliography

Banner, Michael C. *Christian Ethics: A Brief History*. Oxford: Wiley-Blackwell, 2009.
Berkouwer, Gerrit Cornelis. *Man: The Image of God*. Grand Rapids: Eerdmans, 1962.
———. *Sin*. Grand Rapids: Eerdmans, 1971.
Brubaker, Rogers. *The Limits of Rationality: An Essay on the Social and Moral Thought of Max Weber*. London: Taylor and Francis, 1984.
Chilton, Bruce, and James Ian Hamilton McDonald. *Jesus and the Ethics of the Kingdom*. London: SPCK, 1987.
Cunningham, David S. *Christian Ethics: The End of the Law*. London: Routledge, 2008.
Ellul, Jacques, and Marva J. Dawn. *Sources and Trajectories: Eight Early Articles that Set the Stage*. Grand Rapids: Eerdmans, 1997.
Hatab, Lawrence J. *Ethics and Finitude: Heideggerian Contributions to Moral Philosophy*. Lanham, MD: Rowman and Littlefield, 2000.
Hobbes, T. *Leviathan*. New York: E. P. Dutton, 1950.
Hoose, Bernard. *Christian Ethics: An Introduction*. London: Continuum International, 2000.
Illies, Christian. *The Grounds of Ethical Judgement: New Transcendental Arguments in Moral Philosophy*. Oxford: Oxford University Press, 2003.
Jeremias, Joachim. *The Sermon on the Mount*. Philadelphia: Fortress, 1970.
Jones, Gareth. "The Authority of Scripture and Christian Ethics." In *The Cambridge Companion to Christian Ethics*, edited by Robin Gill, 16–28. Cambridge: Cambridge University Press, 2001.
Kierkegaard, Søren. *Fear and Trembling*. Radford, VA: Wilder, 2008.
Kliever, Lonnie D. "Moral Argument in the New Morality." *The Harvard Theological Review* 65, no. 1 (1972) 53–90.
Liu, Xiusheng. *Mencius, Hume, and the Foundations of Ethics*. London: Ashgate, 2003.
Melden, Abraham I. *Ethical Theories*. Alchester, UK: Read, 2008.
Niebuhr, Reinhold. "The Relevance of an Impossible Ethical Ideal." In *From Christ to the World: Introductory Readings in Christian Ethics*, edited by Wayne G. Boulton and Thomas D. Kennedy, 241–47. Grand Rapids: Eerdmans, 1994.
Oudtshoorn, Andre. "Constructing a Non-Foundational Theological Approach to Christian Ethics." *Herv. Teol. Stud.* 71, no. 3 (2015) 1–8.
Outka, Gene H., and John P. Reeder. *Religion and Morality: A Collection of Essays*. New York: Anchor, 1973.
Pollock, John L., and Joseph Cruz. *Contemporary Theories of Knowledge*. London: Rowman and Littlefield, 1999.
Ramsey, Ian T. *Christian Ethics and Contemporary Philosophy*. London: Macmillan, 1966.
Ramsay, Paul. *Basic Christian Ethics*. Library of Theological Ethics. Louisville: Westminster John Knox, 1950.
Robinson, Norman Hamilton Galloway. *The Groundwork of Christian Ethics*. Grand Rapids: Eerdmans, 1972.

Ruse, Michael. *The Darwinian Paradigm: Essays on Its History, Philosophy and Religious Implications*. London: Routledge, 1989.
Sell, Alan P. F. *Testimony and Tradition: Studies in Reformed and Dissenting Thought*. London: Ashgate, 2005.
Stassen, Glen Harold, and David P. Gushee. *Kingdom Ethics: Following Jesus in Contemporary Context*. Downers Grove: InterVarsity, 2003.
Velásquez, Eduardo A. *Love and Friendship: Rethinking Politics and Affection in Modern Times*. Lanham, MD: Lexington, 2003.
Weber, Max, and Talcott Parsons. *The Protestant Ethic and the Spirit of Capitalism*. New York: Courier Dover, 2003.
Williams, Rowan. "Making Moral Decisions." In *The Cambridge Companion to Christian Ethics*, edited by Robin Gill, 3–15. Cambridge: Cambridge University Press, 2001.
Willis, Robert E. *The Ethics of Karl Barth*. Leiden: Brill Archive, 1971.
Wogaman, J. Philip. *Christian Ethics: A Historical Introduction*. Louisville: Westminster John Knox, 1993.

www.ingramcontent.com/pod-product-compliance
Lightning Source LLC
Chambersburg PA
CBHW05084823O426
43667CB00012B/2198